low Homo
3ecame Sapiens

How Homo Became Sapiens:

On the Evolution of Thinking

Peter Gärdenfors

Lund University
Cognitive Science
Kungshuset
S-222 22 Lund
Sweden

OXFORD
UNIVERSITY PRESS

OXFORD

UNIVERSITY PRESS

Great Clarendon Street, Oxford OX2 6DP

Oxford University Press is a department of the University of Oxford.
It furthers the University's objective of excellence in research, scholarship,
and education by publishing worldwide in

Oxford New York

Auckland Cape Town Dar es Salaam Hong Kong Karachi
Kuala Lumpur Madrid Melbourne Mexico City Nairobi
New Delhi Shanghai Taipei Toronto

With offices in

Argentina Austria Brazil Chile Czech Republic France Greece
Guatemala Hungary Italy Japan Poland Portugal Singapore
South Korea Switzerland Thailand Turkey Ukraine Vietnam

Oxford is a registered trade mark of Oxford University Press
in the UK and in certain other countries

Published in the United States
by Oxford University Press Inc., New York

A catalogue record for this title is available from the British Library

Library of Congress Cataloging in Publication Data

Data available

Typeset by Newgen Imaging Systems (P) Ltd., Chennai, India
Printed in Great Britain
on acid-free paper by Biddles Ltd, King's Lynn

ISBN 0 19 852851 5 (Pbk: alk. paper)   978 0 19 852851 7 (Pbk: alk. paper)

10 9 8 7 6 5 4 3 2 1

Preface

The fundamental question of humanism is: what is a human being? From a biological point of view, human thinking is unequalled. My aim in this book is to describe how uniquely human thinking has emerged. I view knowledge as biologically grounded and I will start from the theory of evolution. However, as I shall argue, the biological foundation does not conflict with a humanistic outlook. On the contrary, I want to show that much of a humanistic worldview can be derived from an evolutionary story of our origins.

I have dual objectives for the book. On the one hand, I want to present my own theory of the evolution of thinking. The theory is a synthesis of material from several scientific disciplines. On the other, I want to tell a story about how the cognitive capacities of *Homo sapiens* were shaped in a way that is accessible to a general audience. For the latter purpose, much of the academic material has been banished to footnotes and endnotes.

The earlier Swedish version of the book was a result of *The cognitive revolution* project that was conducted at the Institute for Future Studies. I want to thank Professor Åke E. Andersson who initiated the project and the Institute for Future Studies for many kinds of support. The Swedish Foundation for Strategic Research has contributed to a good research environment at the section for Cognitive Science at Lund University, where most of the work on the book has been done. Also Centre Culturel Suédois in Paris was an excellent environment for writing.

The English version of the book has to a considerable degree been updated and revised to bring it in line with the latest developments of research.

I have received help and comments from many people during different stages of the work. I wish to thank Christian Balkenius, Martin Baum, Ingar Brinck, Nils Dahlbäck, Daniel Dennett, Jeanette Emt, Annette Gärdenfors, Ulf Gärdenfors, Agneta Gulz, Magnus Haake, Gisela Håkansson, Lars Hall, Nicholas Humphrey, Petter Johansson, Peter Kitzing, Karina Klok Madsen, Lars Larsson, David de Léon, Jens Månsson, Björn Merker, Mathias Osvath, Mary-Anne Williams, Joanna Rose, Birgitta Sahlén, Sverre Sjölander, Peter Sylwan, Lena Wahlgren, Petra Zücker Björne, and the anonymous reviewers for Oxford University Press. Magnus Haake has congenially drawn many of the illustrations, Ric Fisher and Alan Crozier have been very helpful in the process of translating the text, and Ann Tobin has done excellent detective work in chasing down English versions of the literary quotations I use.

In the book, I am frequently citing the French poet Paul Valéry. Many decades ago, he wrote in one of his aphorisms a strangely close summary of the contents of this book:

> Homo stands on his legs. And he copulates at any season, face to face.
>
> Has an opposable thumb. Is omnivorous. Capable of attention even to objects not before his eyes.
>
> Thanks to what he calls thought, reflection, obsessions, and so forth, he can dream constructively during his waking hours, combining his imaginings with his perceptions and eliciting from them plans of action, co-ordinated movements, a sort of reorganization of his instincts, desires, etc.
>
> He modifies his environments, hoards, keeps what he has got, foresees, and innovates. Has means, in short, of "getting there."

Contents

CHAPTER 1

Thinking from an evolutionary perspective

All our knowledge is ourselves to know.

Alexander Pope

In all times, humans have pondered upon their origins. This is witnessed by the creation stories found in every culture. When Charles Darwin presented his theory of evolution in 1859, a new answer to the question of our origins was given: humans are animals among others and have evolved from ancestors that we have in common with the apes.

In the light of Darwin's theory, the question about our origin instead becomes: what is it that has made humans *different* from other animals? We very much want to identify a characteristic feature that makes us unique. There are many proposals for such a feature: Humans are the only animals who have a symbolic language. Animals have a will, but only human beings have a free will. Humans are also said to be alone in having humour.

When Linnaeus in the 18th century classified all things in nature according to his system of one family name and one species name, humans were called *Homo sapiens*—the knowing Homo.[1] In line with the Linnean definition, this book focuses on our capacities to *think*, to gather *knowledge* about the world, and to be *conscious* of the thinking of ourselves and others. The fundamental question is how these capacities have emerged in the course of evolution.

In this book I will tell my version of the story about the evolution of human thinking. According to Darwin's theory, natural selection is the driving force behind the appearance of new species as well as changes within the species. The individuals who are the fittest in their environment are favoured, and their

---

[1] It is interesting to note that Linnaeus placed one more species in the family Homo, namely *Homo troglodytes*, referring to the chimpanzee that was the only ape known to him. Later the chimpanzee was classified in a different family and is now called *Pan troglodytes*. Thus Linnaeus, long before Darwin, associated humans and chimpanzees, although he did not believe in any evolution of species.

traits spread in later generations. To understand our unique cognitive capacities, the evolutionary forces that have generated *Homo sapiens* must be identified. It is a difficult reconstruction, since during most of the period thinking has not left any direct traces.

The riddle to be solved is how humans developed their capacities to think and their consciousness. Tackling this riddle means solving the world's longest detective story. As clues, volatile thoughts are of little help to prospective evolution detectives. The traces left by thoughts have, until very recent time, only been indirect. To understand how the uniquely human form of thinking has evolved, one must solve a jigsaw puzzle with pieces from a variety of areas—a puzzle where most of the pieces will be lost forever. I will mainly borrow my pieces from other researchers, and I will fit them together in the pattern that I find most coherent. But the riddle is far from solved—future evolution detectives will most likely answer it in different ways.

On the temple in Dephi in ancient Greece was written 'Know thyself!' An investigation of the evolution of thinking is, in my opinion, the best way of understanding what is involved in being human. I thereby agree with what Darwin wrote in the margin of his notebook from 1838, long before he published *The origin of species*: 'Origin of man now proved. Metaphysics must flourish. He who understands baboon would do more towards metaphysics than Locke.'

My main thesis in this book is that the development of an ever-richer *inner world* has provided us with an increasing number of cognitive faculties. In turn, this has led to the evolution of language, to an increasingly more advanced transmission of knowledge between generations, and to culture. I shall argue that most of what is uniquely human can be derived from the mechanisms of our inner worlds.

1.1   The human family tree

In biological taxonomy, humans belong to the greater apes, which in turn are one of the groups of primates.[2] The other species of greater apes are chimpanzee, bonobo (pygmy chimpanzee), gorilla, and orang-utan. Our closest relatives are chimpanzee and bonobo.

Orang-utans are tree dwellers, while the others mainly live on the ground. The apes are predominantly vegetarians, but the chimpanzees also eat some meat and insects. All except the orang-utans live in hierarchical troops dominated by

---

[2]   The lesser apes are the gibbons.

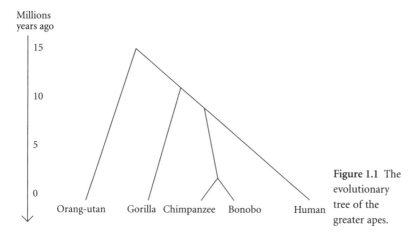

Figure 1.1 The evolutionary tree of the greater apes.

one or several males. One interesting difference between apes and monkeys is that among the former (including Homo), the females move out of the troop in which they were born to join a new troop; among the monkeys and many other social animals it is the males who change troops.

The branch of the evolutionary tree that was to develop into the modern human being diverged from the branch that was to become chimpanzees at least six million years ago.[3] With regard to the biological development, we know quite a lot about how human anatomy has changed since then. We have been able to use various skeletal finds to reconstruct the broad contours of the evolution of the brain and the rest of the body.

During Homo's development from the ancestors we share with the chimpanzees, there has been a gradual growth in the complexity of thinking in which new aptitudes are constantly developing from old ones. Hence there is no clear dividing line we can point to and say, 'That is where *human* thinking began'.

The human forebears on the branch of development that diverged from other apes are called *hominids*. Assumptions about the various hominids are based on archaeological finds that mainly consist of fossilized pieces of skeletons and stone tools. Because of this meagre material, scientists often disagree about species classification and dating—very much is still speculation. A new find of a skeletal piece often leads to a disruption of the previous classification.

---

[3] However, a new find in Chad (see Brunet *et al.* 2002) may push back the separation yet a couple of million of years.

One general apprehension is that a new type of ape emerged on the savannahs. That evolution has been thought to take place in East Africa, so the development is sometimes referred to as 'the East Side Story'.[4] Between approximately eight and five million years ago, the climate in this region became much drier, and many areas that had been rain forest turned into savannah.

Life on the savannah requires good mobility on the ground, so the apes living on the savannah increasingly walked on two legs (instead of using their knuckles like the chimpanzees). One explanation for this is that walking on two legs requires less energy when moving about on open ground. The lower 'hands' develop into 'feet' that are miserable for grasping but better for maintaining balance when moving rapidly on two legs. Another possible explanation is that our ancestors began walking on two legs to reduce the amount of body surface exposed to the sun. Out on the savannah, in contrast to life in the forest, the first hominids were exposed to much more direct sunlight. Today we speculate that we have become less hairy and better at perspiring thanks to the need to regulate body temperature in that climate.

Beasts of prey constitute a greater hazard on the savannah than in the rain forest, and gradually the hominids gathered in bigger groups for better protection and to acquire food more effectively. Over time the brain grew in size in order to cope with the harsher way of life and the increased social complexity. Natural selection saw to it that walking upright (and later, running) became more natural by reshaping the bones of the pelvis, resulting in a smaller and narrower pelvic girdle. In order for the head of a newborn to pass through the pelvis, hominid children were born increasingly underdeveloped. (The brain of a newborn chimpanzee is about 60% of its adult weight, while that of a newborn human child is about 24%.) This in turn meant that the mothers had to be committed to their young for a longer period before they became sufficiently developed to take care of themselves. In addition, human babies are the only ones among the primates that cannot cling onto their mothers by themselves. Their mothers, consequently, became more dependent on other members of the group for food. And increasingly, the father of the child assumed this responsibility.

The earliest known hominids were the *australopithecines* (the name means 'southern apes'), who lived between ca. four and two million years ago.[5] Different fossil finds over large parts of Africa indicate that there were several

---

[4]   Again the new finds in Chad may cast doubt on this story.
[5]   It is unclear whether the new find in Chad should be classified as a hominid, as an early chimpanzee, or as some third branch.

different species.[6] The most famous find from this period is the nearly complete skeleton known as 'Lucy'. She was about one metre tall. One can clearly tell from Lucy's feet and pelvis that the australopithecines walked upright. We conjecture that they had a form of family structure in which food was shared, and a division of labour in which the males were more involved in gathering food and hunting than were the females.

1.2   Enter Homo

The first species traditionally assorted under the Homo family is *Homo habilis*, 'the handy one', who existed between 2.5 and 1.7 million years ago.[7] It is in association with skeletal remains from this species that we have found the earliest, roughly fashioned stone tools. There are certain interesting differences between the australopithecines and the species that belong to the Homo family. The australopithecines have a comparatively small brain and large molars, whereas Homo has a larger brain and smaller molars. The chests of the australopithecines are conical, but Homo chests are barrel-shaped. This is attributed to Homo's having developed the breathing technique required when running, while the australopithecines probably could not run for long distances.

The first clearly human species, *Homo erectus*, 'the upright one', existed between 1.7 million and 300 000 years ago. The designation is not strictly correct because even the australopithecines walked upright. *Homo erectus* had an appreciably larger brain than the earlier hominids. This species was also taller than its predecessors, measuring about 150 centimetres. It emigrated from Africa and colonized substantial parts of the Old World. The so-called Peking man as well as the Java man belong to *Homo erectus*.

In the vicinity of finds of this species we come across considerably more advanced tools of various kinds, particularly well executed, symmetrical stone hand axes. *Homo erectus* also had seasonal dwelling places, which indicates a more highly developed way of life. Their diet was distinctly more based on meat than that of the earlier species. We assume that they could use fire, at least during the later period of their existence (the first traces are about 500 000 years old).

---

[6]   An alternative theory is that the australopithecines did not develop in Africa, but in what is now southern Europe and the Middle East, and that they wandered into Africa while there was a land connection with that continent. A nine million-year-old jaw of a species that has been given the name *Ouranopithecus macedoniensis* has been found in Greece. This species may be an ancestor of the australopithecines.

[7]   However, some modern anthropologists want to place them among the australopithecines.

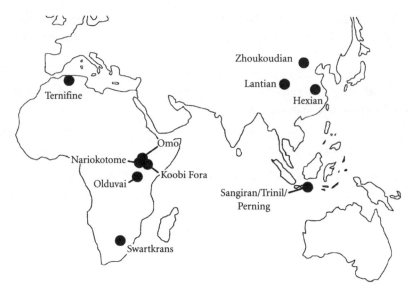

Figure 1.2 The known extension of *Homo erectus*.

Homo sapiens, 'the knowing one', emerged about 200 000 years ago. Its brain was another 20% larger than that of *Homo erectus*. Another anatomical difference, important for theories about the origins of speech, is that *Homo sapiens'* larynx lies low in the throat but high up in the throats of the other hominids and apes. This has been taken as a sign that spoken language developed in connection with the genesis of this species. Culture developed—rites and myths were probably born at a rapid pace. We know that at least 40 000 years ago cultural art forms like cave paintings and engravings appeared.

The Neanderthal man, *Homo neanderthalensis*, who presumably disappeared about 40 000 years ago, has been regarded as a subspecies of *Homo sapiens*. However, more recent genetic studies suggest that this species derived from *Homo erectus* about 500 000 years ago. The Neanderthals were larger and stronger than *Homo sapiens*, but probably less intelligent, and in time they were driven out of competition by the modern human being.

The brain has grown constantly from australopithecines up to *Homo sapiens*. Above all, the cerebral cortex has grown, and especially the frontal lobe. But it is only with *Homo erectus* that we find a brain substantially larger than that of the apes. The increase accelerated additionally with the appearance of *Homo sapiens*. The brain is an energy-consuming organ and requires a nutritious diet. The hominids satisfied the brain's energy requirements by becoming more carnivorous. In order to acquire enough meat, they developed the organized

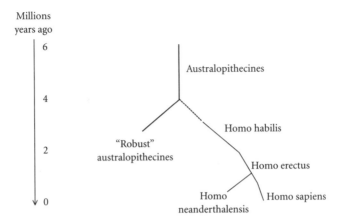

Figure 1.3 A simplified evolutionary tree of the hominids.

hunt. The early hominids probably also fed on carrion and, like the hyenas, made use of the game that other predators had killed.

Neurobiologist Terrence Deacon points out that, from an anatomical point of view, the human being is just one more ape.[i] About 98% of our genes are the same as those of gorillas and chimpanzees. But when considering the *mental* aptitude made possible by a larger brain, we are essentially new in evolution. The question is what the evolutionary powers were that drove the gradual growth of the brain. The size of the brain was naturally significant for the development of the thinking capacity of the hominids. But we cannot know anything directly about their world of ideas; we must draw conclusions from what is known about how our ancestors lived.

The main objective of this book is to tell a story, as coherent as possible, about how the modern human being's way of thinking has come into existence. Most of our thinking capacity, however, is based on what already exists among other animals. Therefore, to understand how humans think we will largely have to consider how other animals do it. To provide better understanding of what is uniquely human, along the way I will make use of what we know about the capacity of other animals (and primarily the primates) to think and to solve problems.

When I was preparing the material for this book, I wanted to gain a little more first-hand knowledge about how animals think. Since I knew there would be many comparisons with monkeys, I decided to acquire one. After a bit of searching, I located an obscure pet shop in Gothenburg that had an old rhesus monkey for sale. The unique thing about this monkey was that it had

Figure 1.4 Egon.

learned to talk—although all the ethologists say that it cannot be done. How Egon, as he is called, learned to do it is still a mystery to me. He says that when he was little he was taken care of by a woman who taught him to speak, but I suspect that there is more to the story . . . .

The store was just about to sell Egon to a circus when I turned up and offered him a more pleasant retirement in my home. Even though Egon has a number of obstinate habits, we have become well acquainted and pretty much agree about things. He likes to sit on my shoulders and poke about in my hair while I sit in front of my computer and write. I customarily read aloud from my manuscript for him, mainly to hear how the text works.

"And remember to write that I am smart," says Egon when I read this to him.

"Of course," I assure him.

As you will notice, Egon has been immeasurably helpful as I have worked on this book—you can even say that he has collaborated with a certain vested interest in the content.

1.3   What is to be explained: the components of thought

> On Earth there is nothing great but man;
> in man there is nothing great but mind.
>
> Sir William Hamilton

Egon sits on the desk and picks his ear. There is a shrewd look about him.

"If you had to choose between being the donor or the receiver during a heart transplant, which would you choose?" he asks.

"I'd want to be the receiver, of course," I reply, somewhat taken aback by the nature of the question.

"Why?"

"That's pretty obvious," I say, somewhat irritated. "The one who donates a heart can't live anymore, but the receiver has a chance."

"But what about a *brain* transplant? Would you want to be the donor or the receiver?"

The question stops me. I am about to answer that in this case I would want to be the donor, because all consciousness is determined by the activities in my brain. But I realize that Egon is up to something, so I say nothing. He works on his other ear.

The most popular opinion today is that your consciousness arises in your brain. If your brain is moved over to another organism, your *self* goes with it. But Egon's question made me wonder about the basis for that opinion.

Brain transplants are still in the realm of science fiction, but given the rapid development of medical technology they may not be far off in the future. The possibility of transplanting hearts has triggered a number of ethical problems. For example, we have switched the criterion for being officially declared dead from cardiac death to brain death. When it becomes possible to transplant brains, or parts of brains, we will face difficult considerations touching on consciousness and personal identity. Related questions have already arisen in the abortion debate (when is a fetus conscious?) and in discussions about animal rights (can a lobster feel pain?).

Philosophers have long tried to describe the nature of thinking and how it relates to the body and its functions. This has often resulted in speculative theories illustrated by quite abstruse hypotheses. But now the edifice of medical technology has almost caught up to the philosophers' castles in the air. Therefore, in order to take a stand on the ethical consequences of various kinds of operations on humans and animals, it is increasingly important to understand consciousness. I will show how an evolutionary approach can offer many clues.

Why does there seem to be a crucial difference between transplanting a heart and transplanting a brain? The explanation is that most of the theories in the contemporary philosophical debate assign thinking exclusively to the brain. Conscious thinking is viewed as the body's guidance system. One popular analogy is that the brain functions something like a computer, and the brain's activities are run by something that resembles a computer program. If you transplant a brain, you transplant all the thoughts that arise in it.

"But what exactly is it you can do when you can think?" asks Egon.

"Hang in there with me a minute, and I'll show you that there are a lot of things."

The philosopher René Descartes maintained that only human beings have a consciousness. According to him, animals are only mechanical automatons.

"Talk about a guy who's living in a world of his own," snorts Egon.

Darwin said that humans were just another of the animals. One result of his theory of evolution is that most people nowadays agree that you can talk about thinking and consciousness even among animals whose brains do not have all the functions of human brains. Since thinking is a complex phenomenon, there is no simple 'Yes' or 'No' answer to the question of whether an organism (or an artificial system) can think; one should talk about *levels* of thinking. Obviously we can distinguish a number of *components* or *functions* in human thinking. These functions did not come into existence all at once—they have appeared and developed gradually during the course of evolution. The components of thinking that I will be sketching are not sharply demarcated, and probably do not constitute a complete list. But I will try to show that they have appeared in the evolution of the animal kingdom by and large in the order in which they are presented below.

Sensations

The philosopher David Hume says that consciousness is nothing more than:

> a bundle or collection of different perceptions which succeed each other with an inconceivable rapidity, and are in a perpetual flux and movement.... The mind is a kind of theatre, where several perceptions successively make their appearance; pass, re-pass, glide away, and mingle in an infinite variety of postures and situations.[ii]

Even if Hume is simplifying, it is obvious that the capacity for *sensation* is a central component of consciousness. If we could not experience sensory perceptions, the other cognitive functions would be meaningless. The author Milan Kundera writes that Descartes' thesis, 'I think, therefore I am', is an asseveration by an intellectual who underrates a toothache.

We actually have more than the so-called five senses, because the sense of touch, for example, can be divided into sensations of temperature, pressure, and pain. It should also be pointed out that the signals deriving from sensory receptors are processed and transformed before a sensation appears in consciousness. The signals from the different senses are treated by separated parts of the brain until, in a later stage of the process, the signals are integrated into an overall experience.

Many species of animals have different types of receptors for phenomena in the world around them, sensory receptors for which we have no equivalent. It is, for example, an intricate question whether the bat's sonar orientation or the bird's reading of magnetic fields mean that they 'experience' the world in a radically different way than we do.[8]

"Yes, it must be hard not to be able to grasp things with your feet," interjects Egon superciliously.

Among the sensations we should also include the *proprioceptive* sensations, i.e. those that inform us about the location of the parts of our bodies and their movements in relation to each other, so that we know where our arms and legs are even in the dark. We are not normally actively aware of these sensations, yet they are naturally important for our daily routines. The philosopher Mark Johnson maintains that our bodily experiences constitute a foundation for all types of conscious thinking.[iii]

Attention

Signals pour in from our sensory receptors. What we call *attention* in everyday practice deals with the ability to focus on a part of the information, to pick and choose from the continuous flow. For example, we focus our gaze on a small part of our surroundings while the remainder of our field of vision plays a subordinate role. We can also control our hearing so that we pay attention to just one voice out of all the chatter that goes on at a party. A useful metaphor is that consciousness is like a poorly lit building where work is going on simultaneously in many places, and attention is like a flashlight that we can point at different parts of the building.

Emotions

Consciousness also contains *emotions*, like fear, anger, joy, and disgust. Emotions are difficult to define and measure. Unlike the case with sensations, there are no special receptors that give rise to feelings.[9] Yet the experiences we classify as feelings are closely connected with different physiological reactions. Although it may be hard to draw a sharp line between the different types of feelings, they all belong to the inner phenomena that we can be conscious of and that are essential for how we live our lives. In contradiction to what Descartes said, that animals are only automatons, it is obvious that animals too have emotions, even though they may not be as rich and varied as ours.[10]

---

[8] The philosopher Thomas Nagel discusses the possibility of 'understanding' the experiences of animals in his 1974 essay, '*What is it like to be a bat?*'

[9] However the two amygdala in the brain seem to be crucial in the creation of emotions.

[10] Darwin (1872) was one of the pioneers in the study of animals' feelings.

Memory

Without *memory* our thinking would not get very far. But there are several different kinds of memory. Psychologist Endel Tulving distinguishes among three main types:[iv]

1. *Procedural* memory, which allows the organism to remember the connections between stimuli and responses of different kinds. When you learn to drive a car, for example, the sensory signals that tell about the location of the pedals, what happens when you turn the wheel, etc. stick in your memory. Later, when you use these memories while driving a car, you do it automatically, routinely, almost unconsciously. Most acquired motor programs build on such memories.

2. *Semantic* memory, which means that we can imagine things that are not perceptually present. This memory makes it possible for the organism to construct a 'mental model' of the world.

3. *Episodic* memory, which allows us to remember individual events and the order in which they have occurred. This type is the conscious memory we use when we think of previous episodes and experiences we have encountered, or when we elicit from our memory facts we have learned from books. Without episodic memory we cannot relate or recount anything.

In Chapter 3 I will show that semantic and episodic memory are required to be able to create an *inner world*. Tulving claims that the order in which memory types are presented here corresponds to the order in which they have emerged in the evolution of the animal world. As we will see, it is probably only human beings that have an episodic memory.

Thoughts and imagination

Thinking is the most central feature of consciousness. There are many ways to think—we can reason, plan, daydream, summon up memories, and so on. We experience an inner world where thinking goes on. Yet we actually know very little about how such processes operate in the brain. So we employ various metaphors to describe thinking—we say that thoughts are 'clear' or 'brilliant', that we can 'follow' a line of reasoning, etc.

Among primitive animals, the nervous system reacts directly to what occurs in their immediate vicinity. Certain organisms, for instance, are drawn to light; this is known as phototaxis. In more highly developed animals, especially in humans, the brain creates its own inner environment that it can use for various kinds of thinking. A dog that chases a rabbit down its hole can imagine that it is there, even though the dog has no direct sensation of the rabbit.

"How can you know whether an animal is thinking or not?" Egon challenges.

"Of course, I cannot know with absolute certainty. But if an animal solves a particular type of problem, for example how to find its way in mazes, in a flexible and systematic manner, I can be reasonably certain that there are cognitive processes in its brain that not only depend on what is given by the animal's senses. In other words, the brain uses *representations* of the world to find new solutions to problems."

"What is a representation?" Egon asks.

"Representations are the building blocks of the inner world. I will discuss this notion in greater detail in the following chapter."

You could say that during the course of evolution, the brain's activities have become increasingly *detached* from the immediate vicinity. I will show that more advanced kinds of thinking are possible only when the brain's activities become unmoored from their anchorage in the surrounding world. By following how the inner world has developed step by step, I will try to explain the evolutionary advantages provided by such a detachment.

To *imagine* means to form mental pictures in an inner world. Imagining is not necessarily goal oriented, but can be viewed rather as *playing* with the possibilities offered by the inner world. A special case of imagining is *daydreaming*. Regarding ordinary dreaming, philosopher Daniel Dennett argues that dreams are *experiences* of the same type as those from our senses.[v] These processes can go on without the need for sensory perception to be engaged, but they presume that there is an inner world.

Planning

If we would lack the capacity to *plan* we would be at a serious disadvantage. Planning means to try to work out a series of actions that will lead to a desired *goal*. In order to plan, we also need some kind of *temporal awareness*: 'First I will do A and then B.' The better we can foresee *when* something is going to happen, the better we can adjust our actions and thereby succeed in our planning.

Planning presumes an ability to imagine. Higher animals seem to be capable of a certain amount of planning, but they can only plan to satisfy needs that they have at the moment. Only humans can consciously foresee that they are going to be hungry tomorrow and thus plan for their *future needs*.

"Whaddya mean, 'higher'?" mutters Egon. "Who's doing the ranking around here?"

"Sorry," I reply, blushing slightly. "When I write about 'higher' and 'lower' species of animals, I by no means imply 'better' or 'lesser'. I'm just going along with the traditional hierarchy. Every animal has its way of life and its way of evaluating the world. A dog that was given a human's sense of smell would surely feel severely handicapped. It is by no means certain that *Homo sapiens* is the jewel in the crown of creation—on the contrary, perhaps our galloping brain will lead us into an evolutionary cul-de-sac."

"Very likely," says Egon with something resembling a wry smile.

Nevertheless, there are some important cognitive differences between primates and other mammals. Psychologist Michael Tomasello and primatologist Josep Call argue that primates are the only mammals that understand 'tertiary relations'.[vi] The term is borrowed from the psychologist Jean Piaget's theory of cognitive development, and it means to understand interactions and relations among objects or individuals in which the observer is not directly involved. As we shall see, primates can, for example, use knowledge of the dominance order in their group for various kinds of actions and they understand the kinship relations between other individuals.[11]

Self-consciousness

It appears that some animals possess *self-awareness*. Chimpanzees, for example, can recognize themselves in a mirror or in a photograph. But that does not mean that they have a self-consciousness in the sense that they can reflect on their being conscious. It is almost certainly only humans who have this ability to consciously focus on their inner processes. Consciousness of death seems to go a step further; for that you must have perceived that your body is going to die, and that your consciousness will probably disappear when your body ceases to function.

Free will

We plan, and we act accordingly. But we also feel that we have *free will*, that we 'could have done it differently'. Philosophers have struggled for centuries with the problem of what this free will actually is, and how it might be reconciled with a physicalistic world-view. It is clear, however, that the experience of a free will is one component in our thinking.

Language

The *ability to use language* as such does not belong to thinking—we are not conscious of what happens when we understand what someone says, or what

---

[11] On the other hand, several researchers have argued that the cognitive abilities of apes are superior to those of the monkeys (this may be a form of anthropomorphism, since apes are more similar to us than are monkeys). Tomasello and Call (1997), pp. 349–50, review the evidence for these claims and find that it is very weak and that much more research is needed. At best there are differences of degree of cognitive capacities.

we ourselves do when we produce spoken sentences. On the other hand, we often experience an inner monologue (or dialogue), that presumes that we have a language faculty. Language, viewed in terms of evolution, is a very recent addition to human abilities. As I will try to show, this is explained by the fact that language presupposes the existence of the other cognitive functions in the list presented here. Not all researchers, however, share my view that language was last to appear among all the powers of thinking.

Each and every one of the components of thinking presented above has an evolutionary function. The question we will be focusing on hereafter is: *What are the evolutionary forces that led to the appearance of these components?* To address that question, I will have to provide a reasonable explanation—for each of the cognitive functions—of why animals (or hominids) with that function enjoy greater fitness and are therefore favoured in the process of natural selection.

I submit that the different functions appear in evolution in approximately the order in which they are presented above. In the rest of this book I will proceed from certain basic functions and move on to discussing the emergence of the others, one by one—especially those that distinguish human beings from other animals. My main concern will be to spell out the functional dependency between different cognitive capacities. A central thesis of this book is that none of the new functions can develop if the others are not already present: you cannot plan if you do not have an inner world, you cannot deceive without being able to plan, you cannot have self-consciousness without being able to deceive, and you cannot have a fully developed language faculty without having self-consciousness. Evolution is a tinkerer and builds on the structures that are already available. Metaphorically, the functional hierarchy of human thinking can be viewed as a cake, in which the lower layers must be finished before you can apply the next layer. One permeating thesis of this book is that the higher you build the cake, the greater becomes the freedom of thought.

Most discussions about brain transplants assume that the brain has sole rights on thinking. But not all thinking occurs in the brain. The brain does not function in splendid isolation: it is highly dependent on the body in which it is located. In order to be able to choose among different plans, you have to be able to *evaluate* the implications of doing one thing or the other. The body's *physiological* reactions play a major role in this task.[vii] If we happen on a dangerous thought, our body reacts—the heart pounds or the legs shake. These reactions are based on physiological systems that are evolutionarily much older than our conscious planning. The philosopher Daniel Dennett says that the brain can reach a wise decision by using the older physiological systems as a sounding board.

Thinking cannot be restricted to the brain, but is located throughout the organism. A brain transplanted into a new body would no doubt feel quite lost. Contrary to prevailing opinion, we should stop regarding the brain as the boss, and view it rather as a *servant* working in the interest of the body.

There is a trend in cognitive science, the theory of *situated* cognition, that goes one step further. The idea is that the brain requires not only the body but also the surrounding world to be able to function. There are many areas where the boundary between sensory organs and the surrounding world is blurred. The submarine commander sees with his periscope, not with his eye. Blind people feel with their canes, not with their hands. In similar fashion, we *think* with our road signs, calendars, and pocket calculators. No clear dividing line can be drawn between the thinking done in the head and that which goes on outside. Consciousness leaks out into the world.

1.4 Four sources of empirical support

"But how can you *know* anything at all about the evolution of thinking?" asks Egon. "Isn't it just a lot of guessing—where you are the one who saws out the pieces of the puzzle?"

"No, not only. I told you that this is a detective story, you know."

In my role as an evolutionary detective I will utilize materials and theories from four different areas. Nevertheless, the available empirical support for the development of thinking is very meagre, so naturally any attempt at reconstruction will contain a goodly dollop of speculation.

1. By studying the behaviour of different animal species, and combining that with knowledge about the species' evolutionary development (known as *phylogeny*), one can establish to a certain extent the components of think- ing to which they have access. It is, of course, difficult to determine what an animal experiences, but by using physiological measurements in combina- tion with behavioural studies one can at least formulate hypotheses that can then be tested. For example, one can argue that certain animals can plan and that they show compassion. Since primates, and particularly apes, are the animals most closely related to *Homo sapiens*, most of my comparative material will be taken from these species.

2. One can acquire another type of evidence by studying how the human brain is constructed, i.e. using material from *neurophysiology*. The brain is usually compared to a walnut when one wants to describe its anatomy. But

a better analogy is to see the brain as an onion: the different layers manage different control functions. The innermost parts are the oldest and answer for the most primitive functions, while the outer layers are younger. In this onion we can then roughly locate the various functions of consciousness. Basic feelings, such as hunger, are managed by the so-called limbic system, which is one of the oldest parts of the brain. This can be used as support for the thesis that feelings are a fundamental part of consciousness and that they exist in a large class of animal species. On the other hand, associative thinking, advanced planning, and a sense of time take place primarily in the frontal lobe, an evolutionarily novel part of the brain that is well developed only in humans. This supports the thesis that advanced thinking and planning exist only among *Homo sapiens.*

3. The third type of empirical evidence derives from studies of children's development—*ontogeny.* It is customary to say that ontogeny reflects phylogeny, i.e. that the growth of the embryo of a species of animal and the time after its birth pass by and large through the same stages as the evolution of the species. Proceeding from this assumption, one can apprehend the order in which various thinking abilities have appeared during the course of evolution. Naturally one does not assume that the ontogenetic development is exactly parallel with the phylogenetic, but in combination with material from the other two areas, studying children's thinking can contribute further pieces to the puzzle of evolution.

4. Finally, *archaeological* (and anthropological) material is of course a source of knowledge about how human thinking has developed. We can draw conclusions about how the human brain has changed by studying the fossils of skulls that have been found. And starting with the period when the hominids began making tools out of stone and other durable materials, we can find further clues that can be utilized in working on the puzzle of human thinking. Yet there is a giant step from skulls or stone axes to the thinking of hominids, so the conclusions are seldom certain.

Even if the archaeological material can be dated, the big problem is to decide when the different cognitive functions, e.g. speech, come into existence. Researchers in the area are often in serious disagreement.[12] But the exact

---

[12] I largely follow the time scale presented by psychologist Merlin Donald in his book *Origins of the modern mind.* In addition to Donald's account, which I find attractive, there are other such stories about the development of consciousness, e.g. in Chapter 7 of Dennett's book *Consciousness explained,* Part III of his *Darwin's dangerous idea* and in Noble and Davidson's *Human evolution, language and mind,* but it turns out that our reconstructions are quite different. An older, more biologically oriented analysis of a similar nature can be found in Konrad Lorenz, *Behind the mirror.*

dating is not particularly important for my purposes—what is important is to get the evolutionary *order* of the different cognitive functions right.

1.5   Early stages in the evolution of thought

The poet Paul Valéry says in one of his aphorisms that the task of a mind is to create a future. Many analyses of different types of consciousness deal precisely with how rich their images of the future are.

In *Darwin's dangerous idea*, Dennett presents a four-step model for the development of consciousness. The lowest level is *Darwinian beings*, which consists of all systems guided by natural selection, which is to say all organisms.[13] The most primitive of these systems have no future except for that which lies in the possibility of reproducing themselves.

For those who want to look farther into the future, it is wise to see farther off in *space*. Many Darwinian beings have reached that stage of development. Organisms that have different systems of perception, e.g. sight or hearing, can apprehend things that happen at a distance and thus have better possibilities of fleeing from danger, finding food, and locating a partner. They can *prepare themselves* and thereby win decisive points in the evolutionary arena.

Even relatively 'simple' species of animals must be said to have sensations. They possess receptors that send signals to the organism, which are processed by their nervous systems and have an influence on behaviour. Probably sensations from the body also turn up at a comparatively early stage in the development of the animal kingdom, conveniently along with a certain capacity for *attention*. Attention can be viewed as a tool for directing the organism to the information of most relevance for what it should do next. Organisms are also *motivated* to do what they do because certain needs must be satisfied. Normally we are totally unaware of our needs, but they do guide our behaviour.

It is easy to explain why sensations are evolutionarily valuable: every organism that wants to interact with its environment depends on sensations in order to do that efficiently. It must be able to distinguish between food and non-food, to avoid being injured or devoured, and to find a partner if it is an organism that propagates sexually. The development of sensitive sense organs in an animal species has very largely contributed to increasing the 'fitness' of individuals, i.e. their ability to survive and propagate. In what follows, I will assume sensation, attention, and motivation as a nucleus for thinking, and then inquire into what

---

[13] The other three levels, which will be introduced later, are Skinnerian beings, Popperian beings, and Gregorian beings. *See also* Dennett (1996).

it is that has led to the development of such a 'protoconsciousness' into increasingly more complex systems.[14]

An organism that harbours a protoconsciousness does not necessarily possess a capacity for *learning*. This does not mean that organisms on the Darwinian level cannot carry out very complex patterns of behaviour. But these are genetically programmed. A female wasp of the family Sphex who is 'programmed' to lay eggs first digs a hole in the sand, then goes out looking for a caterpillar from a large white butterfly, anaesthetizes it with a sting, lugs it back to the hole, checks that everything is as it should be, pulls in the caterpillar, lays her eggs in it, and then covers the hole with sand.

The chains of actions that are 'pre-programmed' in this fashion are called *tropisms*. The wasp cannot adapt her pattern of behaviour or otherwise re-learn it. For example, if you move the caterpillar a couple of centimetres while the female is inside checking out the hole, the first thing she does is lug the caterpillar back to the hole and then go in to check it out once more. If you move the caterpillar again, the same procedure is repeated over and over again. Here we can say definitely that the Sphex wasp has no 'planned' conduct.

Another intricate example is how termites build their stacks. Termite stacks are complicated structures with many vaults and passages. Yet there is no architect who draws up a blueprint and no construction foreman in charge. The termites have no 'picture' whatsoever of what they are doing. They roll their clumps of mud that, from the outset, were randomly laid out. The balls of mud, or clay, contain a fragrance that is irresistible. The termites like to leave their balls where the fragrance is strongest. Actually, this is the only thing that guides them.

What happens then is interesting. A ball that is already on the ground smells strongest. Thus the new balls are most often placed over the old ones. In this way small pillars of mud arise. But if two pillars come close to each other, the odour from the other pillar affects a termite that was about to place a ball on the one side, meaning that the ball comes to lie a little closer to the other pillar. The higher the pillars rise, the more they come to influence each other. As a result, they begin to lean towards each other, and—presto!—the termites have quite mindlessly constructed an arch. One arch is followed by others, and after an enormous number of mud balls the gothic form of the termite stack has grown up. The termites observe one single principle: put your mud ball where the fragrance is strongest! The physical laws of the surrounding world see to it that the result is an architectonically sophisticated stack that provides suitable protection for its builders.

---

[14] For those who want to know more about the evolutionary background of the functions in the protoconsciousness, I recommend Nobel Prize winner Konrad Lorenz's book *Behind the mirror*.

Higher animals can also demonstrate tropisms that can express themselves in routine actions. A dog can turn round and round in its bed for quite a while before lying down, even though there is no grass to tramp down. A weaverbird in captivity, although it lacks building materials, can go through the entire pattern of behaviour for weaving a twig into the nest. It acts as though it were 'hallucinating' the twig.

The disadvantage of pre-programmed patterns of behaviour is precisely that they are *inflexible*. An organism that can use experience or changes in its environment to vary its behaviour has an advantage in the process of natural selection.

"When I do something," says Egon, "I don't think very much. I just do what feels best at the moment."

The next component in the list of what consciousness contains is emotions. How can feelings be valuable in the struggle for existence? One reasonable answer is that sensations of changes are not enough in a changing environment; a successful organism must also be able to quickly and efficiently *evaluate* what is happening in its surroundings. If a predator approaches, you must be able to discern that it constitutes a danger and tell your body to prepare itself physiologically for escape. Or, if an organism's territory is endangered, one generally advantageous strategy is to exhibit threatening behaviour. It is no coincidence that the feelings we experience are coupled to a cascade of physiological reactions that prepare our bodies for different types of behaviour. When you suddenly find yourself in a dangerous traffic situation, for example, the rush of adrenaline through your body is clearly perceptible.

Basic physiological needs guide the behaviour of simple organisms. But the mechanisms of the needs are relatively slow processes. Feelings complement them by quickly evaluating different aspects of the surroundings and how acute the needs are. A feeling of hunger can be counteracted by the fear an animal feels when confronted by hostile surroundings, thus heightening its ability to adapt. Somewhat abstractly, we can describe feelings as parameters for behavioural strategies. The strengths of different feelings are weighed against one another to decide on a suitable action. An animal with feelings that function in this way demonstrates much more flexible behaviour than if the animal were guided exclusively by needs.

1.6   Skinnerian beings

Still more flexible (or 'open', as Konrad Lorenz calls it) is an organism that can adapt the strength of its feelings in line with the *experiences* it accumulates.

The insect that seems scary on a fox cub is perhaps actually good to eat, so it would be advantageous to be able to break the habit of fear. But to be able to accumulate experiences, the organism must be able to *learn* something, and not just blindly follow the genetically transferred patterns of behaviour. Being able to adapt one's reactions to feelings in line with what one has experienced is of course valuable from an evolutionary perspective.

The second level on Dennett's ladder is called *Skinnerian beings* after the behaviourist Frederic Skinner. Such organisms have the ability to learn from their experiences. Behaviour that yields positive results is reinforced and will with higher probability be repeated in the future, whereas unsuccessful behaviour will be avoided. Through such learning, the organism will become better equipped to confront the future.

One elementary form of learning, found even among primitive animals, is becoming accustomed to a stimulus, which is called *habituation*. For example, careful studies have been conducted of how individual nerve cells in sea hares (*Aplysia*) accustom themselves to electric shocks.[viii]

But a more interesting form of learning is the *conditioning* that has been studied by psychologists and ethologists ever since Pavlov's famous experiments in which dogs learned to salivate when a bell rang. By repeating different combinations of stimuli and rewarding the desired behaviour (or punishing undesirable behaviour), one can use conditioning to get animals to learn complex patterns of behaviour. For the branch of psychology called behaviourism, it is only the couplings between stimulus and response that are regarded as suitable for scientific study. Everything involving thinking and consciousness is not considered proper science in this research paradigm. The evolutionary value of learning through conditioning is obvious: an animal that learns that food is often available at a certain place or at a certain time, for example, is better adapted than another animal that more randomly searches for food. Expressed in terms the behaviourists would never accept, you could say that conditioning creates *expectations* in the animal.

"In my younger days, some other rhesus monkeys and I spent several years in a cage in a laboratory full of devout behaviourists," says Egon. "After a while we got pretty good at conditioning."

"You mean that you monkeys learned what the psychologists wanted you to learn?" I wonder.

"That's just what we did. We actually learned a lot faster than the white coats expected. But we soon realized that if we adapted ourselves at a reasonable pace, we got more peanuts and bananas than if we learned quickly. As long as our learning curves confirmed their theories, we reinforced their reward behaviour."

"Aha, you mean that it was the monkeys who conditioned the behaviourists and not the other way around."

"You finally got it," sighs Egon.[15]

The behaviourists' approach to learning makes the form of behaviour called *trial-and-error* comprehensible. By testing new behaviours, an animal can discover 'unexpected' consequences and it benefits from *remembering* the behaviours that produce success in some respect. This kind of learning is by and large the sort of conditioning studied by Skinner and other behaviourists. Consider for example the great tit that pecks at just about anything. In England these birds have learned to peck a hole in the caps on the milk bottles delivered to the front steps of houses to get at the top cream. Without learning in the form of conditioning, trial-and-error behaviour would not work. New behaviours are discovered through *curiosity* and *play*, and this gives rise to a broader spectrum of learning possibilities.

The abilities I have introduced up to now, i.e. perception, attention, emotions, and learning via conditioning, provide a behavioural system that contains the level of behaviourism and a bit more. The behaviourists did not want to include feelings or attention in their models because these factors were difficult to describe as couplings between stimulus and response.

Various advocates of behaviourism, especially Skinner, have maintained that learning via conditioning is all we need to consider, even with regard to human beings. They hardly tolerate any discussion of thinking and consciousness. Even if we do not accept their methodology, it seems that the form of memory that arises via conditioning is in general not 'accessible' to consciousness. Hence we have 'knowledge' that we cannot elevate to a conscious level.

Yet stimulus–response learning does not account for all forms of learning. Many animal species conduct themselves intelligently in new types of situations where they have had no opportunity to be exposed to conditioning; 'intelligent' in the sense that they can utilize previous experiences and *adapt* them to the conditions of the new situation. To explain this ability we need to assume a more advanced form of learning and a different mechanism than conditioning. Another limitation of conditioning as a method of learning is

---

[15] This anecdote is not entirely unrealistic. Savage-Rumbaugh and Lewin (1994), p. 64, write about the language training of the chimpanzees Sherman and Austin: 'As teachers holding up objects, we assumed that the object we were showing the chimp would serve as the 'stimulus object' since it preceded the response. The chimps, however, were assuming that the symbol-key they selected served as the 'stimulus' for us to give them food. They looked for a link between the symbol they depressed and whether or not we elected to give them food—and if so, what sort of food. They paid no attention to the 'stimulus item' we displayed.'

that it is *time-consuming*: usually a stimulus must be repeated many times and the response rewarded or punished every time before the real coupling can occur.[16]

Notes

i. Deacon (1997), p. 23.
ii. *A treatise of human nature*, Book 1, Part IV, Section VI.
iii. Johnson (1987).
iv. Tulving (1985).
v. Dennett (1978), Chapter 8.
vi. Tomasello and Call (1997), pp. 370–4.
vii. Damasio (1995).
viii. Hawkins and Kandel (1984).

---

[16] However, there are cases where the connection between stimulus and response is established after a single exposure, but such connections seem to work mainly to avoid poisonous food and other biologically fundamental dangers (Garcia and Koelling 1966).

CHAPTER 2

Sensation, perception, and imagination

The most obvious anatomical change during the evolution of the hominids is the body's adaptation to walking upright. But when it comes to thinking, the rapid growth of the cortex is more important news. In particular, the frontal lobe grows and that is what we assume to be the seat of the higher cognitive functions. The function of the cortex is primarily to create *representations* of events in the surrounding world. Roughly speaking, an 'inner' representation is something in the brain that is used instead of the object itself.[1]

I believe that in order to understand how most higher forms of thinking function, we must recall that animals (and humans) represent the world around them and its possibilities in different ways. In my presentation I shall divide the different elements in the consciousness into:

1. *Sensations* that are the immediate sensory impressions.

2. *Perceptions* that are *interpreted sensory impressions*. Perceptions form one category of representations.

3. *Imaginations* (or images) that are not directly governed by sensory impressions. I will also call them *detached representations*. Imaginations and perceptions are the elements from which the inner world is constructed.

I submit that this is the evolutionary order in which the different functions appear. Even simple organisms have sensations—sensory impressions that report what is happening with the body. More advanced animals have perceptions that consist of interpretations of sensations. In particular, perceptions can provide knowledge about what is going on in the animal's immediate surroundings. It is probably only mammals (and perhaps birds) that have imaginations—in their inner world they can direct their thinking towards something that is not immediately present in the surrounding environment.

---

[1] In Chapter 8 I will discuss 'external' representations, i.e. those that people put out in the world to serve as an aid to memory or to communication.

2.1   Sensations: being aware of the world

On my desk are a number of things I have brought home from my various trips—some snails, a razor clam, and a prickly sea urchin. Egon can't help investigating them. Naturally he pricks himself on the sea urchin's spikes.

"Ouch!" he yells. "That hurts!"

The sensation of pain that Egon has is the result of nerve signals from his fingers to his brain. These types of experiences are probably the most original components of the consciousness. The philosopher Karl Popper writes:

> We must assume that consciousness grows from small beginnings; perhaps in its first form a vague feeling of irritation, experienced when the organism has a problem to solve such as getting away from an irritant substance.[i]

Our subjective world of experiences is full of such *sensations*: tastes, smells, colours, itches, pains, sensations of cold, sounds, etc.[2] They provide an *awareness of the world*. One important thing to notice is that I can have a sensation without knowing *what* gives me the sensation. For example, I can detect a scent without recognizing it as the smell of a honeysuckle even if I know very well what a honeysuckle is and how it smells.

My basic assumption is that all components in the consciousness have a biological function. So if sensations are fundamental, what is their function? The psychologist Nicholas Humphrey says in his book *A history of the mind* that the biological role of sensations is to tell about what is *happening right now* to the organism.

The sensations often involve an (unconscious) *evaluation* of whether what is happening is good or bad. This is sometimes referred to as 'raw feels'. They facilitate a decision about what should be done and thus prepare the organism to *act*. These decision processes do not by any means have to be conscious. Sensations are often closely aligned with basic choice of action—eat, fight, flee, or mate. This applies especially to more primitive organisms.

Humphrey formulates a number of criteria that characterize sensations:

1. Sensations belong to the subject: They deal with what happens to *me*.

2. Sensations are localized in the body. You cannot describe a sensation without telling *where* in your body you experience it. When I burn my foot stepping on a hot coal, that is a different experience than when I burn my hand.

3. Sensations are modality specific. We have visual experiences, auditory experiences, etc. and these cannot merge into one another.

---

[2]   This is what philosophers of mind call *qualia*.

4. Sensations exist in the present. They are about what is happening to the body here and now.

Descartes is famous for the thesis 'Cogito, ergo sum'—I think, therefore I am. In other words, he viewed thinking as a criterion for consciousness. But Humphrey proposes that we replace the thesis with 'Sentio, ergo sum'—I feel, therefore I am. A minimum requirement for being conscious is to have sensations.

This idea receives support from the fact that when we are awake, we can hardly avoid receiving impressions from our sense organs. Only intense practice, to which some Buddhists devote themselves, can turn off sensations. Wordsworth expresses it beautifully:

> The eye—it cannot choose but see;
> We cannot bid the ear be still;
> Our bodies feel, where'er they be,
> Against or with our will.

Sensations need not give rise to conscious experiences. This can be established by the fact that experiences assume a kind of *attention*, but not all sensations do so. Where you are sitting (or lying) just now, what is supporting your thighs develops a certain pressure, but you have no experience of this sensation until my text draws your attention to it. The experience does not exist until you focus on the sensation in your thighs. In a certain sense, then, experiences are exercises in attention. Certain sensations are extremely assertive (for example a toothache), but the conscious experience we have depends on how much attention we pay to the feeling. You can significantly reduce the experience of pain by concentrating on something else.

Even the most basic kinds of experience, then, require some degree of attention. But our conscious relationship to the world consists of more than sensations. As I said, I will distinguish sensations from *perceptions* and *imaginations*. In order to explain what I mean by these concepts, I will now execute a brief detour.

2.2   The art of aiming—why chimpanzees cannot throw darts

While preparing to write this book I have made notes on small pieces of paper. Now as I enter these notes in my manuscript, I crumble up the slips of paper and toss them one after the other into the wastebasket. It stands a couple of metres from my desk, so this is a bit of a game. But I hit the target most of the time—at least four out of five tries. Egon thinks that tossing these balls of paper is a cool game. But very rarely does he hit the basket—his wads of paper lie spread out all over the floor.

"You're lousy at throwing," I say to Egon.

"Whaddya mean, lousy? I throw just as far as you do."

"Yeah, but that's not the point. You can't aim—your wads land far from the wastebasket."

"How do you aim?"

The question surprises me. After a muddled discussion I realize that Egon has no ability to aim. He quite simply cannot guide his arm in the direction of a target when he throws. I search the literature and discover that apes cannot aim.[3] Yet this ability was naturally important evolutionarily for the hominids on the savannah when they began to hunt game or when they were defending themselves from predators.

"Come on down to the pub with me and have a beer," I say, "and we can watch the dart players. They can really aim. From a distance of three metres they can throw a dart with great accuracy at a target only a couple of square centimetres big."

"Beer makes me feel strange—I don't know why."

So I assume that it was of great evolutionary value to be able to aim when you throw. The question is how the hominids, in contrast to the other apes, have changed in body and brain to be able to accomplish that.

"What happens when you throw?" wonders Egon, showing real interest for a change.

"Well, you hold an object in your hand while you move your arm so that your hand picks up speed in the right direction and then you release the object at the right moment, often with a flick of your wrist."

"So what's hard about that?"

"The main challenge is to know whether you are steering your arm in the right direction in relation to the object you want to hit."

"So can't you feel that?"

---

[3] One reference is from Jane Goodall, who with exemplary patience has studied chimpanzees in the Gombe reserve in Tanzania. She has recorded that of 44 observed tosses of an object towards other animals, only five hit the mark. Those that did hit were thrown from a distance of less than two metres (van Lavick-Goodall 1968). See also Calvin (1982, 1983). On the other hand, Westergaard *et al.* (2000) have shown that capuchin monkeys can throw stones with considerable accuracy. They also use throwing as a way of sending food between themselves. Interestingly enough, female capuchine are just as good at throwing as males, while in humans males are significantly better. As Corballis (2002), p. 77, remarks, this suggests that 'in humans the sex difference in throwing ability is at least partly biological rather than cultural.'

The throw begins in the cerebrum and is guided by the cerebellum. Naturally, the brain gets feedback from the sensors in the muscles of the hand and arm about the direction they are taking during the throw. This feedback is part of what is called proprioception. The catch is that the signals that come back from the muscles via the nerve fibres are too *slow*. It has been calculated that the loop from the signals that go from the brain to the muscles and back to the brain takes something between 200 and 450 milliseconds. (In that time a 100 metre sprinter runs between two and five metres.) Unfortunately, that is much too long for the brain to be able to check that the arm is moving in the right direction during a throw.

"So you don't have time to feel whether you've thrown in the right direction before it's too late?"

"That's right."

"But so how can you aim?"

This is where the big news comes in. A kind of *simulator* has been created in the brain that quickly estimates what the *anticipated* result of the signals to the muscles will be.[ii] The signals that leave the motor part of the cortex are sent by the cerebellum to both the arm and the simulator. A calculation is made in the brain of what is about to happen in the arm and the result is sent back to the cerebellum, which adjusts the arm's continuing movement.

The calculation loop in the simulator is faster than the loop that goes via the body's muscles. It has been estimated that the brain can actually correct a signal it has sent to the muscles within 70 milliseconds. That is significantly faster than the 200–450 milliseconds it takes for the signal to reach the muscle and return. So the simulator manages to adjust the arm's movements during the throw much more quickly than what one can accomplish with the muscular feedback. The faster you want to throw a projectile, the less time you have to steer your arm. Without such a simulator we would never be able to solve the control problem involved in the art of aiming. But we do not know exactly how the simulator is implemented in the brain.

"But how can you know that the simulator estimates correctly?"

When the body is going to solve a new problem, of course the simulator will guess wrong at first. Anyone standing in front of a dartboard for the first time is not going to throw the darts with much accuracy. But if we assume that the neurons in the brain that are part of the simulator gradually adjust their calculations in accordance with how we have succeeded in previous attempts, the simulator will eventually be able to make precise predictions of the result of a motor signal from the brain.

The simulator *bluffs* in the sense that it has not received any real feedback from the body. But with careful training it can learn to bluff sufficiently believably so that it pays off better for the rest of the brain to 'trust' it than to wait for the slower message from the muscles' nerve fibres. Otherwise we could never learn to aim with anything like precision.

The simulator provides a mechanism with whose help we can guide the direction and force of our limbs' movements with great accuracy. We need this not only to be able to aim when we throw; it is also important for being able to knap a piece of flint into an axe, for example. You need precise guidance of your hand and the right knapping action—and of course a lot of practice—to be able to knap away the right size pieces of flint in the right place so that you obtain a well-formed axe. There are actually great similarities between the movement you make when you throw a stone and what you do when knapping flint. Throwing can therefore be a skill that hominids needed to master before they were able to form stone tools.[4] It turns out that during the hominids' evolution, not only the shape of the hand but also the shoulder section changed in such a way that made throwing much more effective.

People are right- or left-handed (apes too, but less clearly). When right-handed persons throw, they aim much better with the right hand than with the left. The simulator has evidently specialized itself on guidance with one hand. There is an interesting experiment that supports this.[iii] The subjects were asked to drum with their fingers as fast as they could, with both the left and the right hand. It turned out that they could drum equally fast with both hands, regardless of whether they were left- or right-handed. But the rhythm was significantly more *even* in the dominant hand (apes cannot keep the beat at all, as we will see later). The experiment reveals that one has better timing in the dominant hand. And this is probably where we find the explanation for why one aims better with one hand.

2.3   Perceptions: seeing the world

Everything takes refuge in the brain. The 'world' to be and recognize itself ever so little; the Being to meet itself, to communicate itself, and to complicate itself.—The human brain is a place where the world pricks and pinches itself to make sure that it exists. *Man thinks*, therefore *I am*, says the Universe.

Paul Valéry

Sensations relate what is about to happen with an organism *right now*. They often contain an emotional component that evaluates what is going on. But an

---

[4]   Grush (1997) thinks that we should perhaps be thankful that the neurons to and from the muscles are as slow as they are. If evolution had not invented the simulator processes, our thinking could not have developed.

organism that can not only find out what is happening with its own body but also receives signals about *what is going on out there in the world* has better opportunities to foresee the future and thus survive in an inhospitable world. This is the role of the *perceptions*. First and foremost, perceptions provide information about the spatial structure of the world and what physical objects are in it.

My hypothesis is that perceptions build on the type of simulator described in the previous section. There I argued that you become much better at aiming if there is a mechanism that more quickly *fills in* the result of the signals sent to the muscles. Even if I cannot justify it for all of the processes I call perceptions, I assume that there are similar complementing mechanisms for many other types of sensations.[iv] Perceptions are sensations that are *reinforced* with simulations.

"It's a pretty bold assumption that there are simulators for all perceptions," objects Egon.

"Yes, I admit that. But I want to show that the hypothesis can explain a number of features in the evolution of thinking, and that it is interesting for that reason alone.[5] Naturally the assumption has to be supported by experimental studies before I can thoroughly embrace it."

One important property of a simulator is that it does not need to rely exclusively on the signals coming from sense organs: it can also *add on* new types of information that can be useful in simulating. It does not matter much if this information has no direct counterpart in the surrounding world as long as the simulations produce the right result, i.e. lead to appropriate actions. This way the simulator's output will be richer than the influx of sensations.[v] As we shall see, much of our reasoning about *causes* depends on this kind of addition.

In the early 20th century, gestalt psychologists studied the multiplicity of perceptual mechanisms that fill in what is taken in by the senses. They sought to formulate the 'laws' that determine how the perceptions are organized. They called the results of perceptions *gestalts*. The triangle that appears to exist in the picture below is a good example of such a gestalt. Because of the strong dominance of behaviourism, these insights were neglected—after all, they dealt with mental processes, which were taboo for the behaviourists. But with the emergence of cognitive science in the late 1950s, the results of the gestalt psychologists received renewed attention. And now, moreover, we have much

---

[5] A similar theory is proposed by the psychologist Lawrence Barsalou (2000). He introduces 'perceptual symbols' as the entities that carry the detached thinking. Through several examples he shows that different cognitive mechanisms can be explained with the help of perceptual symbols. Barsalou also assumes that related perceptual symbols are organized in 'simulators'. But his notion of simulators appears to be different from the one described here.

Figure 2.1 The Kaniza triangle.

greater capacities to understand the brain processes behind the Gestaltists' constructions.

The brain is full of mechanisms that contribute new information. In particular, there are many well-studied examples of the visual process. When we see an object, we sense that it has *contours*, for example. But if we examine the influx of light that hits the retina, we find nothing that corresponds to such contours—they are part of the information that the visual process *constructs*.

Look, for example, at Figure 2.1.

Our perceptions tell us that a white triangle lies on top of three black circles. Yet in the figure there are no lines marking off the sides of the triangle from the white surroundings. The lines are a construction of our brains. There is a mechanism in the brain that simulates the existence of lines among the segments of the circles.[vi] You could also say that we *represent* what we see as a triangle.

Phenomena such as this are very common and well known from psychophysics. They show that we have plenty of simulators that *complement* the signals provided by our senses. Such complementations create the *representations* with which thinking works, since what we experience is not only that which is presented by our sensory receptors but also that which is recreated, i.e. *represented*, by our simulators.[6] The filled-in representations are what I call perceptions. In other words, perceptions are *constructions* of what is going on around us.

---

[6] For a more thoroughgoing discussion of the concept of representation and a comparison with other definitions, see Gärdenfors (1996a). I regard representations as *theoretical quantities* from the way they are treated in scientific theory. Representations are idealizations, in the same way as the concept 'force' for example is used in Newtonian mechanics to *predict* and *explain* empirical phenomena. See also Lachman and Lachman (1982) for a defense of this view of representations. Thus my epistemological stance is what is usually called instrumentalist.

"Whaddya mean, constructions?" protests Egon. "Are you saying that what I see doesn't exist in the world?"

"No, no. Of course most of what you see also exists outside your head. But your brain fills in what reaches your eyes so you can more easily understand what you see."

"But how do I know I can trust my brain to fill in right?"

"By believing that you are well-adapted to the world you find yourself in. But the constructions our brains supply us with are not perfect. Just think, for example, about all the visual illusions the psychologists have discovered."

"Why should we have a brain that makes up things that don't exist? All that which already exists out there in the world—isn't that enough?"

Our senses don't give us information about everything that exists in the world. The evolutionary point is that the richer representations help us *predict* what the world will look like. They create the future in advance. If I see the front side of a woman, I naturally imagine that she has a back (only the wood nymph has no back). If I hear the roar of a lion, I'm not so dumb that I can't imagine the whole lion. In that way I am prepared for what can happen in the world and thus for suitable action.

If the sensation is weak or incomplete, as in Figure 2.2, it may be difficult to turn it into a perception. For many, it is initially just a number of black blobs on a white surface. However, if I tell you that it is a picture of an elephant, I hope that you can make the blobs fall into a coherent pattern (the right tusk is the protruding line to the left and the tip of the trunk is in the lower left corner). The transition between seeing it as incoherent black blobs and seeing it as an elephant is just the transition between a sensation and a perception. Once you have seen that the pattern depicts an elephant, the pattern 'locks' into a perception and it is difficult to go back to the pure sensation.

The weaker the sensations, the more important it is for the brain to create its own perceptions. In fact, we are so dependent on perceptions that if

Figure 2.2 Incomplete object.

someone prevents us from having sensations, we soon begin to hallucinate.[7] Dreams are in a like category, where sensations are similarly turned off. Dreams do not have to be connected to sensations, and hence they become less controlled. The author Horace Engdahl writes in *Meteorer*: 'Dreams resemble a family dinner where something goes wrong. The waking world is a place where things *keep a straight face*. In dreams they fall out of their roles and become embarrassingly voluble.'

Sensations undoubtedly appeared before perceptions in evolutionary history. Sensations only need signals from the sense organs (sensory impressions) and from the body itself (proprioceptions) in order to function. But because the genesis of different simulators has given rise to perceptions, the sensory organs play a double role. When I smell the scent of a honeysuckle, the sensation answers the question 'What is happening to me?' while the perception answers the question 'What is happening out there?' Humphrey says that sensations give us *egocentric* information while perceptions contribute *allocentric* (outside the self) information. The two types do not exclude each other. One and the same experience, e.g. a scent, can simultaneously be both a sensation and a perception.

The ability to *categorize* is a special case of using representations. When a bird not only sees an object but sees it *as food*, the bird's brain adds to the information about the object seen, which leads to the bird's swallowing it, for example. Since the animal in its perception adds to information that does not come from the surrounding world, *mistakes* become possible. A mistake occurs when the behavioural conclusions derived from categorization turn out to lead to undesirable consequences. ("Pardon me," said the hedgehog, and climbed down off the scrubbing brush.)

2.4   Categorical perception: sorting the world into boxes

We have been endowed with brains that fill in incomplete patterns because such mechanisms improve our chances of surviving. Some of the mechanisms that search for patterns are provided genetically. Others are learned (even if we are not conscious of it). There is a phenomenon called *categorical perception* in cognitive psychology. This means that a reality for which there are no sharp boundaries is sorted into distinct compartments by our perceptual

---

[7]   Sjölander (1984), pp. 43–57, writes that perceptions can be seen as controlled hallucinations— the content comes from within, but is guided by sensations.

mechanisms. When the perception is created, our brains add boundaries that have no correspondence in reality. The boundaries are provided by a system of *categories* that are usually a product of learning.

We can take an example of categorical perception from our apprehension of shapes. Psychologist Robert Thouless conducted a simple study in the early 1930s that has become classic.[vii] He placed a round plate on the table and asked his subjects to look at it from different angles. What they saw was more or less elliptical. Then they were asked to describe how the plate looked from their perspective, either by drawing it or by matching it with various elliptical shapes provided by Thouless. The subjects without exception described their perceptions of the plate as *rounder* than how they actually saw it, i.e. as rounder than the image that fell on their retina. Their knowledge that the object was actually a round plate thus influenced their perception of it. What we think we see is not always what we see. The same type of effect turns up, though much more markedly, with regard to our memories. We remember what we expect to remember.

Another example of categorical perception is the phonetic discovery concerning our apprehension of a spoken sound, what we call phonemes. The sound differences found for example among the consonants in 'ba', 'da', and 'ga' (so-called plosives) vary gradually along a physical dimension. If you create synthetic sounds in the laboratory and have this dimension gradually change, the subjects will still hear the sounds as three separate consonants with no unclear intermediate positions. This example shows that the differences are levelled out in the perceptual classification created by the category system. Two sounds filed in the same category are thus apprehended as more similar to each other than they 'really' are, i.e. if one makes a comparison with the results of physical measurements.

A third example is musical. Using a tone generator it is easy to create sounds with different frequencies. Then, in controlled experiments, you can study how subjects apprehend different combinations of tones. If you play a chord that contains a pure F and a pure C and a third tone that falls between an A flat and an A, the subjects will apprehend the chord either as an F minor chord (here the intermediate tone is experienced as an A flat) or as an F major chord (where the intermediate tone is experienced as an A). The intermediate tone is never experienced as false or as a borderline case because our perception *interprets* it as one of the 12 tones in the scale.

It is important to note that the tonal pattern that is apprehended (interpreted) by our brains is *culturally* conditioned. Just think about how Westerners experience oriental music! Our perception is governed by a scale that contains

12 halftones.[8] There are 17 tones in the Arabian musical scale, and 21 in the Indian. To Western ears trying to sort the tones in an Indian raga or an Arabian love song under our 12 tone scale, such music sounds whiny, because one cannot get it completely 'in tune'. One cannot hear the pattern because the categorical ear cannot break the code. Or as Goethe says in one of his maxims, 'We hear only what we understand'.

2.5 Object permanence: the world outside our sensations

Egon is still troubled by my assertion that the world he experiences is largely a construction.

"Is the world there when I close my eyes?" he wonders.

"Of course it is, you dummy. We wouldn't be able to conduct ourselves very meaningfully if we didn't trust that objects in the world are there even when we don't have any direct sensory impressions from them. But this apprehension is not innate in humans—very little children have no world beyond their experiences."

But let me begin with how animals experience things. A cat chasing a mouse that runs in behind a curtain can predict that it will come out the other side. So the cat can draw conclusions about the mouse even when it is receiving no direct signals from its senses. Such behaviour presumes the cognitive ability called *object permanence* by Piaget. This implies that the cat retains some kind of *image* of the mouse even when its sensory impressions of the mouse are gone. The cat has expectations about the mouse. Wolves hunting in a pack often manage in sophisticated fashion to predict where their prey will turn up. Such an ability also presumes an image of the prey even when no perceptions are available. Those organisms that possess object permanence thus enjoy one more way to build in knowledge about the future in their consciousness.

Various studies of animals show that all mammals and a number of birds, especially the crow family, possess object permanence. It does not seem to exist among reptiles or other 'lower' animals. This ability is not innate; human babies acquire it between the ages of six and nine months (which is considerably later than among other animal species). When the permanence of things is still a novelty for the child, playing peek-a-boo is great fun.

Most of our sensory impressions are very brief. We move our body and our head and are constantly on the lookout for other parts of our surroundings.

---

[8] Although, in certain folk music traditions, e.g. the Swedish one, quartertones also occur.

To be able to relate the different impressions to one another, an organism needs at least some kind of 'resonance' or 'echo' that makes the sensory information remain among the brain's activities a little longer.[viii] Sensations do not survive the present, but perceptions do. There are feedback loops in the nervous system that keep perceptions alive. The so-called primary areas of the cerebral cortex process the incoming sensory signals, while the association areas (the secondary areas) maintain the signals and analyse them further, coordinate them, and categorize them.[ix] These mechanisms may be one component in the simulators that I believe give birth to perceptions. As we shall see in the next chapter, an 'inner model' of the world strengthens how we retain the perceptual information.

Object permanence can be seen as a form of simulation of the same kind as that involved in controlling a throw effectively. When the cat no longer has sensory impressions of the mouse that disappeared behind the curtain, it simulates a vicarious object that takes the place of the mouse and can be used to figure out where the real mouse is. The cat creates an *image* of the mouse—in other words, a representation. (A more precise description is that the simulated mouse runs constantly in parallel with the real one, i.e. even when the cat does receive sensory impressions from the mouse. I shall discuss the significance of this parallelism in the next section.)

2.6   The art of chasing a mouse

"You're stuffing a lot of funny things in my head," says Egon. "What's the point of representations, anyway?"

"OK, granted, if the behaviourists are right, there's no need to use the concept of representation to understand the behaviour of animals and humans."

In many situations, of course, this concept is completely unnecessary. Many kinds of behaviour among animals, like phototaxis (an organism seeking light), are decided entirely by psychophysical mechanisms that transfer signals from the surrounding world for immediate action. Another example is the escape behaviour of the cockroach.[x] When a predator approaches, the cockroach instantly disappears from the scene. It has no notion of *what* is approaching—it solves the problem of disappearing by methods that are quick, cheap, and dirty. Within a few milliseconds, the cockroach reacts to the air movements caused by the predator; it can distinguish such air movements from normal puffs of air, and it does not run randomly: it employs its familiarity with its own position, nearby obstacles, light conditions, and wind direction. It observes what cognitive scientist Andy Clark calls the 007 principle: know only what's necessary to do what's necessary! The subsequent behaviour is a very economical solution. When its entire nervous system consists of only a few thousand nerve cells, the cockroach has to use cheap tricks—tricks that exploit how the world looks right at the moment.

In these cases, no representations are involved. The actions that succeed from sensory impressions are *reflexes* that directly connect the signals the animal receives to its behaviour. The biologist Jakob von Uexküll articulates the difference between animals that have representations and those that do not in the following drastic formulation:[xi] 'When a dog runs, it's the animal that moves its legs. When a sea urchin runs, it's the legs that move the animal.'

There are experiments that convincingly demonstrate that simple behaviouristic models are inadequate.[9] Among the higher animals, there is a lot of behaviour that cannot be explained by stimulus–response connections. Such behaviours are best explained by assuming that the animal employs *representations* of an object when it solves its problem. Animals use sensory impressions as clues to perceptual mechanisms that add in information to what has been received from its receptors. A noise that sounds like the roar of a tiger can be more than sufficient to make a deer have a *perception* that there is a whole tiger in the vicinity, and not just a sound. I do not want to assert that this conclusion is based on any 'consciousness' in the deer, but the result of the sound it hears is that it imagines a tiger—it 'thinks about' a tiger. The deer's behaviour will definitely be influenced in accordance with this conclusion.[10]

Von Uexküll maintains that as soon as an animal can reproduce the spatial structure of its environment through a corresponding structure in its nervous system, the animal constructs:

> a new world of excitation originating in the central nervous system that is erected between the environment and the motor nervous system. [...] The animal no longer flees from the stimuli that the enemy sends to him, but rather from the mirrored image of the enemy that originates in a mirrored world.

Von Uexküll refers to a mirror world when he talks about the representations that control an animal. Naturally, this should not be interpreted as meaning that an animal with representations does not interact with the world outside.

---

[9] The debate is not dead, however. Robert Epstein, one of Skinner's successors, maintains in a 1982 article that behavioural models can also explain everything that can be explained by using the concept of representation. And there are modern neo-behaviourist models based on artificial neuron networks that are more in line with experimental findings (Balkenius and Morén 1998).

[10] When I talk about 'conclusion' I by no means presume that the material is presented in any explicit way, in speech or in some other symbolic form (see Gärdenfors 1994). Nor do I assume that animals are aware that there is a process that contributes information.

On the contrary, the mirror world should be viewed as a bridge between sensory perceptions and actions. This mirror world corresponds nicely to what is controlled by the simulators I talked about previously. According to von Uexküll, the representations in the mirror world are 'tools in the brain prescribed by its organisational plan. The tools are always ready to be activated as responses to appropriate stimuli from the world outside'.[xii]

In order to illustrate the significance of representations for animal behaviour, we can compare how snakes and cats chase mice. (I have borrowed this example from ethologist Sverre Sjölander.[xiii]) Both snakes and cats employ a combination of senses during the hunt, but they do it in entirely different ways. When a snake strikes at a mouse, it uses its sight or, in certain cases, heat detectors located in its head. After the strike, the mouse usually runs some distance before the poison acts and it dies. To find the dead mouse, the snake utilizes only its sense of *smell*. Even if the mouse should happen to drop dead right in front of the snake, the snake will follow the mouse's scent in order to find its prey. Finally, when the mouse is to be swallowed, the snake has to find its head, since that is the only direction in which the mouse will go down the snake's throat. The snake could have accomplished this by using sight or smell, but it only uses *touch* to solve the problem. So: the snake uses three different senses to catch and eat a mouse. But there is no communication among the senses that are employed in the various stages of the process. The snake reacts only to its *sensations*. It has no perception of the mouse as an object, and hence no representation of it.

Now compare the snake's behaviour with how a cat hunts a mouse! The cat *simultaneously* utilizes signals it receives from several different sensory receptors— eye, ear, nose, whiskers, and perhaps also paws. The cat has object permanence and can therefore predict that a mouse that runs under one side of an armchair will come out the other side. A snake could never manage that. The cat can 'think' of the mouse even when it is receiving no signals from its senses: it can, for example, wait outside a mouse hole. A snake never does that. The decisive difference is that the cat has a representation—a *comprehensive image* of the mouse—that *combines* the input from its various senses. The representation is in the cat's head even when it is not receiving any direct sensations from the mouse. It is this representation that makes the cat's way of hunting much more flexible and efficient than the snake's is.

2.7   Going between the senses

The example of the cat's hunting method shows that it is important for the brain to *coordinate* input from the different senses when it is going to create usable representations of objects. After all, the brain handles impressions from the different receptors in rather well separated centres, at least in the initial stages of the processing. Sometimes we speak of a *modal* treatment of impressions. But for successful hunting, the preparation of food and for making tools, vision, hearing, and the sense of touch must be able to work together. Apes, and especially humans, are much better at using their hands than are other animals. To be able to control your hand precisely, you have to be able to coordinate sight and touch with the proprioceptoric sensations from the hand's muscles. In order to be able to meet such challenges of coordination, the human brain has developed representations of its surroundings, objects, actions, and so on that are *independent* of sensory modalities. The literature refers to such representations as being *crossmodal*.[xiv]

Sensations are modal, i.e. they are tied to a certain sensory domain: visual, auditory, etc. Humphrey says that one can move around constantly in each modality, but that there is no bridge connecting them—it is as though the modalities had separate owners.[xv] You can imagine a sensation that glides from sour to sweet, from the note F to the note A, and from red to blue. But you cannot imagine a sensation that goes from white to sweet or from round to pain.

In contrast, perceptions are crossmodal. The explanation is probably that because the perceptions deal with what exists in the world, they are more useful to an animal if they are accessible for all thinking processes, and not bound to some special sensory modality. Davenport explains the evolutionary value of crossmodality as follows:

> First, it appears that multimodal information extraction of environmental information is likely to result in more veridical perception, and may facilitate cognitive functioning. Second, in my view, cross-modal perception requires the derivation of modality-free information, a 'representation'. That an organism can have the same representations, concepts or percepts, regardless of the method of peripheral reception, confers great advantage on that animal in coping with the demands of living.[xvi]

I can detect that there is a badger in the neighbourhood with my senses of sight, hearing, or smell. One sensation suffices to produce an association to a badger (which in turn produces associations to the other sensations to which a badger gives rise).

Because we have well-developed crossmodal representations, humans are good at connecting information from different senses. Other species of animals seem generally worse at it.[xvii] A number of experiments have shown that apes can transmit information from touch to sight and vice versa, but it does not appear that other groups of animals can do that. In an experiment, a chimpanzee, for example, is allowed to touch some object that it cannot see (under a blanket), and then it is rewarded if it can identify a similar object (e.g. by stretching its hand out to it) among several objects in front of it that it can see but not touch. Chimpanzees can even connect objects in photographs to tactile sensations. On the other hand, it is unclear to what extent monkeys and apes can go from *hearing* to sight or vice versa. If you send a Morse signalling sound, the task would be to identify the corresponding visual pattern.[xviii] Experiments of this kind show mixed results. In contrast, human children show both visual–tactile and visual–auditory crossmodality in the first few months of their lives.

The development of progressively larger association areas in the frontal lobe and other parts of the brain during the course of human evolution has resulted in our having a greater ability to go between the senses than have other species of animals. This probably makes it easier for us to discover different kinds of connections between phenomena in the world. As we shall see in the following section, humans seem to be particularly unique in their ability to see the connections between causes and events.

2.8   Causal reasoning: finding the invisible threads

Humans have a vigorous inclination to look for *causes* in the world. Kant calls this disposition one of our basic categories, i.e. a pattern of thought that we cannot abandon. There are good evolutionary reasons why we cannot help looking for causes, since they help us understand how the world works. But I shall argue that our thinking about causes consists of several subcomponents. When it comes to the understanding of cause and effect, I shall distinguish four different kinds of thought processes:

(a) Being able to foresee the physical effects of one's own actions.

(b) Being able to foresee the effects of others' actions.

(c) Understanding the causes of others' actions.

(d) Understanding the causes of physical events.

I have arranged these abilities in the order I believe they appear in evolution. Many animal species can manage level (a), at least for many kinds of actions. Without this ability there would of course be no point in having an inner world—one could not plan anything if one could not foresee the probable consequences of one's own actions. Level (b) is necessary for co-operation as well as for deception. This will be the topic of Section 4.6. One way of managing level (c) is to identify the *intentions* that drive the actions of others. Level (d), which seems to be the typical case of causal reasoning, turns out to be surprisingly difficult for animals other than humans. However, the available data on how other animals handle the different kinds of causality is scant and much more research is needed in this area.

In contrast, humans can easily manage all four levels of cause and effect. The primatologist and child psychologist David Premack has shown that even very small children have an ability to distinguish between effects caused by 'natural' (physical) forces and those caused by 'arbitrary' forces.[xix] The latter comprise movements and events caused by animals and humans. Premack suggests that different nervous systems in the brain are involved when we recognize the two types of causality. His finding provides some support for separating levels (c) and (d).

"It is strange that you don't understand physics," I say rather absentmind- edly to Egon.

"Thank you very much, I am doing fine," he rebuts offended. "Humans are not very good at physics either. They think that a heavy cannon ball falls faster than a light one and they believe that if a running person drops a ball, it will fall straight down."

"You are right that even well educated people have problems in grasping the consequences of scientific physics, let alone understand the equations they learn by heart at school. But I am interested in everyday reasoning about phys- ical processes, what is sometimes called folk physics."

"But chimps use different kinds of tools. Does this not show immediately that they can understand physical mechanisms, that they have ape physics, if not folk physics?"

"No, this only shows that they can represent the effects of some of their actions, which is what I call level (a). Understanding physical principles means that one is able to reason about what are the causes of different events."

Primatologists Elizabetta Visalberghi and Daniel Povinelli and their col- leagues have run a series of experiments that almost unanimously indicate that monkeys and apes cannot understand even simple physical causes.[xx] In some of the experiments a peanut was placed in a transparent Plexiglas tube with a trap in the middle. Visalberghi's capucin monkey subjects were provided with sticks that could be used to push the peanut that was inside the tube. They had already shown that they were able to push out peanuts from ordinary Plexiglas tubes. But in the trap tube the stick had to be inserted into the tube opening farthest from the peanut, otherwise the peanut would be pushed into the trap and could no longer be reached. After 140 trials one of the monkeys had learned how to solve the problem—the rest performed more or less randomly.

Figure 2.3 The trap tube used in the experiments. (From Povinelli 2000).

They do not seem to understand that something (we call it 'gravity') causes the peanut to fall down into the trap if it is pushed there.

James Reaux and Daniel Povinelli tested the same tube problem on four chimpanzees. One of the four, Megan, learned to solve the problem (after about 60 trials), but the other three, again, performed randomly. To test whether Megan had understood what happened or had just learned to put the stick at the end that was farthest away from the peanut, they ran a variant of the experiment where the trap was turned upwards so that there was no risk that the peanut would fall into it. But Megan continued to insert the stick at the end that was farthest away. Thus it seems that she had mechanically learned a rule for how to obtain a reward and not at all understood the underlying physical mechanism.

Another example involves vervets. When they catch sight of a python or a leopard they emit warning cries. To test whether they can interpret a *sign* that there are predators in the vicinity, i.e. reason from the effect of a predator to its cause, Dorothy Cheney and Robert Seyfarth made a false python track in the sand for a troop of vervets. They did not react to this, even though pythons are highly dangerous to vervets. A group of vervets was once observed passing a real python track without reacting—until they came across the snake, when panic broke out. Nor did the monkeys react when the scientists hung up a dead antelope in a tree, despite the fact that this was a clear sign that there was a leopard in the vicinity. In brief, these experiments and observations indicate that monkeys and apes *cannot infer physical causes from their effects.*

The psychologist Wolfgang Köhler ran a series of experiments concerning chimp's ability to plan already in the 1910s. He hung a banana in the ceiling of a big cage and placed some wooden boxes in the cage. Some of the chimpanzees succeeded in stacking the boxes on top of each other and they could thereby climb up and get hold of the banana. These classical experiments have been presented as support for the hypothesis that apes can plan and have 'insights' concerning how a problem is to be solved.

As Povinelli points out, Köhler's chimpanzees were in fact not so successful. Even if an ape had once solved the problem of stacking the boxes, it could often not repeat the exploit. They simply had problems placing one box on top of another, making peculiar mistakes like pulling away boxes underneath themselves so that the entire stack, including the chimpanzee, collapsed.

"I've done that too," says Egon with a grin. "It is great fun!"

To test the apes' understanding of physics, Köhler placed some stones underneath the banana, which would make a box placed on top of it unstable. If the animals had any idea of a 'stable' placement of a box, they would remove the stones before placing the box. But no—the apes tried in the most awkward ways, placing the boxes on top of the stones. Povinelli interprets these observations as indicating that the apes have the ability to *visualize* a tower of boxes with the aid of which they can reach the desired banana, but they have no understanding of the physical principles that govern the behaviour of the boxes.

The upshot is that monkeys and apes have great difficulties with level (d), i.e. understanding the causes of physical events. As we shall see, monkeys and apes may be more qualified to understand causal mechanisms when social relations are involved. Povinelli summarizes his experiments on the apes' understanding of physical causality as follows:

> This, then, is our most important theoretical conclusion: the principles
> of chimpanzee folk physics are founded upon things that can be directly
> perceived, including action sequences that can be generated from imagination
> or held in memory as visual imagery.[xxi]

And Tomasello gives the following explanation for why monkeys and apes cannot understand causal mechanisms and intentionality in others:

> It is just that they do not view the world in terms of intermediate and often
> hidden 'forces', the underlying causes and intentional/mental states, that are
> so important in human thinking.[xxii]

Even very small human children, in contrast, show strong signs of interpreting the world with the aid of hidden forces and other causal variables. A fascinating illustration of how children infer causal mechanisms comes from an experiment ran by the psychologist Thomas Shultz.[xxiii] Two electric blowers were directed at a candle, but the candle was shielded on three sides by a Plexiglas box. One blower was turned on (and left on), but it did not blow out the candle because of the Plexiglas that was in between. Then the other blower was turned on and at *the same time* the experimenter turned the box so that the open side was facing the first blower, thus blowing out the candle. Note that if one reasons by temporal contiguity, the turning on of the second blower should be connected with the extinction of the candle. But even 2- to 4-year-olds chose the first blower as the cause, thus indicating that they have some understanding of the *forces* that lie behind the events. Psychologist Alison Gopnik claims that:

> other animals primarily understand causality in terms of the effects of their own actions on the world. In contrast, human beings combine that understanding with a view that equates the causal power of their own actions and those of objects independent of them.[xxiv]

My interpretation of this crucial difference between humans and other apes is that the inner simulators we use to understand the physical world are much better at using hidden variables to make predictions about the future. The causes are not part of our sensations, but the simulators that generate our perceptions fill them in. In this way we *perceive* the causes. These causal fillings produce in humans' inner worlds a much more fully formed toolbox for reasoning about the future than exists in other apes.

"So these weird things you call causes only exist in our heads?" Egon asks.

"Yes, that's correct."

"Why do you look so pleased?"

"Because this is a position that will upset many philosophers who believe that causes are part of the physical world."[11]

The tendency to look for hidden mechanisms is so strong in humans that one can speak of a *causal drive*. For the most part, this drive is beneficial for our planning capacities, yet sometimes we take it to extremes. We crave causal connections also in cases where there is none. Even purely random events, such as winning a lottery, are interpreted as the result of having 'luck'. There is no such thing as luck; the fact that we talk about luck is just a reflection of our incurable drive to find causes.

"And all this talk about gods," Egon adds. "That's something I've never understood."

"Yes, that could be based on the same mechanism. We have a strong desire to find meaning in the world."

---

[11] In philosophical jargon my position could be described as neo-Kantian, i.e. I believe that causation is one of the categories of our thought, but the contents of this category may vary from culture to culture.

2.9 A room with a view

Egon sits playing with my video camera. He pans around the room with it. Then he puts the camera down and shakes his head slowly.

"Why are you shaking your head?" I ask. "Is something wrong?"

"I'm not shaking my head, I'm turning it. What's funny is that when I turn the video camera, the room moves on the view finder, but when I turn my head the room stands still."

"That's a very good point," I agree. "The explanation is basically that the room you see with your eyes is an advanced kind of representation."

"You and your representations! What's that got to do with it?"

"Well, the egocentric room you experience is created by a simulator of the type I talked about earlier."

"Whaddya mean, *egocentric* room? The room I see is the one that's out there, right? It's just as much yours as mine?"

"Yes indeed, the simulator that is connected to sight functions very well and it tricks us into believing that we see the world as it really is. But if you close one eye and press gently with your finger beside the eyeball of the other eye, you'll see that your room moves."

Egon does as I say.

"Yech, it's rocking. I feel dizzy."

This simple experiment proves that the room Egon experiences is created by the visual processes in his brain—the room is a *perception* in the sense I defined earlier. When we turn our heads and let our eye follow along, the image that reaches the retina changes very rapidly—in other words, what is presented to our sight varies. But, just as quick, our brain calculates a representation of the room that remains still *in relation to the direction of our body*. When we press on our eyeball, we step outside the normal simulation process and our perception changes.

"Isn't there any room out there then?" wonders Egon uneasily.

"Yes of course, but what you experience is not the room in itself, to use Immanuel Kant's terms, but your brain's *construction* of it. That's why I called it egocentric."

"Why does it stand still when I turn my head? Why doesn't it move like on the camera's view finder?"

"The point is that you need to see to be able to *do* things. And normally you carry out actions with your hands and the rest of your body. What you see is your *field of action*. As long as you move only your head and not the rest of your body, there is no change in your possibilities to act. Since it is primarily your hands that are to be guided, it's better if your brain creates a room that is constant in relation to *their* possibilities. The representations we create in our heads are generally constructed so as to support the actions we need to take."[12]

It turns out that the experience of space is not innate but must be learned through *interaction* with the world around us.[xxv] The simulator that creates our three-dimensional perception space from the two-dimensional images provided by our eyes must learn how the sensory impression can be used to create a meaningful field of action. (Actually the image on the retina is upside down and it is turned 'right' by the brain.) When you get a new pair of glasses, for example, the conditions for this process are altered, and it takes a while before the simulator in the brain has adjusted itself and can provide the perceptions we need for carrying out precise actions, for example like walking up or down stairs. The brain is very flexible, though: if for a couple of weeks you have to wear special glasses that turn the world upside down, you will gradually adjust and *perceive* the world as right side up again. (Although what hits your retina is right side up—in contrast to the normal upside down projection.)

"I still think it is a heavy assumption that there are simulators for all kinds of perceptions in the brain," Egon maintains.

"I have tried to give some examples of how they work. But I admit that it is still a rather programmatic hypothesis."

2.10 Imagination: detaching the senses

> Man shoots an arrow into the future with a cord attached. The arrow fixes
> itself in an *image*, and he hauls himself toward it.
>
> Paul Valéry

A war is raging. A general stands in front of a big map of the combat zone at head-quarters. The map contains different kinds of markers to show the positions of friendly and hostile forces. Now and then orderlies come in with new information about the enemy troop movements. The general moves the corresponding

---

[12] Grush (1997), p. 24. This view of how perceptions arise can be compared with philosopher Merleu-Ponty's (1962) concept of 'motility'. He writes that 'bodily space and external space form a practical system, the first being the background against which the object as the goal of our action may stand out' and that 'movement is not limited to submitting passively to space and time, it actively assumes them, it takes them up in their basic significance which is obscured in the commonplaceness of established situations' (1962, p. 102). Merleau-Ponty thus regards perception as an ongoing activity that makes the agent's surroundings *meaningful* for him or her.

markers around on the map. He tries moving some of his own units into new positions, steps back to survey the map, changes the enemy's positions, shakes his head and tries another rearrangement. After a few minutes he gives his orders and dispatches the orderlies. He has already moved the markers for his own troops to the new positions, though he knows it will take time before the order is carried out. But he counts on their really being moved there.

"But why are you talking about war?" Egon asks. "I thought you were writing about the brain."

"This is a metaphor for what happens in the brain when it commands the body."

"I've always had a hard time with metaphors," mutters Egon.

The orderlies' messages are what reach the brain from the sense organs. The general's orders correspond to the nerve signals sent out to the muscles. His planning with the markers can be viewed as a simulation. The time scale is of course different—a body reacts faster than an army does.

The great difference between what happens in the brain and in war is that there is no general in the brain. There is nobody sitting there and giving orders. The commands to the body are produced through a complex interplay among different parts of the brain. No individual part of the brain functions as a central command post.

But I want to focus on the role of the map in the metaphor. The map is not the real war, but it provides a *picture* of the war. The reports coming in from outside make the picture change bit by bit. When the general moves his markers on the map, his troops do not similarly jump around on the battlefield. Through his rearrangements, the general can *test* various developments of the battle and choose to give the order that he thinks best in relationship to his picture of what will happen. Of course, there is no guarantee that the reality will be as he foresees it, but he has no other options.

The general does not reach his decision on the basis of direct knowledge of the world, but by using a *representation* of the world, namely his map. His interaction with the map and its symbols corresponds to the kind of simulator I talked about in connection with what happens when you guide your arm when throwing. Note that the general uses the markers on the map *both* as presentations of how the battlefield looks *and* as representations when he tries various alternatives. So the representations are tools that can suitably be used to *anticipate* the consequences of different possible actions. Above all, it is much easier and quicker to move the troop markers around on the map than to move the troops in reality (which would correspond to the Skinnerian beings' trial-and-error behaviour).

The point of the metaphor is that certain animals' brains, especially humans', utilize representations of this kind—things that we can move around in our heads before trying to move them in reality. Naturally, we do not literally have maps and markers in our heads, but there is something there that *functions* in the same way.

The evolutionary explanation for the emergence of a nerve complex that simulates the movements of the arm when throwing is that it provides faster and thus more effective control of the throw. Similar simulators have undoubtedly also been developed for a number of other control problems confronting the body. In the short run, the simulator works independently of feedback from the rest of the body—it simply does not have time to wait. Eventually it will require feedback to learn whether or not the guess it simulated produced the desired result.

Yet there is nothing that says there has to be any feedback from the body. Actually, it is only a little extra step for the evolutionary process to let the simulator work without any signals being sent to the body at all—the simulator is *detached* from the sensory and motor systems. This is what happens when the organism creates for itself an *image* of what will happen if a certain action is undertaken. In the remainder of this book I shall argue that the power of imagination is completely decisive for the development of all higher thought processes.

Imaginations are naked since they come without sensations. The philosopher John Locke, in *An essay concerning human understanding*, writes that 'the pain of heat or cold, when the idea is revived in our minds, gives us no disturbance; which when felt was very troublesome'. The thought alone is not sufficient for it to be painful. Or as Bolingbroke says in Shakespeare's *Richard II*:

> O! who can hold a fire in his hand
> By thinking on the frosty Caucasus?
> Or cloy the hungry edge of appetite,
> By bare imagination of a feast?
> Or wallow naked in December snow
> By thinking on fantastic summer's heat?

On the other hand, the founding father of psychology William James writes already in 1890: 'The commonly received idea [about imagination] is that it is only a milder degree of the same process which took place when the thing now imagined was sensibly perceived.'[xxvi] Although James did not have much evidence for this position, there is now quite strong support from brain research that the same mechanisms are involved in controlling the body as in imagining controlling it. The neurophysiologist David Ingvar and his colleagues were in the vanguard in using the flow of blood in the brain to survey what parts are working during different types of activities. It turned out that the same parts of the motor cortex are involved when an action is carried out as when one only imagines the action. The so-called motor imagining ability has since been investigated thoroughly by the brain researcher Marc Jeannerod.[xxvii]

Now I am ready to make a distinction between two types of representations in the brain—*cued* and *detached*.[xviii] In cued representation there is a perception: it stands for something that is *present* in the surrounding situation. The categorical perceptions that were presented earlier, for example, are cued representations. A detached representation, on the other hand, is an imagination: something the individual can utilize *regardless* of whether what it represents is present or not. A detached representation can even stand for something that does not exist at all. For example, our imaginative worlds are full of centaurs, unicorns, elves, and trolls—about which we easily communicate although they do not truly correspond to any sensory impressions we have received. One common feature of both types of representations is that they are evoked by the kind of simulator mechanisms I have described.

Being able to use a detached representation requires that one can *suppress* the sensations one has for the moment; otherwise they will come into conflict with the representation. Memory researcher Arthur Glenberg says that detached representations put reality in quarantine. That places new demands on mental capacities. The suppression of information coming in from reality is probably managed by the frontal lobe of the brain, which is the part that is in charge of planning and fantasizing and the so-called 'executive functions' of self-control.

Glenberg presents a theory of how memory works in which he distinguishes between 'automatic' and 'effortful' memory.[xxix] The automatic memory is the one that is used to fill in sensations so that they become perceptions. When I recognize a person in a crowd it is because I blend what I see of the person with my memories. Sometimes there is a mistake—I overlay my memory of one person on top of the sensory impression I receive of another person.

The effortful memory is the one we use when we create images. Images do not appear from nowhere—they build on our previous experiences. What we usually call remembering is only a special kind of image that we think corresponds to something that has actually happened. But memory is also used in fantasies: you cannot imagine a centaur (if you have not seen a picture of one) without memories of horses and people. But images must not be confused with perceptions.[13] An effort is required to ignore sensations. That is why we

---

[13] Except when we pretend. See Section 3.3.

often close our eyes or look up at the ceiling when we want to remember something or when we fantasize. This effort can be investigated since, for example, it is more difficult to carry out some action at the same time as we are remembering or imagining.

"According to what you're saying, there seems to be a lot of make-believe in the brain," interjects Egon. "But how can you *know* that someone has detached representations?"

"People can use language to describe what they are thinking about," I reply evasively. "And what we talk about in language is often things that are not present in the here and now, as I will show later."

"But how can we know that animals have such representations?" asks Egon. "After all, they can't talk."

"No, here it gets harder. We have to rely on indirect signs."

"How do you know that you're not just making that up about animals thinking? My old psychologists in the lab didn't believe in such figments of the imagination. They wanted to have solid connections between a stimulus and a response—stuff you can observe."

The advantage of the behaviourists is that they were so assiduous at gathering data about animal behaviour in a lot of different laboratory situations. Innumerable rats and pigeons have been painstakingly trained to do the most remarkable things. But parts of the behaviourists' conclusions about animal behaviour are very difficult to explain unless one presupposes detached representations; i.e. that animals have an imaginative capacity. For example, rats are good at learning to find their way through labyrinths. Psychologist Edward Tolman discovered way back in the 1930s that if you altered a labyrinth so that the rat could take a short cut to the goal, it did so *immediately* without having to learn anything new. Tolman interpreted this behaviour as meaning that the rats have acquired an *inner map* of the labyrinth that they can use to find the shortest path.[14] Such a map is a prime example of a detached representation.

"Whaddya mean, map?" Egon protests. "Surely there can't be any such thing in a rat's head!"

"No, that is of course also a metaphor," I reply. "But there is something that *functions* like a map. How this function is neurologically implemented in the rat's brain is unfortunately still an unsolved problem."[xxx]

---

[14] His conclusion, however, did not receive attention until much later. The reason is that it was very difficult to explain with the behaviourist view of learning that dominated at the time. See also Vauclair (1987) for an analysis of the concept 'cognitive mapping'.

It is possible to further subdivide the detached representations. Sometimes representations are *dependent* on an external referent, even if the object is not immediately present in the surroundings. The mental maps that Tolman proved were constructed by rats are naturally dependent on the labyrinths they have been running around in. But 'the map' exists even when the rat is back in its usual cage.

The other type of detached representations is those that are *independent* of any external referent.[xxxi] *Desires* and *fantasies* about things that do not exist or events that have never occurred are obvious examples of referent-independent representations. If there were no such representations, we would have no fairy tales. Albert Einstein describes these representations in the following way:

> The psychical entities which seem to serve as elements in thought are certain signs and more or less clear images which can be 'voluntarily' reproduced and combined. . . . This combinatory play seems to be the essential feature in productive thought—before there is any connection with logical construction in words or other kinds of signs which can be communicated to others. The above-mentioned elements are, in my case, of visual and some muscular type. Conventional words or other signs have to be sought for laboriously in a secondary stage, when the mentioned associative play is sufficiently established and can be reproduced at will.

As we shall see in the following chapter, detached representations are necessary for planning and for all other higher cognitive functions. Many species of animals can plan, which supports the assumption that they have access to detached representations—at least in the form of referent-dependent representations. Yet certain examples suggest that at least apes also have referent-independent representations. In addition to the material about the language acquisition of apes that I will discuss later, one can consider how they use tools. One example occurs when a chimpanzee that wants to get at eating termites in a termite stack goes away from the stack to break off a twig from a nearby tree and peels off the leaves. It then returns to the stack and uses the stick it has manufactured to 'fish up' the termites. In this case, it would seem that the image of the peeled stick was a referent-independent representation that existed in the chimpanzee's head even before it went out to make one. The representation has not been triggered by anything in the chimpanzee's surroundings.

(Egon yawns.)

"Yes, I know, you are not terribly interested in philosophical distinctions. But I have to go through this inasmuch as the concepts will be required when I analyse different types of cognitive functions in what follows."

My hypothesis is that cued representations precede referent-dependent detached representations in the evolutionary perspective, and that the latter in

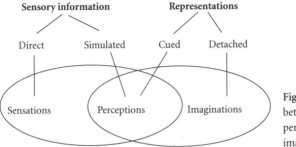

Figure 2.4 The relations between sensations, perceptions, and imaginations.

turn precede referent-independent detached representations. As we shall see, this hypothesis can be applied in several different areas. One permeating idea of this book is that the development of thinking can be described as the detachment of more and more representations.

(Egon goes to sleep.)

Figure 2.4 summarizes the classification of the three kinds of thinking I have described in this chapter: sensations, perceptions, and imaginations. Representations (perceptions and imaginations) are created by simulators. For perceptions, the simulators are coupled to sensory impressions, but for imaginations, no direct contact with the surrounding world is required.

Tulving's three types of memory—procedural, semantic, and episodic—can be associated with different levels of representations.[xxxii] You need no representations to remember a procedure such as how to ride a bike. It is sufficient to have sensations and responses that are connected to the various kinds of conditioning studied by the behaviourists. The procedural memory determines what action should be carried out when an organism receives a certain stimulus. The semantic memory, however, is tied to the categories that an organism has created. This requires at least cued representations in the form of perceptions. Semantic memory presents the world in a way that supports the selection of appropriate actions. Finally, episodic memory presumes detached representations and a personal identity that combines the individual episodes of memory. In order to think about a previous event, you have to be able to produce representations that are not bound to the current situation. At the same time, you have to *suppress* the perceptions you have at the moment to avoid a conflict with the memory you have evoked.

If this association among different types of memories and different levels of representations is correct, it follows that the semantic memory comes evolutionarily later than the procedural memory, and that it is only the higher animals (probably only humans) who can have episodic memories.

Notes

i. Popper (1972), p. 250.

ii. Grush (1997, 1998), Kawato (1999).

iii. Hammond (1990).

iv. See also Hesslow (2002) for a related theory.

v. See Grush (1998).

vi. See, e.g. Månsson (2000).

vii. Thouless (1931) as presented in Humphrey (1993), pp. 89–90. See also Mitchell (1997), pp. 146–9 for a description of follow-up studies.

viii. See Humphrey (1993), p. 176.

ix. Cf. Deacon (1997), p. 292.

x. Clark (1997), pp. 4–5.

xi. Von Uexküll (1985), p. 231.

xii. Von Uexküll (1985), p. 234.

xiii. Sjölander (1999), p. 278.

xiv. See Sjölander (1993).

xv. Humphrey (1993), p. 120.

xvi. Davenport (1976), p. 147.

xvii. See Davenport (1976), Murray (1990), and Tomasello and Call (1997) for a review of the research.

xviii. Davenport (1976), p. 146.

xix. Premack (1996).

xx. The experiments are reported in Povinelli's book *Folk physics for apes.*

xxi. Povinelli (2000), p. 307.

xxii. Tomasello (1999), p. 19. Also see Povinelli (2000), p. 298.

xxiii. Shultz (1982).

xxiv. Gopnik (1998), p. 104.

xxv. Held and Hein (1963).

xxvi. James (1890), p. 68.

xxvii. Jeannerod (1994).

xxviii. See Gulz (1991) and Gärdenfors (1996a).

xxix. Glenberg (1997). See also Gärdenfors (1997) for a commentary on Glenberg's theory of memory.

xxx. See Balkenius (1995) for some models based on neural networks.

xxxi. See Brinck and Gärdenfors (1999).

xxxii. Tulving (1985), p. 388.

CHAPTER 3

The world within

3.1 Popperian beings

> Daydreaming got us where we are today; early on in our evolution we learned
> to let our minds wander so well that they started coming back with souvenirs.
>
> Terry Pratchett

Skinnerian beings can acquire knowledge through trial-and-error—they try something and see what happens. One drawback of this form of learning is that it is *time-consuming*—most often the animal must try many different actions before it finds one that works. Furthermore, trial-and-error is often directly *dangerous* for the animal. A deer that tries to leap across a ravine to take a short cut runs a great risk of not having a second chance. Evolution inexorably eliminates failed efforts.

If, on the other hand, an animal can represent the world in an *inner world*, it can foresee the consequences of different actions.[1] In this way the animal can *simulate* the consequences of behaving one way or another. The future is perceived in this inner world. One can so to speak cross-examine the alternative actions before they are carried out in reality. The body is the referee that uses different reactions, e.g. fear, dizziness, and trembling, to indicate that what one was considering doing is probably not such a great idea.

After such a simulation, one can choose the path that seems best and execute an action in the outer world. For example, when you think about lifting a stone and then become aware that even if you carry it over and place it under a tree you still won't be able to reach up to the fruits, you have gained a lot compared with actually carrying the stone and then realizing your failure.

Back in 1943, psychologist Kenneth Craik had a similar idea:

> If the organism carries a 'small-scale model' of external reality and of its
> own possible actions within its head, it is able to try out various alternatives,

---

[1] Dennett (1978), p. 77, calls this construction an inner environment: 'the inner environment is simply any internal region that can affect and be affected by features of potential behavioral control systems'.

conclude which are the best of them, react to future situations before they arise, utilize the knowledge of past events in dealing with the present and future, and in every way to react in a much fuller, safer and more competent manner to the emergencies which face it.

For an animal that has detached representations, we can define its inner world as a set of all such representations and the dynamic processes in which they can be involved. The dynamic processes are necessary for being able to calculate the consequences of different imaginable actions. My hypothesis is that these processes are made up of the simulators discussed in the previous chapter.

The evolutionary point of such an inner world is that it exempts the animal from the trial-and-error behaviour that is so fraught with danger—it can conduct its trials in its inner world.[2] In Popper's words we can say that our inner world allows our hypotheses to die instead of us. The organisms that have an inner world reach a third level of development that Dennett aptly calls *Popperian beings*.

The behaviourists' program was based on showing that all animals are Skinnerian beings. Yet in fact, all mammals and possibly also birds are Popperian beings. Tolman's rats in the labyrinth proved that they have an inner world, at least in the form of a virtual map of their surroundings.

The behaviourists tried to explain how rats made their way through labyrinths by using a complex system of stimulus–response connections. But by employing representations in the inner world, animals gain a much more *effective* method for handling the world around them than by learning all the relevant connections between different stimuli and responses. The step from Skinnerian to Popperian beings yields a profit in the economics of learning that is evolutionarily valuable. The price the Popperian beings have to pay is a brain that is capable of keeping track of detached representations, which requires mechanisms over and above those that handle sensory information.

To return to Valéry's suggestion that the task of a consciousness is to create the future, we can note that the inner world makes it possible to look over an *imaginary future* before it actually falls upon us. To the extent that we manage to foresee the consequences of our choices we enjoy better possibilities of guiding the future.

---

[2] Jeannerod (1994), p. 187, says that 'actions are driven by an internally represented goal rather than directly by the external world'.

The success of the simulations in the inner world of course depends on how well they are *adapted* to the mechanisms of the outer world. If the consequences portrayed in the inner world coincide sufficiently well with what would happen in reality, the individual improves its survival value. But a monkey that hallucinates a branch where there is none will soon be a dead monkey. So in the long run, an individual with a maladjusted inner world will be eliminated by natural selection.

(Egon grunts uneasily in his sleep.)

But this does not imply that the inner world is a copy of the outer world. The brain has neither the time nor the energy sufficient for recreating the real world. Thus it is likely that the inner world is a simplified and somewhat reconstructed model of the outer world, with many random and cobbled-together constructs. As I have explained earlier, the different simulation processes can supply new variables and make a number of simplifications so that the simulations can flow smoothly, i.e. so that the actions the simulations lead to will be decided on as quickly and economically as possible.

It is often more convenient to act upon what happens in the inner world than to be constantly considering the outer world. A typical example is that once a rat has learned its way around a labyrinth, it runs along according to its inner map, only occasionally checking to see that it coincides with reality. In other words, it acts in accordance with what its simulator generates rather than with the sensations it receives. As a result, when you introduce a new obstacle in the labyrinth, the rat will at first run right into it, even though it could have detected it with its sensory organs. But it quickly learns to avoid the collision. This example shows that an organism must continue to check that what is going on in the outer world can be made to tally with what is happening in its inner world. As the poet Olav Hauge writes: 'Reality is a stony shore for a dreamer drifting with the waves.'

I have defined the inner world of an organism as the system of all its detached representations and the dynamic processes in which they are involved. I do not take it for granted, however, that the organism is conscious *of* its inner world. That would correspond to a form of self-consciousness that will be discussed in Chapter 5. But one is conscious *in* one's inner world in the sense that the representations provided by perceptions and imaginings and included in the simulations *are* a part of consciousness.

As with all theories of consciousness, 'the inner world' is a metaphor. Metaphors are neither true nor false, but they can be more or less suitable as aids for producing pertinent theories. In what follows I will show that the metaphor of an inner world is useful for explaining the evolutionary value of several different functions of thinking. I shall show that without the inner world, evolution cannot construct a thinking system that can plan or deceive, or have self-consciousness, free will, and language. My underlying thesis is that the inner world has become increasingly richer on the way to *Homo sapiens*.

3.2   Representations and the brain

> The more I think, the more I think.
>
> Paul Valéry

It is difficult to determine when an inner world comes into existence during evolution, but it would appear closely connected with the development of the cerebral cortex, the so-called neocortex. Mammals have a neocortex, but not fish or reptiles. Among birds, a corresponding structure, the hyperstriatum, has developed for functions that resemble what the cortex achieves for mammals.

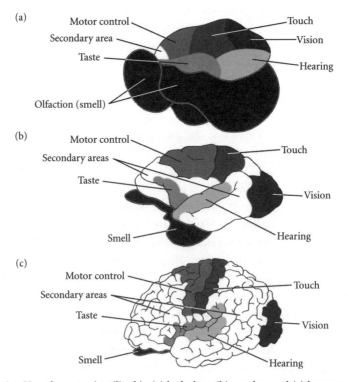

Figure 3.1 How the cortex is utilized in (a) hedgehog, (b) monkey, and (c) human.

The cortex has not only grown in size; its use has also changed over millions of years. Almost the entire cortex of a primitive mammal, for example a hedgehog, is primary; i.e. it handles sensations directly. The hedgehog's sense of smell is decidedly dominant. But among higher mammals, the cortex becomes increasingly secondary; i.e. it works with crossmodal *coordination* of sensory information. In humans, the secondary cortex is much larger in size than the primary, which suggests that it devotes much energy to crossmodality.

There are a number of interesting differences between mammals and reptiles that support the hypothesis that the genesis of the cortex can be related to the existence of an inner world. Mammals *play*, but reptiles do not.[i] Play primarily exercises patterns of movement, but some kinds of play can be seen as a way to *construct* an inner world that can subsequently be used in new situations. Above all, while playing you learn about the *consequences* resulting from different kinds of actions. This knowledge is necessary for being able to plan successfully.[3]

(Egon's front hands twitch in his sleep.)

Another difference is that mammals probably *dream*, whereas reptiles do not.[ii] Mammals have the same kind of rapid eye movement while sleeping as occurs among humans only when they are dreaming. And a dream, even a daydream, takes place precisely in the inner world. In other words, dogs can dream about hunting, but snakes cannot. Neurophysiologist Rudolfo Llinas and his colleagues have also shown that the activity in the cortex during a dream is nearly identical with what happens while awake, but with the difference that normal perception is controlled by sensory receptors.[iii] There are many theories about what impels dreams, but one that has become popular in recent times is that dreaming is a form of *learning* that compiles and consolidates the impressions one has received while awake.

Further confirmation that the structure of the inner world depends on the cortex comes from patients with certain kinds of brain injuries. One example is a patient who had to have one occipital lobe removed.[iv] The visual centre is located in this lobe and after such an operation only half the field of vision remains. Before the operation, the patient was asked to *imagine* that objects of various kinds were coming closer and closer until there was no longer room for them in the imagined field of vision. After the operation, the patient was asked to perform the same exercise. It turned out that the imagined objects were now experienced as considerably farther away than previously when they

---

[3] In an experiment with chimpanzees involving putting two sticks together in order to solve a problem, those who had been allowed to play with the sticks in advance did much better than those who had not had that opportunity.

flowed over the edges of the field of vision. This implies that the inner world had also changed structure in parallel with the sensory world when the structurally supporting part of the brain was removed.

Studies of the blood flow in the brain have shown that when we perform normal bodily actions, both the motor cortex and the area in front of it are active. When we only imagine an action, however, the motor cortex is not activated, but only the parts located in front of it. A likely explanation is that the simulation of an action occurs in the forward parts, and that when we only imagine the action, the motor cortex is blocked so that the signals are not transmitted to the body.[v]

The anthropologist Kenneth Oakley presents a similar account.[vi] He distinguishes among three levels of consciousness in evolution. The first is *awareness*, which contains basic physical processes, habituation, and conditioning. These processes are controlled by structures that lie under the cortex, i.e. the evolutionarily older parts of the brain. This level corresponds to a consciousness that contains sensations.

Oakley calls the second level *consciousness*, where the organism can integrate sensory information and where the surrounding world is represented. According to Oakley, this level comes into being with the development of the cortex and the hippocampus and is thus mainly found among mammals and birds. The hippocampus, located in the inner part of the brain, plays a major role in our apprehension of space and in different memory processes. This second level corresponds to organisms that have representations (in the form of both perceptions and imaginations).

Oakley's third level is *self-awareness*, which is found only in humans and possibly some of the apes. I will treat this level of consciousness in Chapter 5, but the key idea is that self-awareness presumes that one can process representations *of one's own inner world*. Oakley provides no exact picture of what brain structures are needed for self-awareness, but this level is presumably closely tied to the development of the frontal lobe, which is the part of the cortex that has developed fastest during human evolution.[4]

3.3   Pretence: playing in the inner world

Egon wakes up, scratches himself for a while and then starts to play with the computer's mouse.

---

[4] Tulving (1985), p. 388, points to one direct connection between his three memory systems and Oakley's three levels: procedural memory appears at the awareness level, semantic memory is related to the consciousness level, and episodic memory to the level of self-awareness.

"Quit it!" I tell him. "What do you think the mouse *is*, anyway?"

The ability to imagine something that does not exist in our surroundings (or at all) is more developed in humans than in other animals. This reveals itself, for example, in the differences between how human children and young apes play. Like other mammals, apes play while they are growing up. Mammal offspring wrestle playfully in a laid-back manner, they learn the consequences of different kinds of leaps and they try different ways of getting the jump on someone else. But it is only human children who intentionally *make up* new games by creating new patterns of movements or by introducing new rules for how a game is to be played. Children often *imitate* adult behaviour in their games. To be able to imitate, they must imagine what adults do and try to do likewise. (As we shall see, it is very difficult for apes to imitate.) Human children are alone in using different types of role-play to construct a world where social relationships are important.

Children's play is *pretence play*. The ability to pretend appears already at the age of two. When you pretend, you use *two* representations of the same object—your perception of the object and an imagined version of the object (which is a detached representation). For example, when a little girl pretends that a table with a blanket over it is a house, she naturally knows that it is a table and a blanket but she simultaneously 'sees' the arrangement as a house. By *suppressing* her perception she can use her imagination instead. Her image is a deliberate false representation of the world.

"But cats when they play with a ball of yarn, aren't they pretending that it's a mouse?" wonders Egon.

"No. Of course you can say that the cat represents the ball of yarn as a mouse, but it does not simultaneously have a perception of the object as a ball of yarn. So it has only one representation of what it is playing with. The ball fills only a gap in the cat's hunting system.[vii] The difference between a cat and a child who pretends can be seen in their behaviour: the cat's carrying on is quite predictable, while the child's play is *creative*—it hits on new patterns of behaviour.[5] The cat's actions are not detached from their evolutionary function; their purpose is to practice routines."

Psychologist Alan Leslie argues that detached representations are required to be able to pretend. For example, when a child uses a banana as a telephone,

---

[5] Cf. Mitchell (1997), pp. 166–7. Adults spend much less time on pretence play than do children. One can ask whether there is a special period in life when one is good at make-believe because it helps in constructing an inner world, just as there is a critical period in childhood when one is good at acquiring new languages.

the make-believe representation, the imagination, must temporarily be detached from one part of the perceptual information. The perception of the banana must be suppressed and the performance completed with knowledge about telephones that the child accesses from its memory. Leslie maintains that small children's pretence play 'is an early symptom of the capacity of human thinking to describe and manipulate its own attitude to information. [...] To put it briefly, the capacity to pretend is an early manifestation of what has been called a *theory of mind* [...], i.e. the ability to reflect on one's own and other people's inner worlds.'[viii] What is meant by 'theory of mind' will be thoroughly discussed in Chapter 4.

There are some examples of pretence play that have been recorded in chimpanzees and gorillas that have grown up among humans.[6] The chimpanzee Austin, who was trained by the primatologist Sue Savage-Rumbaugh, often pretended to be eating when he was young, sometimes even with make-believe plate and make-believe spoon. Kanzi, a bonobo, often pretends that a make-believe dog or gorilla is biting him, or that he is pursuing and biting someone. Kanzi's younger sister, Panbanisha, often pretends that she hears a monster in the neighbouring room.[ix] Primatologist Frans De Waal describes a case where bonobos played blind man's buff.[x] One of them covers its eyes and stumbles around after the others.

3.4   Directing thought: intentionality

Human beings look for goals and meaning in their lives. We do not want to regard what happens in the world as merely mechanical processes. Above all, we want to regard other people's (and animals') behaviour as though they have a goal. As we shall see, we are so eager to see goals that we have a tendency to interpret the inanimate world as though it, too, were governed by intention.

Philosophers call what gives our thinking this goal orientation *intentionality*. The philosopher Franz Brentano's description of this concept in *Psychologie vom Empirischen Standpunkt* is a classic in philosophy. He says that every mental phenomenon is *directed* at some object. If I want to have cabbage pudding for dinner, my thought is aimed at cabbage pudding. The intentional is Valéry's arrow that humans throw at the future and reel themselves in after. But the intentional object need not exist in reality, either now or in the future; an imagined object will suffice. If I am afraid of the wood nymph, my thought is aimed at a purely imaginary object.

---

[6]   Mitchell (1994) maintains that dolphins, too, can pretend.

For Brentano, intentionality is characteristic of thinking: all mental phenomena are intentional. But there are other ways of looking at intentionality. Dennett distinguishes three different ways of relating to the objects and beings with which we interact. He calls the first level the *physical* stance. If the object is a computer, for example, this means that it is seen as an object made up of a number of electronic chips that are joined with encapsulated metal wires that go to the keyboard and monitor, etc. It is mostly when the computer does not function as it should that we adopt the physical stance.

The electronics in modern computers are so complicated that a layman can hardly understand them by viewing them from the physical stance. One can use the *functional* stance instead. This can be illustrated with the aid of a computer that plays chess. If I know how the computer is programmed, I can predict what it is going to do by following the programme's instructions step by step. In this way I could figure out what move the computer is going to make in response to the move I am planning. The predictions will come true as long as the computer functions the way it has been designed to—I do not need to be familiar with its physical construction.

But today's chess programmes are so advanced and calculate so rapidly that it is virtually impossible to follow the programme's function. Instead, we must base our predictions on the assumption that the programme is so well made that the computer will choose the most *rational* move in each position. According to Dennett, this implies that we adopt an *intentional* stance towards the computer, and that we thus treat it as though it were *rational*. We attribute 'goals' to the computer that not only imply that it 'wants' to win the game; we also say things like 'by moving the knight to QB4 the computer wants to *prevent* me from castling'. We also say that it 'believes' things like 'in this endgame the computer *believes* that two pawns are stronger than one knight, since it sacrificed its knight'.

Dennett says that the intentional strategy functions as follows:

> Here is how it works: first you decide to treat the object whose behaviour is to be predicated as a rational agent; then you figure out what beliefs that agent ought to have, given its place in the world and its purpose. Then you figure out what desires it ought to have, on the same considerations, and finally you predict that this rational agent will act to further its goals in the light of its beliefs.[xi]

The strategy functions well for humans and animals, but Dennett is generous with how it can be applied:

> The strategy works on birds, and on fish, and on reptiles, and on insects and spiders, and even on such lowly and unenterprising creatures as clams (once a

clam believes there is danger around, it will not relax its grip on its closed shell until it is convinced that the danger has passed). It also works on some artefacts: the chess-playing computer will not take your knight because it knows that there is a line of ensuing play that would lead to losing its rook, and it does not want that to happen. More modestly, the thermostat will turn off the boiler as soon as it comes to believe the room has reached the desired temperature.[xii]

"Philosophers are strange," mutters Egon. "A thermostat can't believe anything."

"No, you're absolutely right: Dennett's strategy is too easy to apply. It seems counterintuitive to say that clams and thermostats have intentions."

"And why is it the one who observes who decides if something believes or wants something?"

"I agree: it's odd that it is the *observer's* attitude that decides whether a system is intentional or not. It would be better to have a test that assigns intentionality to an organism or a system."

Unlike Dennett, I use the theory of representations and an inner world to understand what intentionality means. In my view, the core of the concept lies in the following criterion:

> An organism (or a system) is intentional with respect to a goal only if the organism (the system) has a detached representation of the goal.

This criterion agrees well with Brentano's idea that intentionality is aimed at a mental object. But in contradiction to Dennett's intentional stances my criterion does not attribute intentionality to a thermostat. The thermostat's 'goal' is indeed to keep the room at a constant temperature. But there is no representation in the thermostat that is in any way detached from its surroundings (if it at all can be said to have representations). In the same way, a sunflower whose blossom follows the sun is not intentional even if Dennett or someone else can take the intentional stance and say that the sunflower's 'desire' is to maximize the influx of solar energy. But of course the sunflower has no detached representation of the flow of energy.

On the other hand, a dog chasing a hare over a field is intentional according to the criterion above. Since the dog has the capacity for object permanence, it can create a detached representation of the hare (even if that representation is probably referent-dependent). The dog has an image of the hare even if it temporarily disappears behind a bush, and it can adapt its hunting accordingly.[xiii]

The psychologist Jean Piaget made a series of observations that showed that children become intentional at about eight months.[xiv] Prior to that age, they can learn that different kinds of behaviour produce particular results (stimulus–response couplings). For example, they can learn to pull a string to get a sound out of a rattle. If you take away the string, the child again tries to use the same hand movement to get the sound going, but it tries nothing else that might obtain the goal.

At eight months, the child alters its behaviour and becomes goal oriented. If it wants to get at a toy and you put a pillow between it and the toy, the child tries to move the pillow out of the way or to get around it. Before it reaches this age, the child begins to interact with the pillow instead and forgets the toy, or it becomes frustrated, but it does nothing about the pillow.

The criterion also locates intentionality *within* an organism and not in the eye of the beholder, as in Dennett's intentional stance. Naturally it can be a difficult problem to determine whether an organism really has a detached representation of a goal—especially when we study animals other than humans. As we shall see in the next chapter, such problems become very palpable when we study deception among animals. To intentionally deceive presupposes an image of the goal one wants to achieve, so this is an obvious application of the criterion.

Using the distinction between referent-dependent and referent-independent detached representations enables one to go further and distinguish between corresponding types of goals of intentional agents. An animal that has only referent-dependent representations cannot have a non-existent object as a goal. But if one has access to the more advanced independent representations one really can seek a unicorn. Hence it is probably only humans who can look for the pot of gold at the end of the rainbow—or for 'happiness' for that matter.

3.5   Imitation—why apes cannot ape

In Popperian beings, the inner world is built up through training and experience. Mammals play, and by playing they learn a lot about the consequences of different actions. This helps them to create an inner world that is sufficiently like the outer world so that the future will be approximately as the animal imagines.

Yet this is actually a roundabout way of acquiring an adapted inner world. You don't have time to make all the mistakes yourself—you should learn from others as well. An animal that can *copy* parts of another's acquired inner world can conserve energy and run fewer risks. Dennett calls organisms with this ability *Gregorian beings* after the British psychologist Richard Gregory who analyses such consciousness systems in his book *Mind in science*.

One example of how you can utilize other individuals' knowledge is to follow their gaze, to look where they are looking. By studying the gaze of others, an animal avoids having to invest so much time checking what is happening in its surroundings.[7] Many species of animal have this ability. If an animal stares fixedly in a certain direction, it is a sure sign that there is something interesting in that direction. This is a prime example of how Gregorian beings can benefit from the knowledge of others.

While I am thinking about my next example, I sit here cracking walnuts with a nutcracker. Egon watches attentively and also wants to have some nuts. I hand him the nutcracker. But he does not try to employ it in the intended manner; he uses it to hammer a nut until it falls to pieces. Fragments of shell and nut fly over the whole desk.

"What a mess you make," I say. "Crack the nuts the way I do!"

"But that's what I am doing—I break the shell and get what's inside."

Another approach to learning from the inner worlds of others is to *imitate* what they do. So one interesting issue in determining other species' cognitive abilities is the degree to which they can imitate. The answer, as it turns out, depends greatly on what you mean by imitation.

"Oh, yeah, philosophical nit-picking again," mumbles Egon around a mouthful of walnuts. "Imitate is imitate, right?"

"Just wait a sec and you'll find out what you can accomplish with a couple of quick distinctions," I reply indulgently.

The psychologist Michael Tomasello makes a distinction among three levels of imitation.[xv] He calls the lowest level *stimulus enhancement*. Members of a group may be attracted to objects with which others are interacting, thereby learning things on their own about these objects. For example a young chimpanzee may be attracted to a stone her mother has used to crack nuts and by playing with the stone learn something about how it can be handled. This process often leads to what Tomasello calls emulation learning. An animal emulates another animal when it realizes that the other animal manipulates its surroundings, or a tool, so that a certain goal is achieved, and then learns to reach the same goal in a similar situation. For example, the animal may see a kindred animal dig up a delicious worm in a certain type of terrain, and thus learn to find worms in similar locations. Emulation does not imply that you imitate the other animal's movements, or understand that it has a certain intention in its behaviour. The only thing that is important is the result.

---

[7] I will return to the ability to read the attention of others in Section 4.3.

The second level is *mimicking*. In this type of behaviour, an animal mimics another's behaviour. This can be done by using your body in the same way as the other animal does, e.g. when a bird mimics human speech. Nor does mimicking presume that you can interpret the intentions behind the behaviour. A parrot does not *understand* what it is saying, however skilful it may be at mimicking a human voice.[8]

Tomasello reserves the term *imitation* for the third and highest level. An animal that imitates understands the *intention* behind a certain kind of behaviour and looks not only at the movements the other animal makes or at the outcome. It sees how the behaviour *produces* the outcome.[9] In order to do this, the imitator must:

1. Be able to *imagine the other animal's intentions*, and hence part of its inner world.
2. Combine a complex series of actions.[xvi]

As we shall see in the section dealing with deception, these are an advanced cognitive abilities.

"It's still hair-splitting," insists Egon. "The important thing must be getting the right result."

"Yes, that's true, but you achieve better results if you imitate rather than just mimic or emulate. If you comprehend the purpose of an action, you can *adapt* your way of carrying out an action to your own capabilities and attain your goal more effectively. And effectiveness yields bonus points in the game arcades of evolution."

Using these three levels as background, Tomasello presents a survey of different experiments that have tested the ability of apes to emulate, mimic, and imitate. His conclusion is that apes cannot ape, at least not apes in the wild. The studies of apes' use of tools and gestures seem to show that they can only emulate one another's behaviour. When Egon cracks walnuts, he is emulating my behaviour. He has only perceived that I use the nutcracker as an aid to open the nuts; he has not understood *how* I use the tool, and he cannot imitate my behaviour.[10]

---

[8] Alex, an African grey parrot trained by Irene Pepperberg (1990) has, however, learned to handle a number of linguistic expressions through rigorous conditioning. Among other things, he can count to six, and he can answer questions about colour and shape. He can even take on the speaker's role and ask questions. Yet how much he 'understands' is uncertain.

[9] This assumes that one can understand the connection between cause and effect, and not just see the world as couplings between stimuli and responses as I discussed in Section 2.8.

[10] As we shall see later, the bonobo Kanzi slammed a flint on the floor when he was going to make chips of stone. But he apparently understood how to knap flint—it was simply a lot easier for him to throw it on the floor: see Savage-Rumbauch and Lewin (1994), p. 213.

The difficulties are well illustrated by a simple experiment by Tomasello and his colleagues. They removed a chimpanzee from her troop and taught her two signs that she could use to obtain food from a human. When she was later reunited with her troop and successfully used the same gestures to obtain food, there was not another single chimpanzee that imitated any of her gesticulations, despite the fact that they all could see her signs and they all wanted to have food.[xvii] Seemingly, they did not understand that the signs were *causes* of rewards.

When it comes to encultured apes, i.e. apes that have grown up among humans, the result is a bit different. The chimpanzees and orang-utans that have learned to use signs to communicate can learn what the sign for 'do like this' means. If a human makes a body movement and then the sign for 'do like this', the ape can learn to mimic the movement. But Tomasello is very dubious about the assertion that the apes can imitate, i.e. that they also understand the point of what they are mimicking.

There are some results that to a certain extent contest Tomasello's position on imitation. The psychologist Andrew Whiten constructed an 'artificial fruit' consisting of a Plexiglas box with a food reward inside.[xviii] But to access the food, one had to manipulate several bolts, pins, and handles. The four subjects, who were naturally reared chimpanzees, watched a human experimenter demonstrating how to open the box three times. Then the apes could try the box on their own. Three of the four used the technique that had been demonstrated to them. Whiten argues that this experiment is evidence that chimpanzees can imitate, even if they are not encultured.

The zoologists Bernhard Voelkl and Ludwig Huber ran an experiment with marmosets that also questions Tomasello's general position. The monkey subjects watched a demonstrator removing the lids from plastic film canisters to obtain a mealworm. One of the demonstrators used its hands to remove the lid, while another used its mouth. When the subjects could try the canisters themselves, those that had observed a demonstrator using its hands to remove the lids used only their hands. In contrast, marmosets that observed a demonstrator using its mouth also used their mouth to remove the lids. Furthermore, a third group of marmosets that had not observed a demonstrator prior to testing exhibited a low probability of mouth opening. Since the two demonstrators brought about identical changes in the canisters, the different behaviour of the two groups of subjects suggests that they could imitate the demonstrator's behaviour, at least in the case when the mouth was used.

There are a number of observations suggesting that dolphins can at least mimic, if not quite imitate, the behaviour of other animals. For example, they can mimic how a sea lion swims, how it grooms itself, and how it lies when it sleeps.[xix] Once when a person exhaled a cloud of smoke outside the glass of an aquarium right where a baby dolphin happened to be looking, the little dolphin swam over to its mother, sucked in a mouthful of milk, swam back to where the person was standing, and released the milk in the water so that it looked like a cloud of smoke. Although that is just a singular observation, it is rather suggestive.

It is difficult to construct experiments that unequivocally determine whether a form of behaviour is imitation or only mimicking. Psychologists Richard Byrne and Anne Russon have studied imitation among wild mountain gorillas and among orang-utans that were 'rehabilitated' from a life in captivity to a life in the jungle.[xx] Their results ascribe somewhat more competence to the apes than Tomasello does. Even though the apes cannot imitate individual body movements, Byrne and Russon maintain that they can imitate on a 'program level' rather than on the level of individual movements. A mountain gorilla can understand how another gorilla tears the leaves off a nettle, folds them up, puts them in its mouth, and begins to chew. It can comprehend the *intention* behind the actions and imitate the behaviour program, even if it does not imitate the individual body movements. By Tomasello's criterion this would be a form of intentional imitation, although it lacks the mimicking element. Following the lines of Whiten's artificial fruit experiment, Byrne notes that it has been found:

> that chimpanzees do tend to copy a demonstrated sequence of actions, an ability that would help enable program-level imitation, but that this imitation depends on repeated observations over trials [...]. If repetition is essential for imitation of this kind [...], it becomes less surprising that there exist no compelling field observations of 'before/after' differences that show imitation after a single observation of a skilled model.

The examples of imitation submitted by Byrne and Russon deal with behaviour that is 'meaningful' for the gorillas and orang-utans, such as acquiring food. It is not clear whether their imitating ability can extend as far as to capricious actions. Humans, at any rate, are capable of imitating even 'meaningless' behaviour.

3.6   Planning—why the squirrel does not plan for the winter

When you can represent *different* actions in your inner world, i.e. different approaches to reaching a goal, then *choice* enters the picture. Representations of alternative actions must be detached, and the capacity for a conscious choice therefore presupposes an inner world. An animal dedicated to trial-and-error does not choose—the action carried out is generated unconsciously, without first being represented in the inner world, and to some extent haphazardly. I would like to point out that there is a difference between being able to choose, which can occur unconsciously, and having a *free will*, which presumes being able to reflect about the choices available. As I shall demonstrate later, free will depends on having self-consciousness.

Advanced planning comprises planning not only individual actions, but also *sequences* of actions. 'I have to do this first before I can do that.' First an action is represented in the inner world, and then the consequences are simulated. And in the new environment that thus arises, you represent a subsequent action and then in turn simulate new consequences, etc. Another way of describing planning is that you allow the simulator that guides your body to run, but without having the real behaviour engaged. The motor of thought is declutched from the wheels of the body.

One suitable definition of what planning implies is this:[xxi]

> An individual plans its actions if it has a representation of a goal and of its present situation, and can generate representations of a number of actions that can lead forward to the goal.

From this definition it follows that the representations of actions must be detached; otherwise a stimulus–response chain might just as well decide the behaviour chosen by the individual.

There are several examples of behaviour from the animal world, especially among the apes, that have to be interpreted as conscious planning.[xxii] One such example, as we have seen previously, is a chimpanzee that wants to get lunch from a termite stack, goes over and breaks a twig off a tree, peels the leaves off the twig, comes back to the stack and uses the stick to 'fish up' the termites. This is incidentally also a prime example of deliberate *tool making* as one link in a planning operation. Further support for the thesis that the chimpanzees have detached representations of their needs is that modifications of the tools are seldom made after the first use.[xxiii] Tolman's rats that took short cuts in the labyrinth are best interpreted as having planned their route before starting to run.

Another example of planning is an experiment made by psychologist Emil Menzel with a chimpanzee.[xxiv] The animal was carried around a field and saw how food was hidden in 18 different places. Then the chimp was released and managed to find almost all of the hidden food. But the path it chose was entirely different from and a lot shorter than the route along which it was carried while the food was being hidden. This suggests that the animal used an inner map of the locations when it went looking for the food.

The ability to plan chains of actions does not necessarily imply that the individual has some concept of *time*—it is enough to be able to order one's actions in a sequence. But a concept of time is impossible without an ability to plan, and it probably also requires that the individual has an episodic memory. So *time awareness* is a cognitively advanced capacity with which presumably only humans are gifted. Naturally there are many different kinds of behaviour among animals that are adjusted to the rhythms of the day and the seasons, but such behaviour is purely instinctive. Animals have built-in clocks, but there is nothing to suggest that they are conscious of the passage of time in the sense that they have detached representations of time.

3.7 Ockham's razor

People have always interpreted their pets' behaviour as meaning that they are smarter than can actually be proved. Even in antiquity the Stoic Chrysippus told about a dog that appeared to be able to reason. When it came to a three-way junction, it first sniffed along the first path, then a bit along the second path, and then ran off along the third path without bothering to sniff. Chrysippus interpreted this to mean that the dog *reasoned* its way to deciding the third path was right because the other two were wrong. Yet there are other interpretations much closer to hand that do not presuppose any advanced thinking on the part of the dog. For example, it could have smelled the scent so clearly along the third path that it did not need to do any sniffing. One argument against a dog having reasoning intelligence is the fact that a dog can rarely figure out how to free up its leash when it has run around a post with it. The moral is that we have to be very careful about ascribing cognitive capabilities to animals. Only when we can find no other reasonable explanation for an animal's behaviour should we draw the conclusion that it can plan, reason or intentionally deceive, for example.

The ethologists who study the behaviour of wild animals work with a very restrictive methodology. Generally they proceed from a version of the so-called Ockham's razor, which in this context means that one must not assign a certain cognitive ability to an animal if it is possible to explain the animal's behaviour without assuming that ability. Because of the anthropomorphism typical of human beings, i.e. our readiness to ascribe human characteristics to the world around us, a scientist must really struggle to hang onto Ockham's razor when dealing with animals' thinking.[11]

"Yeah, that's just what I'm saying," Egon points out. "You'd better be really careful with your assumptions about the representations you want to use to construct those inner worlds."

"If you don't behave yourself, I'll follow Descartes and treat you as if you were a machine."

The most classic experiment is the one Wolfgang Köhler carried out with the chimpanzee Sultan and others way back in the 1920s. Köhler put two sticks in Sultan's cage, neither of which was long enough to reach some desirable food placed outside the cage. After several vain attempts, Sultan realized that he could join the two sticks together to make one long one that he could use to reach the food. Sultan's success has often been described as his having achieved an 'insight' or a 'perception', but it can almost equally well be described as the result of trial-and-error. In Sultan's defence, however, one must observe that once the two sticks had been joined together, he immediately 'perceived' that he could now reach the food.

Another example is the following story about a dog that was allowed to be in just one armchair in the home.[xxv] One evening when her master was sitting in that chair and the dog lay on the floor in front of it, the dog whimpered to get her master to turn the chair over to her. When that did not work, the dog stood up and went to the front door. She scratched at the door and thus intimated that she had given up hope of getting to lie in the chair and now wanted to go out. But as soon as her master reached the door to let her out, she ran

Figure 3.2 Also orang-utans manage problems that require insight.

---

[11] This point is argued eloquently by Hauser (2000).

back and climbed into the armchair. This behaviour is probably a form of planning, since the dog perceived that if she went to the door her master would get up from the chair. But this is not intentional deception in the sense that I will describe in the next chapter, since the dog need have no image or representation of what is in her master's mind in order to form her plan. In principle, the dog can see it as though she had *conditioned* her master to go to the door as soon as she herself did.

"That's probably just how it was," Egon breaks in.

"Possibly," I allow.

3.8   Thinking about tomorrow

Our most important thoughts are those which contradict our feelings.

Paul Valéry

Egon is very fond of peanuts. He is willing to do anything—even to betray confidences—to get hold of peanuts. To test his thought capacity I performed a simple experiment. I put peanuts in two piles of different sizes on the table, out of his reach. Egon was given the following instructions:

"Here are two piles of nuts. We can each have one. You point to the one I can have. The other pile is for you."

The outcome of the test was surprising. Egon pointed to the bigger of the two piles and was highly indignant when I took it and shoved the smaller pile over to him. To see whether this was a chance result, I repeated the experiment a few times, but the outcome was the same. He was equally distressed each time.

"Why do you point to the big pile?"

"Because I want it."

"But that's daft," I tease him. "Don't you understand that you would get more nuts if you pointed to the little pile?"

"No, you're the one who's daft for trying to trick me."

Ethologists, who study animal behaviour, appear to be largely in agreement that certain animal species can plan in the sense defined in the previous section. Yet all examples of planning among animals available in the ethological literature concern planning for *current needs*. Apes and other animals start planning because they are hungry or thirsty, tired or frightened. Their motivation comes from the present state of the body. Oakley writes:

Sultan, the chimpanzee observed by Kohler, was capable of improvising tools in certain situations. Tool-making occurred only in the presence of a visible reward, and never without it. In the chimpanzee the mental range seems to be limited to present situations, with little conception of past or future.[xxvi]

Man seems to be the only animal that can *plan for future needs*. We can *foresee* that we will be hungry tomorrow and put by some of our food; we realize that it will be cold and windy in the winter, so we build a shelter in good time. (Chimpanzees build night camps, but only for the coming night.[12]) The cognitive scientist Agneta Gulz calls the capacity to plan for the future *anticipatory planning*.[13] This is yet another example of how human thought has been detached from the present situation.

"But what about animals that gather food for the winter?" wonders Egon. "Aren't they planning for future needs?"

"It might appear that way, but that behaviour is not planning. It is purely instinctive, a tropism. There is no evidence that the squirrel has an image of its cache or of its needs come winter."

In support of this, Sjölander writes that 'if you give a squirrel in a cage a standing tube with a hole at the bottom, and a nut, then the squirrel busies itself all day by putting the nut in the tube, where it falls out again, just to pick it up again, and put it back into the tube etc.'[xxvii]

My experiment with the peanuts, which Egon found so mean, is in fact a variant of an experiment performed with chimpanzees by Sally Boysen and Gary Berntson.[xxviii] The outcome was the same as with Egon: the chimps consistently chose the bigger pile of food. They seem to be incapable of detaching their thoughts from the current situation of choice and imagining the near future when the other party receives the pile that they choose and they are left with the other pile. Boysen and Berntson's experiment indicates how difficult it is to manage even the simplest form of anticipatory planning. Deacon writes that the choice is difficult for chimpanzees since the indirect solution (choosing the small pile) is *overshadowed* by the direct presence of a more attractive stimulus, namely, the big pile.[xxix] They cannot suppress their perception.[14]

If one performs the same kind of experiment with human children, they have no problem choosing the small pile—from the age of two and up. They can *imagine* receiving the big pile when they point to the small one. When children are younger they behave more like chimpanzees. It has also been

---

[12] On the other hand, they have little reason to do otherwise, since they do not know where they will sleep the following night.

[13] See also Bischof (1978), p. 57. Byrne (1998) also writes about 'anticipatory planning', but his use of the term concerns events that lie in the near future and that are determined by the present needs of the planner.

[14] In other words, they lack some of the executive functions that are controlled from the frontal lobe in humans.

shown that persons with autism have difficulties that closely resemble those of chimpanzees and small children.[15]

Sheba, one of the chimpanzees in Boysen's study, was also trained to connect figures with quantities, so that she knew that the figure 5 corresponded to a bigger pile of treats than the figure 3. Once she had learned the meaning of the figures, she was instead allowed to choose between two cards showing figures, and the pile corresponding to the selected figure was given to the other chimpanzee, while she received the pile corresponding to the figure she had not chosen. The results were now better: Sheba could learn to select cards so that she received the big pile. The explanation is that there is no longer a conflict between the stimuli she *sees* and what she has to choose—the cards had no intrinsic value for the chimp.

It is surprising that chimpanzees cannot learn to choose the food they do not want. The psychologists Alan Silberberg and Kazuo Fujita have argued that this is because of a flaw in Boysen and Berntson's experimental set-up: the chimpanzees are *always rewarded* to some extent, regardless of their choice. To check the importance of this factor, Silberberg and Fujita ran a variation of the experiment with Japanese macaques.[xxx] In the first phase of the experiment, a human offered the macaque subjects four treats in one hand and one in the other. When the subjects choose a hand, they were offered what was in the other. This condition was like Boysen and Berntson's test and the macaques performed in the same way the chimpanzees did, choosing the hand with four treats and receiving only one treat. In the second phase of the experiment, four and one treats were presented again, but if the monkey now selected the hand with four, it received nothing at all, while if it chose the hand with one, it received four. In this condition, the macaques changed their behaviour and learned to choose the hand with one treat. The difference is that in this case the cost for making the wrong selection was greater for the macaques, and apparently this is sufficient for them to learn the appropriate rule.

"Why is it more difficult to plan for future needs than for current ones?" wonders Egon.

The answer has to do with the different representations that are required for the two types of planning. When planning to satisfy current needs, one must be able to represent in one's inner world the possible actions and their consequences, and to determine the value of the consequences in relation to the need one has *at that moment*. But no separate representation of that need is required. To plan for future needs, on the other hand, one must also be able

---

[15] Russell *et al.* (1991). I shall come back to the cognitive abilities of persons with autism in Section 4.8.

to *represent these potential needs* (and to understand that some of them will arise). The available ethological evidence suggests that man is the only species of animal with the ability to imagine future wishes and to plan and act accordingly. Deacon calls our thinking front-heavy; anticipatory planning takes place in the frontal lobe, the most recently evolved part of the brain.

Byrne presents a case where a group of old male chimpanzees cornered a mother leopard and a cub in her narrow breeding cave.[16] One brave chimp went into the cave and emerged with the cub that was then bitten and kneaded until it was mortally wounded. Byrne writes that 'in the absence of any immediate reward, their behaviour cannot be explained as conventional animal learning. [...] Perhaps the 'least implausible' explanation is that the chimpanzees had an understanding of the likely effects of their actions in the future.' I don't agree that this is the least implausible explanation. It is natural that chimps show more or less innate aggressive behaviour against leopards— old and young—and if there was no danger they would be happy to eliminate any leopard they encounter. In the observed case, directly attacking the mother would be too dangerous—but bringing out the cub from the cave turned out to be possible thanks to a foolhardy chimp. In my opinion, the event can thus be explained without any reference to the chimps *imagining* the future consequences of their hunt and hence it is not a case of anticipatory planning.

A historically interesting example of anticipatory planning is the art of keeping a fire alive. This art presupposes the following thought components:

1. The insight that the fire consumes the fuel.
2. The conclusion that new fuel must be added if the fire is to go on burning.
3. The awareness that, when the fire goes out, I will be cold (or predators will come close).
4. The insight that this creates a future need which requires me to act now.
5. The conclusion that I must start gathering firewood right now. Once the fire has gone out it is too late.

The crucial step is imagining oneself freezing when the fire dies; or, in more general terms, being able to represent one's needs in a future situation.

3.9   Making tools

The use of *tools* by hominids gives us important clues as to how they thought. Even *Homo habilis* was able to make crudely cut stone tools. The oldest finds

---

[16] Byrne (1998), pp. 119–20.

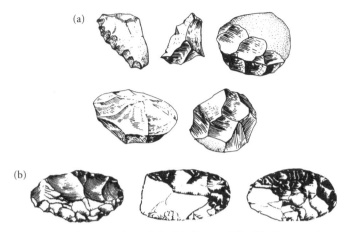

Figure 3.3 Examples of stone tools made by (a) *Homo habilis*, (b) *Homo erectus*.

are about 2.4 million years old. The origin of stone tools is associated with the transition to a diet with a larger content of meat. *Homo erectus*, a later species, used much more advanced tools, in the form of symmetrically worked hand axes of stone.

Tools like these indicate a fairly advanced capacity for thought. To be able to learn how to make hand axes one must be able to *imitate* someone else manufacturing an axe. As I have argued earlier, apes find this difficult. It also requires being able to *remember* a series of actions in the right order. Tool making presupposes *purposeful* training. The shape of the raw material probably determined the form of the tools made by *Homo habilis*. But when *Homo erectus* made symmetrical axes, they had to *imagine* the finished tool while it was being made, and to *plan* the knapping. Imagining a finished axe does not require any language, but it does presuppose advanced *visualization*. As I shall argue later, the art of thinking in images is much older in evolutionary terms than the ability to think in words.

Many animal species use tools in their natural environments. Some birds, for example, use sticks to extract insects from cracks in trees. The chimpanzee, however, seems to be the only animal species, apart from man, that *manufactures* tools and makes several different kinds of tools.[17] For instance, they peel

---

[17] Byrne (1995), pp. 187–90. One possible exception is a female Caledonian crow that has been observed to bend a wire to make a fishing hook (Weir, Chappell, and Kacelnik 2002.)

the leaves from twigs in order to 'fish' for termites in their mounds. They use two stones as a hammer and anvil for cracking hard nuts. Yet chimpanzees make tools only when they need them, and they hardly ever bring tools with them from one place to another. This suggests that they do not imagine that they can use the tools later; in other words, they do not plan for the future.[18]

Apes use stones to crack nuts, but they do not work the stones. The bonobo Kanzi, who will be presented in greater detail later, lives in a research centre where he has been trained to knap stones. His motivation for this is that, if he succeeds in striking a sufficiently sharp flake, he can use it to cut a string tied round a box containing sweets, so that he can get at them. After a great deal of practice, Kanzi learned how to strike reasonably sharp flakes. However, he dis-covered a short cut: by throwing the stones against the cement floor he could split them, thus quickly obtaining the sharp edges he was after.

It takes great strength and precision to be able to knap flint in the right way. Bonobos are much stronger than humans in relation to their body weight, so strength is no problem. But the structure of their shoulders, wrists, and hands differs from that of human, which prevents them from gripping the stones in the right way and from being able to flick the wrist while striking. Moreover, they are not very skilled at aiming. The tool manufacture developed by the hominids is consequently difficult for apes to copy, for several reasons.

The difference between immediate and anticipatory planning is seen, for example, in the way tools are used. Apes and some other animals make tools, but only for their current needs. A human, by contrast, can understand that the tool will be needed the next day and can therefore take it along when mov-ing to a new habitation site. Signs showing that tools were carried are therefore an interesting test of whether there is a capacity for anticipatory planning.[19] The anthropologist Nicholas Toth argues that several of the finds of stone tools manufactured by *Homo habilis* in Kenya and Tanzania were transported over several kilometres. The raw material for the tools was also moved over long distances, which indicates *plans* to make tools later, in another place. In con-trast to this, scientists observing how chimpanzees use tools have found that they carry their tools at most a few hundred metres.[xxxi] The longest time

---

[18] However, chimpanzees in the Tai forest of the Ivory Coast have been observed leaving their stone hammers near a fruiting nut tree and returning to use them again. Hauser (2000), p. 35, suggests that 'they understand the function of these stones and appreciate the importance of retrieving them in the future'. We know very little of what they understand in this context and, in my opinion, the evidence for thinking about the future would have been much stronger if they had carried the stones along to a new place.

[19] This idea has been proposed by Mathias Osvath.

elapsing between the manufacture and the use of a tool by a chimpanzee that has been observed is 17 minutes. There are thus no signs that chimps have anticipatory planning in relation to their tools, but there is a great deal to imply that *Homo habilis* already had this ability. This suggests a significant difference in cognitive capacity between the apes and the early hominids.

The anthropologist Robert Foley notes that humans sweat much more profusely than do other primates. The reason for this is presumably that perspiration helps to regulate body temperature.[xxxii] This makes humans thirsty animals that are dependent on being close to water. Once the hominids had learned how to carry water, they would have had much greater freedom to move over longer distances. Carrying water is a minimal form of planning for the future that nevertheless may have meant a major breakthrough in the lives of the hominids.

It would be interesting to know when the first baskets or water containers (presumably made of skins) were manufactured, since they are used for carrying things from one place to another, and would hence provide further evidence of anticipatory planning. Since artefacts of this kind rarely leave any archaeological traces, however, we do not know when this happened. It is at any rate clear that our long-term planning has become increasingly comprehensive, to the extent that we now constantly carry our future around with us.

3.10 The human dilemma

> Lying awake, calculating the future,
> Trying to unweave, unwind, unravel
> And piece together the past and the future,
> Between midnight and dawn, when the past is all deception,
> The future futureless, before the morning watch
>
> T. S. Eliot, *The Dry Salvages*

The human capacity for planning is the foundation for several functions of our thinking. The ability to plan for future needs is valuable from an evolutionary point of view. Once it has arisen, it will therefore spread in the population by the mechanisms of natural selection. We have now come so far that we cannot help planning for the future.[20]

I believe that this capacity for *planning in advance* gives rise to a fundamental human predicament. Goethe expresses the conflict clearly in *Faust*:

> Two souls, alas, are housed within my breast
> and one would gladly sunder from the other.

---

[20] Paul Valéry says: 'Man is an animal confined—outside his cage. He lives and moves *outside himself.*'

> One clamors for the world, its lust
> is shackled to the joys of brute creation.
> The other struggles to ascend from dust
> to infinity of aspiration.

The dilemma is that the actions required to satisfy future needs often conflict with those that satisfy our current desires. If I do not want to be cold later in the night, I have to go off and search for firewood, but right now I am warm and drowsy and do not feel like leaving the fireplace. We must *choose* between acting for the present or for the future, whereas other animals, whose consciousness does not contain any conceptions of future needs, simply choose for the moment. They are like 'the fowls of the air: for they sow not, neither do they reap, nor gather into barns'.[xxxiii]

Happiness is when the desires for the present and the future go hand in hand—as when you fall in love or when a child is born.

Psychoanalysis emphasizes the conflict between the ego and the superego. I think that these concepts can be better described as the part of the inner world that represents the present and the part that represents future needs and choices. It is also only in conjunction with a detached representation of a goal that *moral* considerations can play any part.[21]

There are great individual differences between how we handle the conflict between our current desires and the future needs we can foresee. The differences are well illustrated by the fable of the ant and the grasshopper. Some people, like the ant, find it difficult to live in the present, instead deriving their greatest satisfaction from planning for the future. They invest in pension insurance at the age of 25. Other people virtually ignore long-term planning. Like the grasshopper in Aesop's fable, they live from hand to mouth and do not worry about tomorrow. This character trait is said to be general among drug addicts. (It is not certain what is cause and effect here.) In the crass terminology of the economists, one may say that they practise rapid discounting of the future.

The conflict between the ego of the present and that of the future is closely related to what Søren Kierkegaard calls 'despair' in his *The sickness unto death*. He formulates this inevitable human dilemma as follows:

> However much [...] the despairer has succeeded in altogether losing his self, and in such a way that the loss is not in the least way noticeable, eternity will nevertheless make it evident that this condition is that of despair, and will nail him to his self so that the torment will still be that he cannot be rid of his self,

---

[21] The id corresponds best to the need-directed unconscious part of our life, which provides us with our immediate wants.

and it will be evident that he cannot be rid of his self, and it will be evident that his success was an illusion. And this eternity must do, because having a self, being a self, is the greatest, the infinite, concession that has been made to man, but also eternity's claim on him.[xxxiv]

In other words, we have no way of extracting ourselves from the conflict between living in the present and thinking ahead; it is precisely this that makes us human. Kierkegaard also points out that the form of 'sickness' that despair constitutes is unique to man:

The possibility of this sickness is man's advantage over the beast, and it is an advantage which characterizes him quite otherwise than the upright posture, for it bespeaks the infinite erectness or loftiness of his being spirit.[xxxv]

Gulz points out that it cannot be taken for granted that man's capacity for anticipatory planning increases our evolutionary fitness.[xxxvi] By living in a world of fantasies and hopes and planning far too much for future needs, one can neglect the opportunities that are available now and thus *reduce* one's fitness.

Valéry summarizes these ideas nicely:

Thought is perhaps no more than a whim of Nature, who has bestowed it on a single species, as she bestowed on the rare or extinct mammals we see in our museums their absurd antlers: weapons or ornaments so curiously ourspread, looped, gnarled, or branching that they are even more perilous than useless to the animal that wears them.

After all—why not? Our heads are cluttered up with speculations and ideas that get caught in the tangles of the forest or hard facts, and keep us in a quandary, proud of our excrescences and doomed to bell, like rutting stags, our poems and our theories—magniloquent and mortified.

Notes

i. Sjölander (1993) and Byrne (1995), pp. 86–8.
ii. See Fagen (1981).
iii. Llinas and Pare (1991).
iv. Farah *et al.* (1992).
v. Grush (1998).
vi. Oakley (1985).
vii. Byrne (1995), p. 88.
viii. Leslie (1987), p. 416.
ix. Savage-Rumbaugh, Shanker, and Taylor (1998), p. 60.
x. De Waal (1995).
xi. Dennett (1981), p. 57.
xii. Dennett (1981), p. 61.

xiii. See Sjölander (1993).

xiv. Piaget (1954).

xv. Tomasello (1996).

xvi. Byrne (1995), p. 66.

xvii. Tomasello *et al.* (1997).

xviii. Whiten *et al.* (1996).

xix. Taylor and Saayman (1973).

xx. Byrne and Russon (1998).

xxi. Gulz (1991), p. 46.

xxii. Gulz (1991), pp. 58–61 presents a number of such examples.

xxiii. Boesch and Boesch (1990).

xxiv. Menzel (1973).

xxv. Dennett (1978), pp. 274–5.

xxvi. Oakley (1961), p. 187.

xxvii. Sjölander (2002), p. 26 (my translation).

xxviii. Boysen and Berntson (1995).

xxix. Deacon (1997), p. 414.

xxx. Silberberg and Fujita (1996).

xxxi. Toth (1985), p. 114.

xxxii. Foley (1996), p. 168

xxxiii. Matthew 6: 26.

xxxiv. Kirkegaard (1989), p. 51.

xxxv. Kirkegaard (1989), pp. 44–5.

xxxvi. Gulz (1991), pp. 136–41.

CHAPTER 4

Reading other people's minds

4.1 Levels of theory of mind

A great deal of the debate about the ability of animals to think has concerned whether they have a 'theory of mind'. The criterion for this is that an individual has representations of other people's minds, what they believe, and what they want (and, of course, that these representations of other people's minds play a part in the individual's thinking and behaviour). The crucial issue is whether an individual has any representation of other individuals' inner worlds.

To determine whether various monkeys and apes (for the debate is mostly about them) have any theory of mind, Ockham's razor is applied. The question is whether their behaviour can be explained solely from the assumption that they have an inner world, i.e. the complexity required for pure planning, without assuming that they have some conception of others' inner worlds. As we shall see, the experiments in this area of research produce a tangle of interpretations from which it is difficult to draw any unambiguous conclusions.

To structure the different possible interpretations and arrive at a clearer understanding of how animals and children think, it is necessary to introduce several levels of mental representations. To achieve sufficient precision in the analysis of the cognitive abilities of animals and children, I shall distinguish between the following six capacities:

1. Having *an inner world*. As we have seen, this is what is required for immediate planning.

2. Having a *theory of emotions*. At this level one can, for example, understand that someone else is in pain. This is what is usually meant by *compassion*. Even though one can understand others' emotions, it does not require that one understands what they believe or want.

3. Having a *theory of attention*. This means that one can understand, for example, what someone else is looking at, but not that this ability presupposes any conception of their inner world.

4. Having a *theory of intentions*. This capacity means, above all, being able to understand the objective that may lie behind another individual's behaviour. This is a particularly interesting form of *causal* reasoning.

5. Having a *theory of others' minds*. This ability has already been defined as having representations of what other individuals believe and want.

6. Having *self-consciousness*. For this level it is required that you have representations of your own inner world, i.e. being able to think about what you yourself believe or want. A special case is the capacity for anticipatory planning, which presupposes that you can represent your future needs.

I submit that these levels make up a series of layers in the cognitive development leading to self-consciousness.[1] The cognitive consequences of having an inner world (level 1) were discussed in the previous chapter. The capacity for self-consciousness (level 6) is, in my opinion, the most advanced and will be kept for the next chapter. Here I shall deal with what we know about capacities 2, 3, 4, and 5. Level 2—having a theory of other's feelings—is an emotive ability and hence relatively independent of levels 3, 4, and 5, which are more concerned with cognitive abilities.

"It seems as if you are happier the more distinctions you can introduce," Egon mocks me.

"Making distinctions is a philosopher's occupational disease," I admit. "But if you can keep quiet while I go through the various experiments that have been conducted, I'm sure I'll be able to convince you that they are necessary."

"I can't keep quiet *that* long."

4.2 Understanding emotions

Since we have so much in common with the apes, their emotional expressions are obvious to us and it is easy for us to feel empathy for them. This makes it difficult to understand how Descartes could claim that animals are just automata; sophisticated automata, admittedly, but with no soul or moral status. Darwin's theory of evolution, however, changed the status of animals: according to him, animals are of the same essence as humans.

---

[1] I have not found any other researcher who makes grades in this way concerning what is involved in a theory of mind. Tomasello and Call (1997), p. 189 and Tomasello (1999), p. 179, distinguish between three levels of a child's development: (1) seeing others as agents (which is common to all primates); (2) seeing others as intentional agents; and (3) seeing others as mental agents. His second and third levels correspond to my skills 4 and 5. Proust (1998) presents a longer list of capacities that are part of a theory of others' minds, but she does not sort them into levels or discuss how they are related.

Before Darwin, philosophers regarded it as a category mistake to talk of animals' emotions—it was like saying that a clock is happy or in pain. After Darwin, however, it became a possible field of scientific inquiry, Darwin himself leading the way with his studies of the emotional expressions of apes.[2] In the apes, emotions are often signalled by highly distinct bodily expressions, above all in the face, but also by sounds. Many of these involuntary reactions are still found in humans—it is hard to suppress a cry of surprise or a laugh.

Kanzi the bonobo, who grew up amongst humans, clearly shows compassion for the people who train him. Once when he tried to open a can of cherries by throwing it on the ground, he happened to hit Kelly, a trainer, on the knee.[i] She screamed in pain and grabbed her knee with her hand. Kanzi did not realize that the can had hit her knee, so he seemed to assume that Kelly had hurt her hand. He looked carefully at it but could see nothing but a scab from an old injury. He moved her hand towards a canteen of water that she was holding. When asked what he wanted, he replied by pointing to the canteen and to the old injury to show that he wanted to pour water on the wound. When she did so, Kanzi tried to clean the wound. Examples of this type indicate that Kanzi can perceive others' feelings.

Bodily expressions of emotions have a *communicative* purpose. The expressions are most obvious among social animals. The evolutionary explanation for this seems to be that the capacity for compassion leads to greater solidarity within the group. This reduces the risk of violent conflicts in which individuals thoughtlessly injure one another. The resulting solidarity increases the chances of survival for the individuals in the group.[3]

"But if you can interpret someone else's feelings, then you must surely have a theory of the other's mind," Egon declares.

"No, not necessarily," I protest. "Having compassion basically means *feeling the same* as the other. It doesn't need to mean that you show *empathy*, which presupposes that you have representations of the other's emotions or other aspects of the other's inner world. To be able to feel empathy, you have to be able to distinguish your own feelings from the other's."

Presumably, compassion functions as follows: the sensory impressions that the other's bodily expressions arouse in me provoke a corresponding emotion

---

[2] Darwin (1872). Even more important is that the recognition of emotions in animals has led to a new view of the use of animals in experiments and breeding. We now have well-argued rules for how animals should be treated in scientific studies and ethics committees to monitor compliance with the rules; and there are associations defending the rights of animals.

[3] This explanation is actually of the same sociobiological type as the explanation of 'reciprocal altruism'. See, e.g. Dawkins (1976).

in me as well.[4] One can then, of course, envisage a more advanced stage at which one also creates an idea of the other's feelings. But the capacity for empathy is an independent stage that means a further step in the expansion of the inner world.

Not all people are good at compassion. One of the central criteria of a *psychopath* is that he (or, in rare cases, she) finds it difficult to feel compassion. Psychopaths do not have the normal blockage against hurting or tormenting other people. Nor can they understand the difference between the rules of behaviour that exist for conventional reasons and those that are intended to prevent us from harming other people.[ii]

Apes, unlike humans, have little detached control over their movements or facial muscles. Those individuals among the hominids who could simulate their emotional expressions or suppress them were more often successful in deceiving others. There has consequently been evolutionary pressure to be able to control one's facial muscles and voice. This is a central part of the 'Machiavellian intelligence' that I shall discuss later.

Modern humans are skilful at blocking their emotional expressions. We can put on a poker face or feign the expression of a different emotion—we *bluff*. Humans are much more expert at deceiving than apes can ever be. Not all of the bodily consequences of the emotions, however, are under the control of the will: a blush or a dilated pupil can reveal a great deal. As we shall see later, the ability to talk also presupposes that we have a well-developed control over our facial muscles and speech organs. Yet it is likely that feigned emotions arose earlier in human evolution.

As more advanced understanding of the other's thoughts evolves, the bodily expressions of emotions become less important as signals. Deacon goes so far as to claim that the coming of language may have blocked the communicative function of the emotions, since the linguistic message competes with that expressed by the body.[iii]

4.3   Understanding attention

Gazes that meet give rise to strange relations.
Nobody could think freely unless his eyes could break lose from the other eyes that follow them.

---

[4] One wild speculation is that since primates have 'mirror neurons' that react to specific actions of others just as they react to the same actions of oneself, there might also exist mirror neurons for emotions. See Gallese, Ferrari and Umiltà (2002).

As soon as the gazes capture each other, one is no longer quite two, and it is difficult to endure alone.

Paul Valéry

Egon sits on the table, having just munched a whole bowl of peanuts. I notice that he has dropped a nut on the rug under the table and I tell him. He swoops down and immediately finds the nut in the long pile of the rug.

"How did you know where it was?" I wonder.

"I saw where you were looking."

For humans, this is self-evident. We are very good at following the *direction* of other people's gazes. Even very small children have the ability to understand where other people are directing their attention. In one experiment, mothers were asked to sit opposite their infants and look in different directions (sometimes the mother did this while turning her head, sometimes not) and then the experimenters followed where the children aimed their gaze.[iv] At the age of just six months a child can follow its mother's gaze if she turns her head at the same time, and at the age of 12 months it can manage this even if she just moves her pupils. Such small children, however, can only follow their mother's gaze if it falls within their own field of vision. It is not until the age of 18 months that they can turn to find a point behind them that the mother is looking at. This task is more difficult since it requires that the child can understand that space also continues beyond its field of vision. This ability calls for a detached representation of space.

Chimpanzees are also good at understanding where others are looking. Povinelli and Eddy tested putting a human opposite a chimp with a transparent screen between them.[v] The apes had no trouble in looking at the spot to which the experimenter was directing his gaze, even if it was behind the chimp. In a variant of the experiment, a screen with an opaque lower half was set up between the human and the chimpanzee. When the experimenter now looked at a point on the opaque part of the screen, the ape would lean forward to try to see what was on the other side. This shows that it is not just the direction of the gaze that the apes follow, but also that they understand that the gaze is directed towards a certain point in the surroundings.

Apes *see that others see* the object. This is called second-order attention: I notice that you notice. As I shall demonstrate, second-order attention is an important component for understanding how intentional deception in animals works.

The experiments with chimps are rather recent; it will be interesting to see which other animal species manage to follow looks in the way tested by

Povinelli and Eddy. Related findings come from the ethologist Carolyn Ristau, who has studied how piping plovers lure predators away from the nest by pretending to be injured.[vi] They let their wings droop and move in a style reminiscent of one of Monty Python's silly walks. The interesting thing is that a plover *adapts* its diversionary manoeuvres according to where the predator is looking. It turns around to look at the predator, and if it is not following, then the bird turns back and limps even more. Ristau also showed that the plover left its nest more often when a predator was looking at the nest than when it was looking away. There was nothing in Ristau's study to suggest that the bird has a theory of the predator's mind, but it is fairly clear that it has a theory of its attention.

A more advanced form of behaviour is *making* someone else notice an object. The primatologist Juan Carlos Gómez tells of a young gorilla at the Madrid zoo that wanted to open a door in a cage that was closed by means of a catch at the top. The gorilla's first strategy was to use the person in the cage as an object: the gorilla nudged the person towards the door and then tried to climb up on him to reach the catch.

At the age of 18 months, however, the gorilla began to use a different strategy: she took the man by the hand, led him to the door while alternating her gaze between the man's eyes and the catch. The gorilla wants to get the man's attention focused on the catch as well. The gorilla's behaviour was intentional, but it does not presuppose that she has any theory of the human mind. It is sufficient that she has learned that there is a link between a person's attention being directed towards a locked door and the actions that humans usually perform when they encounter locked doors.

An even more sophisticated form of attention is to succeed in drawing *joint attention* to an object. If I see that you are looking at an object and you see that I see the same object, we have achieved joint attention. This presupposes that both you and I have second-order attention. The capacity for joint attention will be discussed further later on, since it is intimately connected with the evolution of intentional communication.

To understand another individual's attention, one needs only understand what he or she is looking at, not how he or she imagines the world. A major step towards having an idea of others' minds consists in being able to put oneself in their position to see *how others see the world*. This can be described as detaching oneself from one's own perspective. Small children are incapable of this, as many experiments have shown. A classical example is Piaget's 'three mountain test'.[vii] In this experiment one puts three 'mountains', one of them much bigger than the other two, in a triangle on a table. The child who is to be tested sits in front of the small mountains and can see the big one behind them. A doll is placed on the other side of the table with its face towards the big mountain. The child is asked to draw what the doll can see from its side of the table. A child on the 'pre-operational level' (Piaget's term) draws the scene from her own perspective, regardless of where the doll is sitting. However, a child on the 'concrete operational level' (roughly from the age of seven), can imagine how the doll sees the mountains and draw the scene from the right perspective. When the child has reached this stage, it can *imagine* the world from different angles, regardless of the perceptions it has at a particular moment. Later experiments have shown that small children are better at imagining what others see in a certain situation if they themselves have previously been in that situation.[viii]

4.4 Understanding intentions

> I notice something and seek a reason for it: this means originally:
> I seek an intention in it, and above all someone who has intentions,
> a subject, a doer: every event a deed
> —formerly one saw intentions in all events,
> this is our oldest habit. Do animals also possess it?
>
> Friedrich Nietzsche

Earlier, I distinguished between four levels of causal understanding:

(a) Being able to foresee the physical effects of one's own actions.

(b) Being able to foresee the effects of others' actions.

(c) Understanding the causes of others' actions.

(d) Understanding the causes of physical events.

I argued that monkeys and apes have serious problems with level (d), i.e. causes of physical events. The question is now how they fare on levels (b) and (c). First, it should be noted that *intentions are special cases of causes*. Intentions are those hidden variables in the minds of other agents that can be used to explain their behaviour.

But there may be other ways of understanding the causes of others' actions. Tomasello and Call hypothesize that one cognitive distinction between primates and other mammals is that primates understand third party relationships, i.e. they understand the interactions of others in terms of kinship, friendship, and dominance. They give a list of examples to illustrate this:

> [I]n a number of species, individuals (1) redirect their aggression preferentially toward the kin of their past enemy; (2) simultaneously threaten a dominant

individual while appeasing another individual dominant to the first;
(3) preferentially groom partners that outrank the others present; (4) are
surprised when individuals who should be dominant to other individuals
seem to vocalize in ways indicating submission; (5) understand different
recruitment screams that encode the dominance relations between the
fighting individuals; (6) respect one individual's 'ownership' of other
individuals and objects; (7) seek to prevent certain relationships between
third parties from forming; and (8) encourage reconciliation between third
parties who have just been fighting.[ix]

An example of how Chacma baboons understand some of the causal structure of social interaction comes from primatologists Cheney, Seyfarth, and
Silk.[x] Using a tape recorder, they replayed for their baboon subjects the vocalizations of two baboons, one dominant to the other. When the playbacks were
what the researchers called 'causally inconsistent', where the dominant individual gives a fear bark while the subordinate gives a grunt that is normally a
sound from a dominant, the subjects looked longer in the direction of the
sounds. On the other hand, if the same sounds were played together with the
vocalizations of a third baboon that was dominant to both of the original
baboons, then the subjects took less notice. In this case the sounds were
'causally consistent' since the fear barks from the dominant of the two original
baboons could have been caused by the presence of the third individual. If this
interpretation of the baboons' behaviour is correct, it suggests that they
make use of their internal representations of the dominance hierarchy in the
troop when interpreting the sounds they hear. These representations then
serve as the hidden variables in understanding the causal relations between
the sounds.

Tomasello and Call's list suggest that primates can handle level (c), i.e.
understand the causes of others' actions when the attributed causes come from
their representations of third part relationships. But this does not imply that
they can manage this level when the causes are *mental*—such as intentions. For
humans such an identification of mental causes is so obvious that we do not
even notice it: When we see that something is caused by an agent, our cognitive system *presumes* that there is some purpose behind the act, in other words,
that it is intentional. Humans thus find it very natural to create a representation
of the objective of an action—our simulators fill in intentions as hidden
variables and we see other people's behaviour as being *goal-directed*. This is
probably yet another of our fundamental categories. Again, the simulators
may be wrong: Mostly it is true that other people's actions are intentional, but
it happens that people do things unintentionally.

An illustration of how easily even small children can understand the intentions of others is provided by a series of imitation experiments by Meltzoff.[xi] One group of 18-month-old infants watched an adult successfully acting on an object, for example removing the lid from a jar. The infants readily imitated the adult's action, and could themselves remove the lid from the jar. A second group of infants watched an adult trying but failing to achieve an action, for example failing to remove the lid because their hand slipped off the edge. But even though the infants never witnessed the complete action, they nonetheless reproduced it and extended it successfully, for example removing the lid from the jar that the adult failed to do. The interpretation of this is that the infants can read the actor's intentions and understand that actions are guided by goals. Inferring these goals is part of the imitative process for humans.

"But could the infants not just figure out the target action without watching the adult?" Egon asks.

"Good point," I reply. "You should become an experimental psychologist!"

To control for this, Meltzoff ran a test where infants watched an adult manipulating an object, but without a successful or unsuccessful action, for example just rubbing the back of their hand against a jar. In this test, the infants did not exhibit any goal-directed target action.

It is important to notice that even though one can interpret someone else's behaviour as goal-directed, this does not necessarily mean that one has any conception of the other's mind. It is sufficient that one creates for oneself a *representation of the goal* of the action. This representation exists in the one who interprets the behaviour, and it is far from certain that it agrees with the objective of the person who actually performs the act. The ability to see objectives thus requires a less advanced inner world than the ability to have a theory of others' minds. When one sees that someone else has objectives, one sees that individual as an *agent*, but when one has an understanding of the other's mind one sees that individual as a *subject*.[5] Meltzoff's experiments suggest that even 18-month-old infants have a theory of intention, but, as we shall see in the following section, it is not until children are about four that they develop a theory of mind.

When it comes to the question of whether apes have any theory of intentionality, opinions are divided. The psychologists David Premack and Guy Woodruff had noted that Sarah the chimpanzee was fond of watching commercials on television, which led to the thought that she understood something of the desires and objectives of the actors. In an experiment they let her watch

---

5 This is what Tomasello calls a 'mental agent'.

video films in which a person had to solve various types of problem, such as getting out of a locked cage. The film was stopped in the problematic situation and Sarah had to choose between two pictures, one of them showing a solution to the problem, for example, a key, and the other showing something that provided no solution to the problem, such as a blanket. She always chose the right picture. Premack and Woodruff interpreted her success at this task as that she understood the *objectives* of the human in the filmed situation.

But other scientists have criticized their interpretation, and it is conceivable that Sarah merely made the right *associations* between the pictures and the problematic situations without having any grasp of the human's objectives. Along this line, Tomasello and Call argue that monkeys and apes *cannot* understand intentionality in others:

> If they understood others' intentionality, they should be able to develop
> novel strategies that take into account the intentions or beliefs of others,
> learn novel strategies by observing others' behavior in communicative and
> other problem-solving situations, [...].[xii]

According to Tomasello's definition, an individual who imitates understands the *intention* behind a behaviour. So if Tomasello's diagnosis is correct, it explains why apes cannot imitate in the sense in which he uses the term. Tomasello also observes that the apes' inability to understand intentions explains why:

1. They do not *point to* objects.
2. They do not *hold up* objects to show them to others.
3. They do not *take someone along* to a place to show them something.
4. They do not actively *offer* something to someone.
5. They do not intentionally *teach* other individuals new behaviours.

Tomasello and Call conclude:

> Nonhuman primates are thus able to understand antecedent-consequent
> relations in the behavior of others, but there is no understanding of a
> psychological component in terms of the intentional and mental states of
> others that mediate their interactions with their environments.

In terms of my four levels, 'to understand antecedent-consequent relations in the behavior of others' is level (b), while 'understanding of a psychological component in terms of the intentional and mental states of others that mediate their interactions with their environments' is part of level (c). The upshot seems to be that primates handle levels (a) and (b); they handle level (c) when the causes are based on third party relationships, but not when the causes are intentions; and they are very bad at level (d) (as was argued in Section 2.8). Human children, on the other hand, manage all four levels, including the understanding of intentions, from a very early age.

In line with this, Cheney and Seyfarth hypothesize that most primate cognitive adaptations evolved in the social rather than in the physical domain. Actually, most adaptations in primates still seem to be specific to the social domain, with hardly any generalization to the physical domain. In contrast, humans can generalize their reasoning to the physical domain. But this is an area where systematic investigations have just begun. Much more experimentation that looks for different kinds of causal reasoning is needed.

However, it is probable that our understanding of physical causality is an evolutionary extension of the social intelligence that we have in common with other primates. In this sense anthropomorphism is built into our thinking. Tomasello and Call argue that:

> it is possible that the 'force' component of the human understanding of causal relations, which nonhuman primates do not seem to apply in the same way as humans, may derive from the extension of intentional thinking to the behavior of inanimate objects as they interact with one another. It is certainly the case that in many cultures the explanation of both human and inanimate events is composed of a complex mix of social, physical, and metaphysical forces.[6]

4.5   Understanding what others know

One way to test whether an animal has a theory of others' minds would be to find out whether they understand what others *know*. Unfortunately, this is not easy to determine. A field observation of hamadryas baboons in Ethiopia is interesting as an example of the difficulties of interpretation.[xiii] An adult female spent 20 minutes slowly moving a few metres to a position behind a stone. Behind this stone there was a younger male from the troop whom she began to groom. This behaviour would not have been tolerated by the dominant male if he had been able to see it. From his position, he could just see the head and back of the female, not the younger male and the fact that she was grooming him.

The factor that makes it possible to interpret the female's behaviour as a desire to *deceive* the leader is her careful displacement. It can be described as showing that she did not want the leader to *know* that there was another

---

[6] Tomasello and Call (1997), p. 388. See also Collingwood (1972), p. 322, who writes: 'Causal propositions . . . are descriptions of relations between natural events in anthropomorphic terms.'

Figure 4.1 The female
baboon can imagine
what the leader can see.

baboon behind the stone. This interpretation would ascribe a *theory of others'
minds* to the female baboon, which is a strong assumption. A weaker interpretation would be that she did not want the leader to *notice* that there was another
baboon behind the stone. This interpretation presupposes only that she can
understand someone else's attention. But she must also have understood that
the stone was blocking the leader's vision. We will never know what went on in
the female's head in this situation. To determine how advanced a theory different animals have of other's minds, much more systematic studies are needed.

One of the first attempts to really test chimpanzees' ability to deceive, which
presupposes a theory of others' minds, was made by Woodruff and Premack.[xiv]
They let four chimpanzees become acquainted with two trainers, one of whom
was kind and helpful to them. The other trainer, in contrast, treated the chimpanzees aggressively, wore sunglasses, and covered the lower part of his face
with a cloth.

When the chimps had got to know the two trainers, they were placed singly
in cages in the laboratory. A third person came into the room with a treat,
which he placed under one of two cups and then left the room. Then one of
the two trainers came in. Since the chimp was in the cage, it could not reach
the cups, but it was able to show the trainer where the food was. If it was the
kind trainer and the chimpanzee pointed to the right cup, the trainer picked
up the treat and gave it to the chimpanzee. If it pointed to the wrong cup, the
trainer looked under it and then went out. In this case, the chimp thus received
its reward if it pointed to the right cup.

If it was the nasty trainer and the chimpanzee pointed to the right cup, the
trainer took the food and ate it himself. But if the chimp pointed to the wrong

cup, the trainer looked under it and then went to the corner to sit and sulk. When this happened, the chimpanzee was let out of the cage and could retrieve the treat itself from under the right cup. In this situation the chimpanzee was rewarded if it pointed to the wrong cup.

"Were the chimps able to trick the nasty trainer?" Egon wonders.

"Yes, but it wasn't easy. They had to practise a lot—all the chimpanzees needed at least 50 trials before they could systematically distinguish which behaviour was most appropriate for which trainer. Since it takes such a long time, the question is whether they understand anything about how the trainers *think* when the chimpanzees point. The behaviour can also be explained as a form of conditioning."

Povinelli and his co-workers conducted another even more sophisticated experiment. It was run in two steps. In the first step a trainer came in and hid a titbit under one of two cups, but since these were behind a screen the chimpanzee could not see which one the food was hidden under. Yet the chimpanzee could understand *that* it was hidden, as the trainer's hands were empty afterwards. Then the screen was removed so that the chimp could see the cups. Another trainer came in and the two trainers each pointed to a different cup. The chimp was only allowed to look under one of them.

To begin with, the chimps chose at random, but after a while they more often looked under the cup that the trainer who had hidden the food was pointing to. The long learning time agrees entirely with the results of Woodruff and Premack's experiment.

The second phase of Povinelli's experiment began when the chimpanzees had learned to choose correctly in the first phase. Now *both* trainers were present when the titbit was hidden behind the screen, but it was hidden by a third person. One trainer looked on passively, while the other had a bucket over her head so that she could see nothing. Just as in the first phase, the screen was removed, the bucket was lifted from the trainer's head, and the trainers each pointed to a different cup. What this experiment tries to test is whether the chimps understand that 'seeing is knowing', in other words, that the visual information that one of the trainers had acquired gave him *knowledge* of where the food was.

"So what happened this time?" Egon asks.

The experiment gave slightly better results, if one wants to believe that apes can understand others' minds. Two of the four chimpanzees that were tested were able immediately to choose the cup pointed out by the trainer who had not had a bucket on his head. A third chimp could manage it after a little training.

These tests are important because the criterion 'seeing is knowing' is a minimum requirement for having a theory of others' minds. Povinelli and DeBlois repeated the second part of the experiment with children.[xv] From the age of about three, the children were able to choose the cup pointed out by the trainer who had seen where the reward was hidden. At earlier ages they chose cups more or less at random.

A later experiment, however, casts doubt on whether the chimpanzees' success was due to an ability to link 'seeing' with 'knowing'.[xvi] This experiment utilizes the natural tendency of chimpanzees to beg for food by extending their hands. The chimp sat behind a transparent screen, but it could stick its hand out through a hole towards a trainer. First the experimenters checked that the begging gesture worked by placing two trainers in front of the hungry chimp, one of them with food, the other with a piece of wood. The chimp understood the situation correctly and begged only from the trainer with the food (which was his reward).

The experiment then went on to study whether the apes could distinguish a trainer who *knew* that there was food from one who did not know. One trainer was blindfolded while the other had his mouth gagged. It turned out that the chimpanzees could not tell which of the trainers it was worth begging from. A number of variants of the experiment were tried. In one variant, one of the trainers held his hands over his eyes while the other had his hands over his ears; in another variant one trainer had a bucket over his head while the other had a bucket on his shoulder; in a third form the two trainers sat with their backs to the chimp, but one of them was looking over his shoulder and could see the food. In none of these cases could the chimps determine which trainer it was best to beg from.

After continued training the chimpanzees were able to distinguish the trainers correctly. Yet it seemed as if the only significant factor was whether the trainer's face was visible or not; it did not matter whether the trainer's eyes were open or shut. Despite the successes in the first experiment, the probable conclusion is that the chimps cannot understand that 'seeing is knowing' and that they therefore do not have a theory of others' minds.

Further evidence that monkeys cannot take into account the knowledge states of conspecifics comes from an experiment by Cheney and Seyfarth. In this experiment macaque mothers were first shown either a predator or food. The predator or the food was then hidden before their offspring were released in the adjoining cage. In spite of the fact that the information was highly relevant for the youngsters, the mothers failed to warn them about the predator or direct them to the food.[xvii]

It is easier to test whether small children can understand that 'seeing is knowing', since one can communicate with them through language from a fairly early age. In one experiment children aged between three and five were asked whether another person knew what was in a box.[xviii] Some of the people had looked inside the box while the others had not. In the same way, some of the children were allowed to see what was in the box while the others were not. None of the children had any problem saying whether a particular person had looked in the box or not. But when the question concerned whether the person knew what was in the box, the three-year-olds consistently replied that the person knew if they themselves had seen what was in the box, and that the person did not know if they had not seen what was in the box. Whether the person had looked or not made no difference. The four- and five-year-olds, on the other hand, were able to connect 'seeing' with 'knowing'. This is one of several experiments suggesting that a theory of others' minds develops in humans at the age of about four.

Another type of test of children's understanding of other people's minds concerns whether they can understand that someone else has a *false* belief about what the world is like. The best known of these experiments was about an oblong Smarties tube. The test was carried out on children aged between three and five. The children are first shown the tube and then asked what they think is in it. All the children reply 'Smarties' (or 'sweets'). When the tube is opened it is found to contain pencils. Then the tube is closed. The children are now asked what Bert, who has not yet seen what is in the tube, will say that it contains. The three-year-olds generally answer 'pencils' whereas most of the older children say 'Smarties'. The older children understand that Bert *does not have the same knowledge* as they do. They thus realize that he has a false belief about what is in the tube. This is a clear example that they have a theory of another's mind. The younger children, on the other hand, do not appear to be able to distinguish between their own minds and other people's.[7]

In an extension of the experiment, the children were also asked what they thought was in the tube when they had first seen it.[xix] Most small children replied 'pencils' while the oldest ones said 'Smarties'. The older ones could remember, i.e. *create a representation* of having originally thought differently. Regardless of age, there was a strong correlation between the children who answered 'pencils' when asked what Bert would say was in the tube and those

---

7   Perner *et al.* (1987). Lewis and Osborne (1990), however, showed that the Smarties test is sensitive to the way the questions are formulated. When the children were instead asked 'What will Bert think before he opens the tube?' many more three-year-olds managed the test.

who answered 'pencils' about what they first thought was in the tube. This type of test once again supports the thesis that children develop a theory of others' minds at about the age of four.[8]

4.6 Deception

> He that deceives me once, shame fall him;
> if he deceives me twice, shame fall me.
>
> English proverb

Many animal species are social beings. The theories that explain why co-operation between individuals is valuable for evolution and why animal societies arise in some species but not others are interesting in themselves.[9] But here it is above all the significance of social interaction for the development of thought that I want to discuss.

When a social animal reacts it must also consider how other individuals in the group will react. When an animal plans it therefore takes into account the actions of the other animals, to decide what it should do itself. The best way to predict what other individuals will do is to know what they are thinking about. As long as there is no language, it can be difficult to get at other individuals' thoughts. But if one can *imagine* the others' inner worlds with some accuracy, one has come a long way. Planning that uses representations of the other animals' inner worlds will be more successful than planning that only accounts for their behaviour. Such representations will also facilitate *co-operation* between individuals, since it gives a greater potential to predict what others will do.

The ability to imagine others' inner worlds involves a significant expansion of one's own inner world. This ability adds yet another level to thinking. It leads to a new form of Gregorian beings with greater opportunities to learn from others' knowledge.[10] When one can imagine others' inner worlds, however, it is not just new forms of co-operation that become possible, but also deliberate *deception*.

"People are good at deceiving each other," says Egon. "Is there really trickery among other animals too?"

---

[8] Mitchell (1997), pp. 162–5, gives some examples showing that if children *actively* take part in the deception, they find it easier to cope with problems of false beliefs.

[9] The political scientist Robert Axelrod's book *The evolution of cooperation* presents a fascinating account. Sociobiology has contributed many new ideas in this field (see, e.g. Richard Dawkins's book *The selfish gene*, 1976).

[10] They could be called Machiavellian beings (see the next section).

"Do you mean deception that utilizes a theory of others' minds?"

"Mm."

The ethologists Andrew Whiten and Richard Byrne have collected a multitude of examples of deception among apes from various field studies.[xx] Unfortunately, most of the available evidence is of an anecdotal character. The problem is that it is difficult to design a *test* that shows that animals really have a theory of what the other believes and wants. The instances collected by Whiten and Byrne are not sufficient, since one cannot control the situation in which the deception took place.

It should be stressed that a great deal of what animals do to deceive each other is not even planning. Harmless insects that mimic other, dangerous insects' wing markings or bodily patterns naturally have no idea that they are deceiving. The appearance is genetically determined, a product of natural selection that protects individuals which sufficiently resemble dangerous ones. Likewise, the partridge that pretends to have a damaged wing in order to lure the fox away from her chicks does not deliberately plan to deceive; her behaviour is purely instinctive.

One example from Whiten and Byrne's material deals with a group of gorillas walking along a path.[xxi] One of the females suddenly caught sight of a bunch of fruit hanging a few metres above the path. If the others were to see it too, there would be a struggle for the fruit. So, without looking at the others in the group, she sat down and began to groom her coat. She went on doing this until the others had passed by and disappeared from sight. Then she quickly climbed up the tree, broke off the branch, and ate up the fruit before catching up with the rest of the group.

Jane Goodall tells of a male chimpanzee that had found a hiding place with bananas that she had placed there. Chimpanzees usually emit a food cry when they find food. The cry attracts others in the troop, often relatives, who can share the find. This time, however, the chimpanzee did not want to share. The problem is that chimpanzees have poor volitional control over their own voices—the food cry and other cries are instincts. To avoid revealing his find, then, the chimpanzee held his hand over his mouth so that his involuntary call would not be heard.

There are isolated observations of apes bluffing about their emotions. The following example is based on the fact that gorillas normally vocalize while mating. On one occasion Byrne observed (and even managed to photograph) how the female gorilla Papoose, by using sidelong glances and head movements, enticed Titus, who was not the highest-ranking male, to come with her.[xxii] When they reached an out-of-the-way place, they mated *in silence*. But Beetsme, the leader, was justly suspicious and went to look for Papoose. He ended up breaking off the couple *in flagrante delicto*.

Another example is when the chimpanzee Yeroen has injured his hand in a fight with Nikkie.[xxiii] Later Yeroen passes Nikkie, limping pitifully, but as soon as he is out of Nikkie's sight he walks normally again. Yeroen limps in this way for almost a week after the fight.

"But is it certain that the animals who deceive know what is going on in the heads of the ones they deceive?" Egon wonders.

"No, and that's a very important question," I agree.

These examples show that apes in their planning can at least take advantage of the way other animals *react*. However, to determine whether they can really imagine others' minds, one must apply Ockham's razor and for each example search for alternative explanations of the animals' behaviour that assume as little as possible about their cognitive abilities. Whiten and Byrne perform a careful analysis of various types of deceptive behaviour in monkeys and apes. Their definition of a deceptive act is:

> Acts from the normal repertoire of the AGENT, deployed such that another individual is likely to misinterpret what the acts signify, to the advantage of the AGENT.[xxiv]

The key word in the definition is 'deployed'. Whiten and Byrne deliberately chose this word in order not to presume that the deceiving animal has a theory of the other animal's mind. They do presume, on the other hand, that the deceiver's behaviour is *intentional*, since they want to go beyond a behaviouristic definition and ascribe an intentional interpretation to the deception.

Most examples of deception in Whiten and Byrne's collection do not presuppose that those who deceive have a theory of others' minds. It seems as if the observations can be explained in terms of the deceiver's simulating the other animal's behaviour as a stage in its planning. Animals are behaviourists: other animals are treated as if they just respond to a certain stimulus. If this interpretation is correct, the examples are at the same cognitive level as immediate planning.

There is a *stronger* form of deception that means that the one who wants to deceive has a representation of how the intended victim will interpret the deceptive act. In other words, deception in the strong sense presupposes that the deceiver's inner world contains a *representation of the other individual's inner world*. Strong deception requires a theory of the deceived individual's mind, and this type of thinking should therefore appear much later in the evolution of thought than the ability to plan.[11]

---

[11] This thesis should primarily be interpreted as a statement about phylogenetic evolution, but it can also be applied ontogenetically, that is, as a statement about children's development.

The question now is whether there are examples from the apes of the stronger form of deception, i.e. actions that presuppose that the deceiver can imagine the other's inner world. Psychologist Cecilia Heyes has studied the experiments conducted in this field, and her conclusion is that there are no unambiguous signs that apes have any theory of others' minds.[xxv] In her view, they are therefore unable to deceive in the stronger way.

Take Goodall's chimpanzee, for example. He knew that a food cry would attract the other members of the troop and that he would then be forced to share the food, but he was not necessarily able to imagine their inner world to be able to work this out. This can be interpreted as an example of deceptive planning, but scarcely deception in the stronger definition.

Yet the issue is still disputed. Heyes has been harshly criticized by the primatologists who carried out the field studies. Nor does she distinguish between the different levels of a theory of others' minds as I do in this chapter.

To see the difficulties, consider the following example from Byrne concerning baboons searching for food. The juvenile Paul came across an adult female, Mel, who had just finished laboriously digging up a corm. Paul would no doubt have been incapable of digging up one for himself. He looked around and noted that there were no other baboons in the vicinity. He then screamed loudly as if he needed help. His mother, who was higher ranking than Mel, came running like a protective mother and chased Mel away. As soon as both the females had disappeared from the area, Paul started eating the abandoned corm. Byrne later saw Paul repeat the behaviour, but never when his mother was nearby (for then his bluff would have been revealed).

Figure 4.2 A strong interpretation of how Paul imagines the consequences of crying out.

A strong interpretation of this is that Paul could imagine that his mother would *believe* that he was in danger. If this is the case, Paul is deliberately deceiving.

"Maybe Paul did not have any purpose at all with his cry," Egon suggests.

"That's plausible," I admit.

The weaker interpretation is that the first time he cried might have been a case of trial-and-error behaviour. When this then proved successful, he naturally learned to try it on other occasions. On this interpretation, he did not need to have any representation of what his mother would think when he cried out. In some way, however, he was smart enough to realize that the cry would not work if his mother were in the vicinity, where she could *see* that he was not in any danger.

In opposition to Heyes, Byrne claims that there are clear examples of intentional deception in the stronger sense.[xxvi] Above all in situations where *counter-deception* occurs, it is difficult to avoid the interpretation that the countering individual has a theory of the other's deceptive thoughts.

"To deceive a deceiver is no deceit," Egon remarks smugly.

One example of counter-deception comes from a series of experiments conducted by Menzel with chimpanzees.[12] The female Belle was allowed to see where food was hidden within a large enclosed area. During this time, the other chimpanzees in the group were locked up outside the enclosure. She was then placed back in the group and all the chimpanzees were allowed into the enclosure. Belle led the group to the place where the food was, and all were able to share it. When the experiment was repeated, however, the male Rock, who was stronger than Belle, began to take all the food for himself. (The food was hidden in different places each time.) After this, Belle did not reveal where the food was hidden if Rock was nearby. She sat further and further from the place where the food was hidden, and it was only when Rock was looking in another direction that she went to the hiding place. Rock, however, countered this by pretending to go away and then turning just as Belle was about to reveal where the food was. Byrne points out that Rock's behaviour in pretending to go away and suddenly turning round is abnormal for a chimpanzee. His interpretation is that Rock has an understanding that Belle is trying to deceive him.

As a possible counter-argument to this interpretation, Tomasello and Call note that the experiment with all its steps lasted several months so Belle and Rock may have successively learned something about how to predict the

---

[12] Menzel (1974). Similar observations have been made by the primatologist Frans Plooij among wild chimpanzees in the Gombe National Park in Tanzania.

behaviour of the other without really being able to understand the thoughts behind the behaviour. This line is supported by a later experiment with mangabey monkeys run by Sabine Coussi-Korbel.[xxvii] She basically repeated Menzel's study, but performed a detailed day-to-day analysis. One of the informed mangabeys, step by step in four days, learned the strategy of leading her main competitor away from the food.

To sum up, it seems as if the limit of the cognitive ability of apes lies somewhere between seeing intentions and having a theory of others' minds, i.e. between levels 3 and 5. As my survey has shown, ethologists do not always agree about what apes really can manage, so the exact limit is still unclear. Some researchers, such as Tomasello and Hauser, apply Ockham's razor strictly and are cautious when drawing conclusions from field observations and experiments. Others, such as Byrne and Premack, are bolder in their interpretations.

"And you are even more speculative, it seems to me," Egon ironizes.

"Well, I come from a philosophical upbringing..."

"...and philosophers are like swifts who can stay aloft almost forever without touching empirical ground," he interrupts me.

"I am now in cognitive science and I do try to account for the data I know of," I reply offended. "But you are right that I am more concerned with filling in the jigsaw puzzle where so many pieces are missing so that we can see a total picture than with supporting each piece with firm experimental data."

4.7 Machiavellian intelligence

In 1532 Niccolò Machiavelli published his book *The prince*, which is about the art of acquiring influence. He had no illusions. According to Machiavelli's *realpolitik*, a popular leader had to give the impression of being sincere, trustworthy, and merciful. To retain his power, however, a prince can set himself above all moral rules and use cunning, lies, and force. Machiavelli writes: 'But men are so simple, and governed so absolutely by their present needs, that he who wishes to deceive will never fail in finding willing dupes.' Skill in deception and maintaining alliances are two of a prince's most important properties.

"Now that's my type of guy," Egon interjects.

It might be hoped that this bleak description of the struggle for social power applies only to humans, but similar patterns occur frequently in the animal world. The zoologist Frans de Waal, in his classic book *Chimpanzee politics*, describes how clever high-ranking chimpanzees are at manipulating others. A typical example is the story of Yeroen, who had long been the dominant male in the troop, but who was dislodged by Luik and later also defeated by the young Nikkie. Instead of retiring in bitterness, Yeroen now formed an alliance with Nikkie. Together they defeated Luik, who had sole right to the females. With the new ranking order—Nikkie at the top and Yeroen in second place—the crafty Yeroen could use his position to mate with some of the females. Nikkie could not protest with any vigour against this since he was dependent on Yeroen's support in the struggle against Luik. However, as I pointed out in the previous section, it is far from certain that Yeroen's manipulation was intentional.

Chimpanzees, and in even larger measure bonobos, keep very close track of social ranks within the group and who is allied with whom. They know that if you start a fight with someone, his allies will rush to his assistance. Many animals can learn which animals are their offspring, relatives, or members of the same group, but it is maybe only monkeys and apes that can keep track of how other animals relate to *each other*. This ability, that Tomasello and Call call knowledge about third-order relations, is the core of social intelligence.

To test what monkeys know about social relations, Verena Dasser carried out an experiment with macaques.[xxviii] The monkeys that were tested were shown a pair of photographs of members of the troop, and their task was to identify another pair of photographs which 'matched' the first one. The first pair could be, for example, a mother and a daughter, two sisters, or two unrelated individuals. The macaques quickly learned to identify the right kinship patterns, even for pairs of photographs that they had not previously seen. The experiment indicates that they do not just recognize their own offspring and siblings, but that they also keep track of other individuals' kinship relations. And Cheney and Seyfarth argue that vervets conduct vendettas: they prefer to attack relatives of the individuals who have attacked their own relatives. Here is one example: One female, Newton, makes a violent lunge at another, Tycho, when they are competing for fruit. When Tycho runs away, Newton's sister, Charing Cross, comes to help with the pursuit. In the meantime, Wormwood Scrubs, another of Newton's sisters, runs up to Tycho's sister Holborn, who is sitting 20 metres away eating, and hits her on the head.

There are also many forms of reciprocal exchange of food and sex among chimpanzees. The apes keep a close account of favours given and returned. If a chimpanzee fails to return a favour, the consequence is punishment. The psychologist Robin Dunbar claims that the rapid growth of the human brain during the evolution of the hominids is above all due to the evolutionary importance of keeping track of social relations and intrigues within the group. As further evidence for this I shall later present Dunbar's 'gossip theory' of the origin of language.

In a commentary on the work of Whiten and Byrne, Dennett notes that deception leads to an 'arms race' in reading one another's minds.[xxix] If the one who is deceived can read the deceiver's intentions, he can take counter-measures; but if the one who wants to deceive understands that the victim has taken counter-measures, he can choose a more sophisticated strategy, and so on. This escalation of deceptive strategies and counter-moves creates a long-term evolutionary pressure that makes individuals better able to interpret each other's intentions. This deception race may be one of the main reasons why hominids' brains grew so large.

The psychologists Leda Cosmides and John Tooby even maintain that humans have a built-in deception detector.[xxx] To support this they show that humans are particularly good at *reasoning* about social relations. Logical thinking is not something that works for all questions, but if it is important to work out who did what to whom, then there is nothing wrong with our logical capacity.

The anthropologist Camilla Power argues that sexual selection also rewards the ability to read others' minds.[xxxi] In all mammals, the females expend a great deal of energy on their offspring through pregnancy, nursing, and so on, whereas the males in principle do not need to contribute anything more than the mating act. For those (more or less) monogamous species where the females are dependent on the fathers' assistance in looking after the young, it is essential to be able to expose unreliable males. The ability to acquire an understanding of others' thoughts thus has an indirect effect on the offspring's chance of survival.

Certain aspects of Machiavellian intelligence can be discovered even in small children. There is, for instance, a connection between being good at deceiving others and having a high social status. The psychologists Caroline Keating and Karen Heltman studied pre-school children and first determined the different children's social dominance by means of a set of sociological criteria.[xxxii] They then tested the children's ability to deceive by giving them two glasses of orange juice, one of which contained quinine, making it taste very bitter. When the children had recovered from the shudders after tasting the bitter drink, they were asked to try to convince an assistant, while they drank the juice, that both the bitter and the ordinary juice tasted good. Many children found it difficult to avoid grimacing as they drank the bitter juice, but some of them managed it very well.

The experiments were filmed and shown without sound to an independent panel of judges who did not know which juice the children were drinking. The judges had to guess whether the children were lying or telling the truth.

The result was that there was a clear association between those who managed to fool the judges and those who were socially dominant. This association was independent of the age of the children.

"That's what I've always said," declares Egon. "You can't be ambitious without being calculating."

"Now you're being cynical," I object lamely.

"You know yourself that if you're going to succeed at poker, you have to bluff sometimes. And life is more like a game of poker than a Sunday school."

There seems to be a similar association between social competence and the ability to pretend. In an experiment by Jennifer Connolly and Anna-Beth Doyle, the researchers first assessed the social competence of a group of pre-school children by weighing up what the teachers said, how popular the different children in the group were, their verbal skills, and how much they engaged other children in conversation.[xxxiii]

As regards the ability to pretend, the researchers distinguished between two types. The first was to pretend that an ordinary object was something else—a stick became a gun, a pinecone became a cow, and so on. The other type was role-play of various kinds: families and cops and robbers are the most typical. Connolly and Doyle assessed how imaginative the children were when it came to using the objects in make-believe games and how creative they were in their various simulated roles. These skills were weighed together to give a general rating of the children's ability to pretend. The result was that the children who were deemed to have the greatest social competence were generally most skilful at pretending.

A third finding along the same lines is that there appears to be a developmental link in children between the acquisition of a theory of mind and the degree of *self-control*. The psychologists Josef Perner and Birgit Lang have compiled a number of studies indicating such a correlation.[xxxiv] They compare different theoretical hypotheses that might explain the correlation, for example that self-control depends on a theory of mind or, conversely, that theory of mind development depends on self-control. But the available experimental evidence does not seem to strongly favour any of the hypotheses.

4.8   Autism: when there are gaps in the inner world

Autism is a functional disorder characterized by a complex of symptoms. The boundaries are fuzzy, and there are degrees of autism. People with autism generally have difficulty with social relations, they find it hard to understand other people's feelings, and it is difficult for them to communicate, both verbally and non-verbally.[13] They usually have an uneven mental development curve. As children they do not play the way other children do, and they find it hard to change their routines. They have difficulties in generalizing, i.e. going outside the information available to them.

It is not clear whether there are any injuries or changes in the brain that can be linked to autism. There have been suggestions about damage to the frontal lobe or in the cerebellum, but as yet there is no agreement about the physiological or neurological causes of the syndrome. One complication is that a large majority of the individuals with autism also have other mental handicaps.

One hypothesis which has become popular in recent years is that there are strong—albeit not unambiguous—links between autism and the ability to have a theory of others' minds.[14] People with autism find it difficult to engage in joint attention and they have problems seeing something from another person's perspective. They generally cannot manage the Smarties test or other tests about false beliefs, even if they are at a level of linguistic development above that of a five-year-old. It is interesting by way of comparison to note that children with Down's syndrome manage these tests at the same age as other children.

By analogy with this, Wendy Stone and her colleagues have shown that children with autism find it difficult to imitate.[xxxv] They have greater problems in imitating body movements than in imitating actions with objects. Imitation of body movements is linked to children's linguistic skills, whereas the imitation of actions with objects is connected to their ability to play.

Children with autism find it difficult to deceive. In an experiment some autistic children were told a story about a wicked thief who wanted to steal their sweets. The sweets were placed in two miniature chests and the children taking part in the experiment knew which of the chests it was. Clinically normal children from the age of four could lie to the thief, but the children with autism told the truth. It appears as if they have difficulty in understanding how a lie works.[15]

It has also been shown that children with autism have problems with a variant of Boysen and Berntson's test with chimps (that was presented in Section 3.8).[xxxvi]

---

[13] This is known as Wing's triad (see, e.g. Frith 1994 and Gillberg and Peeters 1998).

[14] See Baron-Cohen, Leslie, and Frith (1986). For a survey of the research see Mitchell (1997), Chapters 5 and 6, and also Tomasello (1999), pp. 76–7. There are levels of autism, and some people with autism manage problems involving false beliefs, such as the Smarties test, but not problems based on second-order false beliefs, such as tests where you have to understand that someone knows that I do not know (Mitchell 1997, pp. 92–4). There is a link between the ability to pass false-belief tasks and general intelligence.

[15] It might be thought that children with autism were more afraid of the thief than clinically normal children were. To check that this was not the explanation, a variant of the experiment was conducted, in which the children could instead lock one of the chests and thus prevent the thief from getting hold of the sweets. The children with autism had no problems with this task.

In the first phase of the experiment, children both with and without autism were asked to point to one of two closed boxes, one of which contained a piece of chocolate. If the children pointed to the empty box, they were given the chocolate from the other box, but if they pointed to the box with the chocolate, it was given to another child.

Once the children learned that they were rewarded if they pointed to the empty box, the experiment moved on to the second phase, where the children could now see what was in the boxes. In this case too, they were rewarded if they pointed to the empty box. The results showed that clinically normal children below the age of three and children with autism could not help pointing to the box containing the chocolate. They carried on doing so after repeated attempts, even though they always failed to get the reward. In contrast, clinically normal children from the age of five had no problem in pointing to the empty box.

It might be envisaged that the difficulties that children with autism have in false-belief tests are due to general problems with their imagination. However, an experiment performed by the psychologist Deborah Zaitchik shows that it is probably only imagining others' minds that is the problem. Zaitchik put a doll on a mat and then got the children who were to be tested to help to take a Polaroid photograph of the doll. While the picture was being processed the doll was moved from the mat to a box. The children were then asked where the doll was on the photograph. Among clinically normal children, three-year-olds say that the doll in the photograph is in the box, whereas older children generally reply that is on the mat. The surprising thing is that the children with autism (who were over four years old) all correctly replied that the doll in the photograph was on the mat.

People with autism generally find it difficult to pretend.[16] This may provide a key as to where the gaps are in their inner world. As we saw above, one must be able to work with two representations simultaneously when one is pretending. As a perceptual object the doll is made of plastic and does not feel anything if you drop her on the floor, but as a make-believe object (the representation that runs parallel to perception) she is a child whom one can care for and talk to. People with autism seem to be incapable of using parallel representations—there is no room in their inner world for two interpretations of an object, especially not when it is a matter of letting an imagination block a perception.[xxxvii]

To sum up, people with autism seem not to develop some of the expansions of the inner world, above all as regards understanding how others think and feel.

---

[16] Again, there is a correlation between general intelligence and the ability to pretend.

They have gaps in their inner world that also entail that they have problems in communicating in an adequate manner.

Notes

i. The example comes from Savage-Rumbaugh, Shanker, and Taylor (1998), p. 53.
ii. Blair (1995).
iii. Deacon (1997), pp. 428–9.
iv. Butterworth and Jarrett (1991).
v. Povinelli and Eddy (1996).
vi. Ristau (1991). See also Hauser (1997), pp. 587–90.
vii. Piaget and Inhelder (1956).
viii. Perner and Lopez (1997).
ix. Tomasello and Call (1997), p. 371.
x. Cheney, Seyfarth, and Silk (1995).
xi. Meltzoff (1988, 1996).
xii. Tomasello and Call (1997), p. 387.
xiii. Byrne (1995), pp. 105–6.
xiv. Woodruff and Premack (1979).
xv. Povinelli and DeBlois (1992).
xvi. Povinelli and Eddy (1996).
xvii. Cheney and Seyfarth (1990a).
xviii. Wimmer *et al.* (1988) and (1991). See also Gopnik and Graf (1988) and Mitchell (1997).
xix. Gopnik and Astington (1988).
xx. Whiten and Byrne (1988).
xxi. Byrne (1995), pp. 124–5.
xxii. Byrne (1995), p. 127.
xxiii. De Waal (1982), p. 47.
xxiv. Whiten and Byrne (1988), p. 271.
xxv. Heyes (1998). See also Bennett (1988).
xxvi. Byrne (1995), p. 206.
xxvii. Coussi-Korbel (1994).
xxviii. Dasser (1988).
xxix. Dennett (1988).
xxx. Cosmides and Tooby (1992).
xxxi. Power (1999), pp. 96–7.
xxxii. Keating and Heltman (1994).
xxxiii. Connolly and Doyle (1984).
xxxiv. Perner and Lang (1999). Self-control is in this context often called executive function.
xxxv. Stone *et al.* (1997).
xxxvi. Russell *et al.* (1991).
xxxvii. See, e.g. Leslie (1987).

CHAPTER 5

Self-consciousness

Consciousness is like a mirror of water where sometimes the sky, sometimes
the depths, invite our gaze; sometimes, too, when its smooth nakedness is
ruffled, it breaks into a medley of mirrors and translucencies, a tangled image
of images.

Paul Valéry

5.1 What is self-consciousness?

Consciousness is a complex phenomenon that engages philosophers, psychologists, and neuroscientists. However, there is a distinction between two kinds
of consciousness that is often neglected in the discussions. One is consciousness as *experience*, i.e. seeing and hearing, feeling joy and pain, etc. The second
kind is consciousness as *reflection*, i.e. thinking about one's experiences. In the
following, I will use the term *self-consciousness* for the reflective sense. In contrast to what Descartes claimed, there are compelling reasons why animals with
a reasonably advanced nervous system are conscious, in the sense of having
sensations and perceptions, but, as will be argued in this chapter, it is most
likely only humans who are self-conscious.

It is also important to note that there are several cognitive processes that are
not experienced and therefore cannot be considered conscious. A great part of
our learning is non-conscious. Furthermore, when we remember an episode,
we become aware of the memory, but we are not conscious about how we
retrieve the memory from the convolutions of the brain. And when we speak,
we are aware of what we say, but, again, we have severe problems in becoming
conscious of *how* we shape the sentences, before they are uttered.

What then is the difference between being conscious and being self-
conscious? According to Humphrey's theory that was presented in Chapter 2,
having sensations is sufficient for being conscious. Different kinds of perceptions make consciousness ampler, but they do not result in self-consciousness.
I wish to advance the hypothesis that self-consciousness actually consists of
perceptions, albeit *perceptions of the inner world* in contrast to perceptions of

the outer world.[1] In words that may sound more mystical than I intend, one could say that self-consciousness consists in seeing with the inner eye, hearing with the inner ear, etc.

Just as we can attend to certain aspects of the outer world, we can also shut off the outer world and 'experience' events in the inner world. To a certain extent, we can also 'act' in the inner world, i.e. imagine the consequences of imagined actions. This kind of 'experience' occurs in many cognitive activities, such as daydreaming, fantasizing, planning, and remembering. A dream at night is also a kind of experience in the inner world.[i] Speaking about 'experiences' in the inner world is, of course a metaphor, but it is a very productive metaphor—our language is replete with visual metaphors for mental phenomena. For example, one says 'I *see* what you mean' and 'I cannot think *clearly*'.

The linguist Wallace Chafe has proposed a similar thesis. He says: '[i]t is tempting to suppose that both vision and consciousness reflect the same basic strategy for information processing.'[2] There is interesting experimental support for this idea. One first presents subjects with different pictures and studies how they look at them using an eye-tracker. If the subject is then asked to tell from memory what was in the picture, it turns out that the order and the content of the stories show striking correspondences with the earlier pattern of eye movements. As a consequence, Chafe presumes:

> that similar principles are involved in the way information is acquired from the environment (for example, through eye movements), in the way it is scanned by consciousness during recall, and in the way it is verbalized. All three processes may be guided by a single executive mechanism which determines what is focused on, for how long, and in what sequence.

The capacity of self-consciousness is closely connected to episodic memory. In order to recall what happened to oneself at different occasions, one must be able to *view oneself from the outside*. The detachment of human thought, from both evolutionary and developmental perspectives, involves becoming ever more skilled at directing one's attention towards the inner world, and at the same time disregarding the impressions from the outer world. Using a pointed

---

[1]   The neurologist Wolf Singer (1999), p. 254, has formulated a closely related hypothesis. He writes: 'The idea is that there are second order processes that treat the output of the first order processes in exactly the same way as these treat the sensory signals.' A similar position is taken by Deacon (1997), p. 448, who writes that 'to be conscious of something is to experience a representation of it'.

[2]   Chafe (1980), p. 16. In the article, he recounts an early study made by Charlotte Baker (her results were never published). Jana Holsanova (2001) has performed several more extended studies of the same kind.

wording, one can say that self-consciousness consists of an *inner* inner world that is used to perceive the inner world of the individual.

"But *who* is it, then, who looks at your inner world?" Egon asks with tilted head.

"It is me, of course," I answer innocently, although I suspect that he is after something.

"So your *self* sits in there studying your inner world," he says and bats his eyelashes meaningfully. "What about the consciousness of your self?"

"You are trying to catch me with a homunculus theory," I accuse.

"How can you imagine anything like that," Egon pouts and looks up at the ceiling. "I don't even know what cumulus is."

"A homunculus is a little man who sits in your head and controls the thinking that goes on in there. The problem with homunculus theories is that one must account for what goes on in the head of the little man."

"Exactly," says Egon. "That's what I meant."

As far as I can see, my hypothesis about self-consciousness does not demand any homunculus—at least as long as normal perception does not require it. When I see something, the nerve signals that emanate from my retinas are spread, via the optical nerve, to the visual cortex at the back of my brain. There the flow of signals is divided into several subprocesses that, roughly speaking, treat colour, shape, and motion in my visual image. These subprocesses are then merged to some kind of unity that constitutes that very perception. But nowhere does one find a little man or any other kind of central control to which the result of the process is reported. The vision process spreads over large parts of the brain and consists of several subprocesses, the interaction among which is not yet fully understood.

Perceptions in the inner world can function in an analogous way. Detached representations can be perceived by an inner 'retina' (let alone that we don't really know what such representations look like) and be processed in roughly the same way as an ordinary visual sensation. So neither does this 'self-perception' require any homunculus who looks at the result. Humphrey formulates the position in the following way:

> No one would say that a person cannot use his own eyes to observe his own
> feet. No one would say, moreover, that he cannot use his eyes, with the aid
> of a mirror, to observe his own eyes. Then why should anyone say a person
> cannot, at least in principle, use his own brain to observe his own brain? All
> that is required is that nature should have given him the equivalent of an
> *inner mirror* and an *inner eye*. And this, I think, is precisely what she has
> done. Nature has, in short, given to human beings the remarkable gift of
> *self-reflexive insight*.[ii]

"What is then the difference between the inner world and the inner inner world?" Egon pursues.

"Hey, you are smarter than you look! That is a very good question," I praise him.

Humphrey puts the emphasis on seeing the inner world as a self-reflective loop. He writes:

> For what consciousness actually is, is a feature not of the whole brain but of this added self-reflective loop. Why this particular arrangement should have what we might call the 'transcendent', 'other-worldly' qualities of consciousness I do not know. But note that I have allowed here for one curious feature: *the output of the inner eye is part of its own input.*[iii]

As Humphrey admits, a self-referential system of this kind may have paradoxical properties. Since the input from the real eye is also part of the input to the inner eye, a consequence of this strong form of self-reflection is that a distinction between the inner world and the inner inner world cannot be maintained. In the words of Valéry: 'The mind is the geometric point... of everything it knows.' But I think this position is too strong. A reflection is not a perfect copy of what it reflects. There is much that goes on in the inner world that is not perceived (yes, it is a perception) in the inner inner world. The inner inner world contains, in turn, simulations of the inner world. Thus I regard them as separate systems.[3] If they are not distinct, there is no point in separating consciousness from self-consciousness. Valéry formulates the position as follows:

> The more 'conscious' one conscience is the more *its* personality, the more *its* opinions, *its* acts, *its* characteristics, *its* feelings appear *strange* to him—*strangers.* It would thus tend to employ that which is most its own and personal to it as exterior and accidental things.

"Hmm, he said that I am smarter than I look," mutters Egon and rigorously examines his image in the mirror.

5.2   Animals for themselves: why baboons do not wear lipstick

> When he awoke in the morning, the first thing he saw was Tigger, sitting in front of the glass and looking at himself.

---

[3] But this does not necessarily mean that there must be a third- and a fourth-order inner world, and so on. At some level, presumably already the second, we cannot construct any further levels or we achieve the form of self-reflection that Humphrey assigns to the first level.

"Hallo!" said Pooh
"Hallo!" said Tigger. "I've found somebody just like me. I thought I was the
only one of them."

A. A. Milne: *The House at Pooh Corner*

We are convinced that other people have a consciousness that is very much like
our own. By talking to each other we learn about the experiences of others. We
also believe that many animals have some form of consciousness, but here
we immediately become uncertain as to how animals experience the world,
including themselves.

"How could one find out something about their experiences when it is
impossible to speak with them," I say to myself.

"Ha!" Egon exclaims. "Humans are experts at fooling themselves. How can
one be sure to find out what they really think by talking to them?"

"Point granted," I admit.

But the questions remain: How can one know whether an animal can
have thoughts about itself? Since they do not seem to be able to plan for future
goals, they cannot be totally aware of themselves as beings in time. But can
they be conscious of their present consciousness?

During the period when behaviourism dominated psychology, questions
about the consciousness of animals were not taken seriously. Problems concerning inner experiences were not considered to belong to the domain of science. But the emergence of the cognitive sciences during the 1960s prepared
the way for a new attitude towards the mental states of animals. In 1970, the
psychologist Gordon Gallup published the results of a series of experiments
that have become paradigmatic for studies of animal self-consciousness.

Gallup's thesis is that chimpanzees have a concept of self. In order to show
this he put mirrors next to the cages of a number of chimps and let them get
accustomed to the mirrors for ten days. Then the apes were anaesthetized and
two non-smelling red dots were painted on an eyebrow and an ear. When a
chimp woke up again, it did now show any signs of noticing the dots until it
saw itself in the mirror. It then became very interested in touching the dots,
and it looked at and smelled the fingers that had touched them. Apparently,
chimpanzees can connect what they see in the mirror to places on their
own body. With his experiments, Gallup wanted to show that chimps are
conscious of the body as *theirs* and that in this sense they have a form of
self-consciousness.

The mirror test has resulted in a separate research tradition within
ethology. Cognitive scientists, psychologists, anthropologists, and ethologists

Figure 5.1 Chimpanzees manage the mirror test. (Photo by Donna Bierschwale, reproduced with permission.)

have proposed different methods for studying self-consciousness in animals and human children in ways that do not presuppose linguistic communication.[4]

Apart from chimpanzees, orang-utans also manage Gallup's mirror test. For gorillas the experimental evidence is unclear. There are indications that macaques might pass the test, but no other monkeys have been observed to pass the original version of Gallup's test.

"Of course, macaques can do it!" Egon says proudly.

Marc Hauser argues that one reason that monkeys have problems with Gallup's mirror test is that staring at somebody else is a sign of aggression among monkeys, but not necessarily so among the apes. Looking at oneself in the mirror is therefore something monkeys would avoid because they regard the image as another individual at the beginning of the exposure.

If this analysis is correct, more dramatic changes to the mirror image may improve the chances of getting a reaction. Hauser and his students ran an experiment with cotton-top tamarins, who have a conspicuous tuft of white hair on top of their heads. They exposed some of the monkeys to a mirror, anaesthetized them, and dyed their tufts in bright colours. When the tamarins woke up from the anaesthesia, most of those with previous mirror experience

---

[4] An excellent collection of articles on this topic is *Self-awareness in animals and humans* (edited by Sue Taylor Parker, Robert Mitchell, and Maria Boccia).

touched their tufts while looking into the mirror, while those who had no prior mirror exposure did not touch their hair. Hauser interprets the observations:

> as evidence that cotton-top tamarins have mirror self-recognition.
> In contrast to Gallup's test, our procedure caused a more salient change in the subject's appearance. This change may have caused an increase in the tamarins' attention to the mirror, a change that is necessary for recognizing the mirror image.[iv]

Still, there is further evidence that apes better understand what goes on in a mirror than monkeys, for example, from an experiment by Menzel and his colleagues.[v] A chimpanzee or a rhesus macaque was placed in a room with a small hole in the wall. On the backside of the wall, out of sight for the subject, food was placed in one of several grid squares. A mirror was placed opposite the wall. By sticking its arm through the hole while looking at the mirror reflection, the subject could navigate its hand to retrieve the treat. The chimps managed this immediately, looking at the movements in the mirror to find the food. But the rhesus macaques failed repeatedly. Actually, the macaques reacted to the mirror image of their arm as if it belonged to a competitor and they produced corresponding threat vocalizations.

"Hrm," Egon mutters.

Some investigations point out that dolphins can recognize their bodies in a mirror.[vi] It is more difficult to perform Gallup's mirror test with dolphins since they cannot move their body parts as freely as apes and monkeys (and they must also be studied in the water). But if a dolphin is allowed to get used to a mirror in its aquarium and one then, under anaesthesia, paints a white spot on the back side of a flipper (that cannot be seen without a mirror), it tries to turn its body while swimming so that it can study the spot in the mirror.

Sue Taylor Parker and her colleagues have explored some variations of Gallup's test. Among other things, apes have been allowed to watch themselves on a TV screen while they are filmed with a video camera. Chimpanzees react to these pictures in the same way as to a mirror image. Again, it is not clear whether gorillas recognize themselves in directly projected video sequences— if nothing else they show signs of being bored by the TV screen.

"Who wouldn't?" says Egon.

Yet another variation is to let an ape see a photograph of itself. This test is considerably more difficult since the animal does not receive feedback from its own movements as it does in front of a mirror or in a directly projected video. It seems that chimpanzees are the only animals that can recognize themselves in a photo. But sometimes the tests give surprising results. The chimpanzee Viki, who was raised among humans, was given the task of sorting photos of humans and chimpanzees in two piles. When she came to the photo of herself, she placed it among the human pictures.

It is debatable whether the different experimental methods really prove anything concerning the conscious experiences in animals. Together with his colleagues Robert Epstein and Robert Lanza, the archbehaviorist Frederic Skinner ran an experiment reminiscent of Gallup's to show that pigeons can also learn the same kind of self-centred behaviour. The pigeons were first trained to peck at stick-on dots placed on various parts of their bodies. Then they were trained to peck at the spot in their boxes where a dot had just been, when it had only been visible to the pigeon through a mirror. Finally, a blue dot was placed on a pigeon's breast and a bib was fitted around its neck so that it could not directly see the dot but only in a mirror. The result was that when the pigeon caught sight of the dot in the mirror, it began bobbing its head as if to peck at the spot on its own breast where the dot was located.

Philosopher Lawrence Davis has argued convincingly that the experiment run by Skinner and his colleagues does *not* show that pigeons have a self-awareness in any interesting sense. What the pigeon learns and its ensuing behaviour can be explained as a case of conditioning—and a laborious one, since the training took a long time. It is not necessary to assume that the pigeon is in any sense aware that it pecks on *itself*. It may seem natural to interpret the behaviour of the pigeon as that it *believes* that 'I am pecking on that part of *my* breast where the dot was located'. But if Ockham's razor is applied, the cognition of the pigeon may as well be described as implying that it believes that it should peck on that part of the breast where the dot was placed.[5] 'The breast' can here be described in terms of the visual perception of the pigeon, since only one pigeon was present. The behaviour does not in any way presume that the pigeon recognizes it as *its* breast. In addition to this argument, it has also proved difficult to repeat the results of Epstein, Lanza, and Skinner.

"But can't you argue in the same way about the chimps?" Egon challenges.

"You are right that Epstein, Lanza, and Skinner propose a similar non-mentalistic interpretation of the apes' behaviour. But one important difference between a chimpanzee and a pigeon is that the chimpanzee requires *no training* to touch the dots. It is interested in the dots just because they were placed on *its* body. But it was necessary to train the chimpanzee to understand that the mirror shows an image of itself. If the dots were first painted on the

---

[5]   This interpretation is, of course, foreign to Epstein, Lanza, and Skinner, since they eschew mentalistic terms such as 'believe' altogether.

chimpanzee and a mirror was *then* placed in front of the cage, it did not show any interest in the dot, but treated the mirror image as if it was an unknown chimpanzee."

Further information about the consciousness of apes can be obtained from those who have been trained by humans to communicate using sign language. Once in a while, a signing ape describes its emotions. The gorilla Koko could, three days after she had bitten a trainer, confess that it was wrong and sign that she did it because she was angry, but she could not answer why she was angry.

(In the Disney movie about Winnie the Pooh, a seam comes apart in his back—remember that Pooh is a stuffed teddy bear. To mend the seam, he uses a mirror so that he can see what he does. When Pooh is finished, he turns to the mirror image and says "Thank you". Even though he understands that the mirror image is useful, Pooh is not quite as advanced as the chimpanzees because he treats it as another individual.)

The kind of self-awareness studied by Gallup presumes that one can direct one's attention towards *one's own body* and understand that there is a connection between one's attention to the body and what happens to it. Chimpanzees and some other animals are conscious of their own bodies in this sense. However, there is yet another level of self-consciousness where one has an understanding of *one's own consciousness*. As far as I know, there are no studies indicating that animals other than humans have such a self-consciousness. For example, even though language trained apes can learn sign for their names or for 'me', there seems to be no case where they talk about themselves or their characteristics in the way that even two-year-old human children do.

"Is that why humans are vain?" Egon asks suddenly. "That is what is called self-conscious."

"What do you mean?"

"You spend a lot of energy adorning yourself—painting your faces and wearing impractical and uncomfortable clothes. What's the point of it?"

Humans care a lot about what impressions we make on other people. Body decorations and the clothes we wear in the modern world are attempts to deceive—we try to make ourselves more attractive than we really are. Such adornments are meaningful only for an individual who has some form of awareness of how *others* attend to how you look. Body decorations occur in all human cultures, but do not exist as *intentional* decorations in any other species.[vii] There are archaeological finds of red ochre that are at least 100 000 years old. Presumably the ochre has been used to decorate the body with red colour.[viii] Nothing in the behaviour of the apes in front of a mirror corresponds to what humans do when they comb their hair or put on a necklace. Indeed, one has never observed baboons wearing lipstick.

5.3   Communication, attention, and consciousness

> Pooh began to feel a little more comfortable, because when you are a Bear of Very Little Brain, and you Think Things, you find sometimes that a Thing which seemed very Thingish inside you is quite different when it gets out into the open and has other people looking at it.
>
> A. A. Milne: *The House at Pooh Corner*

Communication, in various forms, is for spreading information. An important difference between humans and animals is that the signals used in animal communication only concern what happens to the communicator or what happens in the external world here and now, while human language most often refers to our *inner world*, i.e. our imaginations, memories, plans, fantasies, and dreams. Language therefore provides us with an immensely powerful tool for copying parts of the inner worlds of others to our own. This mechanism makes us very successful Gregorian beings.

In *Consciousness explained*, Dennett describes consciousness as constructed from a collection of rather independent systems in the brain. He suggests that these systems cannot form a unified consciousness until spoken language has developed. By speaking to oneself, in an outer or inner monologue, one creates connections between the different subsystems and thereby one constructs a self.

However, Dennett seems to be over-confident as regards the impact of spoken language on the evolution of consciousness. One argument against this model is that spoken language is a very late phenomenon in human evolution. Consequently, most of human consciousness has already been formed before the event of spoken language. Tomasello writes that 'invoking language as an evolutionary cause of human cognition is like invoking money as an evolutionary cause of human economic activity'.[ix] But once the monetary system has developed, it makes economic transactions much more efficient. The same thing applies to language: human beings have been communicating long before language, but language makes the exchange more efficient. The analogy can be extended further: when money is introduced, a more stable system of *prices* emerges. In the same way language will lead to a more stable system of *meanings*, i.e. components in the inner world that the Gregorian beings can trade with one another. Thus language leads to a *common mode* of thinking.

The original function of language is to be a tool for communication *between* people. Tomasello argues that the primary function is to *direct the attention of others.*[x] Dennett defends his theory partly by pointing out that small children often sit talking to themselves when they are playing. He suggests that in this way they practice the use of different linguistic expressions in the appropriate context. But the child cannot practice before it has been involved in or exposed to discussions where the expressions are used. *Dialogue* must precede monologue, in evolution as well as in the development of a child. Valéry expresses it concisely: 'This strange, essential property of being *two*-in-*one*—in contrast to amorous desire—to be *one* through *two*—appears complementary to conscious knowledge... Every monologue is a dialogue.' Donald emphasizes the same point:

> The developmental rule is that symbolic thought first represents external
> action, and only later reconstructs it so that it will occur internally. Every
> function in a child's development thus appears twice: first interpersonally,
> then intrapersonally. Thus the silent thinking skills of adults might be very
> misleading when we want to specify their origins. Given the self-centered
> nature of symbolic cognition in adults, we might easily gain the impression
> that they used their skills in a solipsistic manner from the start. But this is
> wrong. Vygotsky's studies have suggested that when they first appear,
> children's own symbolic performances are completely public, *even to*
> *themselves*. Only later do these operations become internalized, and
> independent of a specific social-mimetic role.[xi]

Language is best seen as an extension of the interaction via shared attention that the child develops from the age of about nine months—an interaction involving linguistic symbols. The neuropsychologist Alexander Luria notes, for example, that in two- to three-year-old children, speech is not well coordinated with their behaviour.[xii] Speech does not control the activity of the child but only runs in parallel. But from the age of four, they can control their behaviour using their own speech. In this context it is interesting to note that Savage-Rumbaugh claims that Kanzi sometimes talks to himself, using the symbols on his board to comment on what he sees or to reveal his travel plans.

In one article, Gómez discusses the connection between the communicative capacities in animals and their self-consciousness.[xiii] One can distinguish two traditions in research concerning animal communication. On the one hand, there is the ethological tradition, which in a behaviouristic spirit avoids talking about the inner life of animals. Within this tradition communication is defined as that an animal influences the behaviour of another without being in direct physical contact with it. This definition suffices for most signalling systems deployed in the animal kingdom. Questions concerning the intentions involved in the communication are considered irrelevant.

On the other hand, there is a more philosophical tradition that seizes on the intention of what is communicated. One theory that is often referred to is that formulated by the philosopher Paul Grice. One element of his analysis is that when a person A, for example, says 'Please pass the mustard' to B, then A *believes* that B *understands* that A *wants* the mustard. Human communication presumes that we can think such embedded thoughts called 'higher-order intentions' by philosophers.

The problem with Grice's definition for researchers studying animal communication is that it presupposes a lot concerning the minds of those who communicate. First of all, A must envision the inner world of B, which is a form of 'you-awareness'. But that is not enough: A must also imagine that B in turn can imagine A's thoughts and intentions. In order words, a third-order intention is required. This makes the theory cumbersome to apply to other animals than man. For most forms of communication between animals, the ethological definition is sufficient. The gulf seems wide between the behaviouristically oriented ethological definition and the more philosophical one involving higher-order intentions.

However, several researchers have argued that there is an intermediate form of *intentional* communication that is more advanced than pure signalling systems, but still does not presuppose any theory of mind.[xiv] The key idea is that animals can *attend to each other's attention*. If I want to tell you something, I want to make sure that you can see or hear what I am conveying—lest it be pointless to communicate. The best way for me to find out what you are attending to is to look at your eyes. The movements of the eye mirror those of the soul.

And conversely, you must watch my eyes to see whom I am contacting. When our gazes meet we can reach joint attention and then the chances of successful communication are the best. Achieving joint attention presumes neither that you are aware of the intentions of the opposite party, nor that you are aware of your own intentions. Hence, communication based on joint attention does not demand so much about a theory of mind as Grice's theory. Gómez' idea is that by experimentally studying how children, apes, and other animals exploit eye contact (and other forms leading to joint attention) we will learn a lot about the mechanisms of communication among humans and animals. Hauser notes that animal mothers almost never look into their infant's eyes and make adoring noises—this uniquely human behaviour may prepare the infants for being partners in joint attention.[xv]

"Take off your sunglasses so I can hear what you're saying," Egon requests.

The most fundamental form of intentional communication is to *manipulate* the attention of others.[xvi] Tomasello writes that in order for me to understand that you want to communicate about an object, I must understand that you *intend* us to *jointly attend* to the object.[xvii] To achieve this requires a second-order intention and a second-order attention. But not even this is necessary to reach intentional communication. Philosopher Ingar Brinck argues that if I aim at manipulating your attention it is sufficient that I *intend* that you and I jointly attend to something.[xviii] This only requires a first-order intention and a second-order attention, since it is not necessary that you understand that I intend to communicate. Such a form of communication can be achieved, for example, by pointing and joint gaze contact—something which children manage from an age of about one year and which presumably also apes are capable of.[6]

The capacity to achieve joint attention seems to be an important preparation for language learning. In one experiment, it was tested how well six-month-old infants could follow the gazes of their mothers.[xix] It turned out that the infants who were best at this also had the largest vocabulary at the age of 12 months.

As we have seen, there is little support for the idea that apes and other animals have higher-order intentions. But as Gómez and others show, apes may very well attain second-order attention. Apart from communication, this capability is sufficient to explain many forms of deception, as shown in the previous chapter.

A more advanced form of communication is established when *symbols*, such as words, are used. But to make something function as a symbol and not just a signal, the communicator must be able to take on the *roles of both the speaker and the listener*.[7] A child, for example, must use a word when addressing an adult in the same way as the adult uses the word when talking to the child. Tomasello argues that this involves a form of imitation.[xx] Considering the earlier results concerning the difficulties apes have in imitating (in the strong sense), the slightly tentative conclusion is that only humans can reach this level of communication.

5.4   It's not rude to point

Not only gazes but also *pointing* can result in joint attention. Apes and other animals do not point intentionally in the wild (pointer dogs just stand still—it is *we* who interpret their posture as pointing). But apes that grow up together with humans can learn to point. The difference is that in order that intentional pointing will pay off, there must be somebody who attends to what

---

[6] Tomasello (1999), pp. 62–5. Gómez (1998), pp. 82–3, argues that gorillas can intentionally communicate with the aid of joint attention.

[7] The distinction between signals and symbols will be discussed in Section 6.1.

you are pointing to. Since animals are no good at this kind of attention, pointing does not arise in the wild.

"What is the point of pointing?" asks Egon.

"You wonder what is the evolutionary explanation for pointing?"

"Man, have you got a one-track mind!"

"Be that as it may, but that's why I'm writing this book."

The psychologist William Noble and the archaeologist Iain Davidson derive the evolutionary origin of pointing from throwing—the arm is directed towards the goal when you have thrown something. But Gómez and Tomasello propose another perspective that seems more plausible.[xxi] They see pointing as a part of a child's communicative development. One can distinguish three stages in a child's development of pointing.[xxii] In the first stage the child stretches towards a toy it desires but cannot grasp. In this phase, the child does not seek eye contact with the adult. This form of 'pointing' is not intentional communication. When the child is older it looks for the adult's attention—it reaches out for the toy and checks at the same time whether the adult is attending to what the child is pointing to, which makes it truly intentional communication. This form of pointing is called 'imperative'.

Tomasello claims that in the second stage children can master intentional pointing without understanding the pointing of others. In order to understand when somebody else is pointing a third level is required where the child grasps that the other *wants* the child to *attend to* what is pointed to. This is a second-order intention which demands that the child has a certain understanding of the intention of the other. At this stage, children can also use pointing just to draw attention to an object. This is called 'declarative' pointing and the communicative function is to indicate the presence of an object.[xxiii] It is interesting to note that children with autism often have problems understanding when others point, even if they can point themselves. Their pointing is, in general, imperative rather than declarative.

Tomasello shows that this mechanism is important for a child's learning of language. An act of pointing is often coupled with a sound so that the child more markedly draws attention to the pointing. Among the first words that children learn are 'there' or 'look'. Conversely, if an adult points to a frog and the child sees what the adult is pointing to and reaches joint attention by shifting its gaze between the adult and the frog, the child will connect the word 'frog' with the perception of the object. Normally, one or two instances are sufficient for a child to learn this connection. And once it has coupled the word with the object, the child can use the word itself to direct the attention of somebody else.[8] Tomasello's claim is that pointing is an essential component in the language learning mechanism and unless the child masters it, the rest of language learning will not work either. This may be part of the explanation why children with autism have communicative problems.

5.5 You and I

> Your words in me
> an endless restless walk
> quivering through labyrinths
> of worlds always awake
>
> Pia Tafdrup: *Transfusion*

Being conscious of one's body presupposes that one can attend to one's own bodily experiences. Being conscious about one's consciousness requires something more: to be able *to attend to one's own inner world*. Attending to one's own inner world is the foundation of *self-consciousness*—a theory of one's own mind. Self-consciousness need not coincide with *you-consciousness*, i.e. a theory of somebody else's mind.

"What comes first in the evolution of mind then, I or you?" asks Egon.

"There are in principle three possibilities," I answer.

"Oh no, spare me from further distinctions!" he sighs.

The first possibility is that self-consciousness comes before you-consciousness. This has been a common position among philosophers. For example, Descartes used 'Cogito, ergo sum' as a stepping-stone to argue that the external world and other minds exist. But this position does not seem to be supported empirically.

The second possibility is that self-consciousness and you-consciousness are two sides of the same coin. As the author Witold Gombrowicz writes: 'I am the centre of the universe, but so are you.' According to this view the two capabilities would arise simultaneously.[9] In connection with the Smarties experiments, Leslie argues that it is *the same process* that is used to distinguish between the representations 'there is a pencil in the box' and 'I *thought* there were Smarties in the box' as is used to distinguish between 'there is a pencil in

---

[8] Tomasello (1999), pp. 114–16, and Bloom (2000), Chapter 3, present a series of experiments that show that if it is not clear from the situation which object is pointed out, the child assumes that what the adult refers to is the object that is *novel* in the situation.

[9] This position is defended by Leslie (1987), Gopnik and Meltzoff (1997), and Frith and Happé (1999).

the box' and 'Bert *believes* there are Smarties in the box'. In the experiments, there is nothing that indicates that children can reflect on their own inner worlds earlier than they can understand the inner world of others. So also from an ontogenetical point of view, the first possibility is therefore not very likely.

Tomasello argues that self-consciousness develops out of the ability to jointly attend.[xxiv] From the age of nine months, the child notes how the attention of others is directed towards *itself*. The child follows how adults look at it and soon perceives the adults as intentional agents. Tomasello claims that this results in a first level of self-consciousness that, among other things, is manifested in that the child becomes *shy*. Shyness presupposes that you can view yourself through the eyes of others. But this form of self-consciousness does not presuppose that the child has any conception of the inner world of others.

The third possibility is the most radical, but, in my opinion, the most plausible: the self presupposes a you. A decisive step in the evolution of thought is that A realizes that B in her inner world can represent that A has plans and thereby that A also has an inner world. Previously I argued that the Machiavellian intelligence has arisen through an arms race in the capacity to deceive. The more your inner world can handle of the series 'I know', 'I know that you know', 'I know that you know that I know', etc., the more skilful you become in deceiving (and in co-operating, as we shall see). The mental weapons of deception become like the anti-anti-missiles that are fired against the anti-missiles that are sent up to shoot down the missiles.

And once you can see yourself through the eyes of others, you can see yourself directly. You can become conscious of your own *consciousness* and not only view yourself as an acting body. With this decisive step we have reached self-consciousness. I submit that the insight about your own consciousness must go via the steps I have indicated here, i.e. through the insight that the members of your species also act intentionally and have inner worlds of their own. Valéry writes: 'Man communicates with—himself, by the same means as he has for communicating with *the other*/Consciousness needs a fictive other—an exteriority—it develops in developing that *alterity*.'

The philosopher Maurice Merleau-Ponty notes that the same applies when we see ourselves in a mirror: 'I understand so much easier that what is in the mirror is my image since I can imagine that this is the way others see me.' The psychologist William James distinguishes between 'I' and 'me'. In my terminology, one could say that 'I' corresponds to my inner world, while 'me' is my experience of a self in my inner inner world. 'Me' emerges when I can view myself through the eyes of others.

The position that self-consciousness is dependent on you-consciousness can be compared to the thoughts of the philosopher of religion Martin Buber in his book *I and You*. According to him, human beings take a double stance to the world. The two stances are determined by the basic words 'I–You' and 'I–It'. According to Buber, these words should be seen as units and not as pairs of concepts. He says about the first basic words that a human being:

> speaks the basic word I–You in a natural, as it were still unformed manner, not yet having recognized himself as an I; but the basic word I–It is made possible only by this recognition, by the detachment of the I.

The former word splits into I and You, but it did not originate as their aggregate, it antedates any I. The latter originated as an aggregate of I and It, it postulates the I.[xxv]

In modern studies of the infants' experiences and cognition, several researchers claim that the striving for experiences of the Other, that is a you-experience, is *innate*. I believe that much of the you-experiences studied within this tradition can be described with the aid of the different levels of theory of mind that were treated in the previous chapter. Several of these powers are arguably genetically prepared so that children who grow up in a normal environment develop them automatically and in this sense they are 'innate' as programs. But I can hardly believe that the very experience of the other is innate.[10]

It is interesting to note that the thought of an innate You can be found already with Buber:

> In the beginning is the relation—as the category of being, as readiness, as a form that reaches out to be filled, as a model of the soul; the *a priori* of relation; *the innate You* [...]

> In the drive for contact [...] the innate You comes to the fore quite soon, and it becomes ever clearer that the drive aims at reciprocity, at 'tenderness'. [...] The development of the child's soul is connected indissolubly with his craving for the You, with the fulfillments and disappointments of this craving, with the play of his experiments and his tragic seriousness when he feels at a total loss.

Buber also emphasizes that a human being cannot consist of merely a self, but the You-relation is also necessary:

> Man becomes an I through a You. [...] To be sure, for a long time it appears only woven into the relation to a You, discernible as that which reaches for

---

[10] The imitation of the behaviour of others that can be found already in newborn children (Meltzoff 1985) can probably be explained as an instinctual behaviour and it need not mean that the newborn has any conception of the thoughts or intentions of somebody else.

but is not a You; but it comes closer and closer to the bursting point until one day the bonds are broken and the I confronts its detached self for a moment like a You—and then it takes possession of itself and henceforth enters into relations in full consciousness.

The last sentences of the quotation are a beautiful description of how the I can only discover itself after having seen the You in relation to itself. An experience of a We is necessary before an I can be reached.

5.6   The mirror of the soul

> In the whole universe there is no well
> deep enough that if one bends over it
> one would not find a reflection of a human face.
>
> Leszek Kolakowski

Consciousness consists of a number of control systems for different cognitive functions: perception, attention, emotions, will, planning, etc. These control systems can in turn be viewed as constituted of smaller control systems for more limited functions, etc. The ants in an anthill can *together* solve a number of sophisticated problems such as gathering food, constructing a hill, taking care of the offspring, even though the individual ant has extremely limited cognitive capacities and they operate according to very simple principles. In a similar way, the brain as a unit can handle a number of difficult cognitive problems by the efficient co-operation of various simple functions.

"But must there then not be a superior control system for consciousness; must there not be an *I*?" Egon ponders.

"Not necessarily. Our experience of a 'I' can be an illusion that *emerges* from the complex system. I consider it to be a mistake to assume a central 'I' functioning as a pilot for the processes of the brain and thereby also for the actions of the body."

"But you just said 'I consider'," Egon protests. "*What* is it then that does the considering, if not your I."

When we try to capture the illusion of an I, it slips away like a ghost in the brain machine. Even Hume had problems with the concept of an I:

> For my part, when I enter most intimately into what I call *myself*, I always stumble on some particular perception or other, of heat or cold, light or shade, love or hatred, pain or pleasure. I never can catch *myself* at any time without a perception, and never can observe any thing but the perception.

When my perceptions are remov'd for any time, as by sound sleep; so long am I insensible of *myself*, and may truly be said not to exist.[11]

Here Hume uses 'perception' as I use 'sensation' in my partitioning of experiences. My view of the self is related to Hume's, but instead of just sensations I start out from the picture of consciousness that I have presented in the previous chapters. Earlier I suggested that what we experience as the I can be described as an inner inner world that is used to look upon the inner world of the individual. This second-order inner world is the dwelling-place of self-consciousness. Yet it does not function as a pilot for the flight of thought, but is one component among many others in a complex system.

Descartes realizes the problems of viewing the I as the pilot of thinking:

> Nature also teaches me by these sensations of pain, hunger, thirst, etc, that I am not only lodged in my body as a pilot in a vessel, but that I am very closely united to it, and so to speak, so intermingled with it that I seem to compose with it one whole. For if that were not the case, when my body is hurt, I, who am merely a thinking thing, should not feel pain, for I should perceive this wounding by the understanding only, just as the sailor perceives by sight when something is damaged to his vessel.[xxvi]

"It thinks inside me: hence the I exists," Egon says with something that looks like a smile.

Deacon says that ironically it is not the real but the virtual events offered by detached representations that result in the experience of an I.[12] In my terminology, self-consciousness is a perception of a virtual reality, i.e. the inner world. He also claims that this is the source of the intuition that our soul is not a part of our body. My ability to manage my inner world—my soul—is experienced as *independent* of the bodily and perceptual sensations.

Or as Paul Valéry expresses it:

> Mystery. A soul in the soul, and to glimpse in the first the other or one's own, and the next in the next and so on; just as one in parallel mirrors sees an object that stands just between them. But what object?—Why, there is no object.

The *unity* of thought arises through meaningful connections between the different parts of the inner world. The representations created by the brain in

---

[11] The quotation comes from *A treatise of human nature*, Book I, Part IV, Section VI. The entire section 'Of personal identity' is well worth reading.
[12] Deacon (1997), p. 452. What he calls symbols correspond to what I call detached representations.

these two inner worlds play a decisive role in such a co-operation. The self-experience thereby becomes an *emergent* phenomenon. It is important that the representations are not just in service of an 'I' but of the whole organism.[13] In other words, the brain is not the master of the body, but its servant.

The theory of the I as an emergent phenomenon is mainly due to the neurologist and Nobel laureate Roger Sperry.[xxvii] The best way of explaining what an emergent property is, is to give an example. The following explanation of a 'virtual governor' derives from Norbert Wiener:[xxviii] Consider a system that consists of a network of AC generators. Each generator has built into it a regulator that controls its speed so that it steers towards 60 Hz at any time. But a generator in isolation does not produce a very steady 60 Hz output. In remarkable contrast, when a large number of such generators are interconnected, they behave much more stably. If a new generator is added to the system, the effects are best explained by saying that the virtual governor causes it to get into step by pumping energy into it, if it lags in phase, or by absorbing energy, if it runs too fast. This 'mutual entrainment' of the generators is an example of *self-organization*. Out of the mutual entrainment emerges what Wiener calls a virtual governor, which is an *equilibrium* property of the entire system that is viewed as having *causal effects* on the individual generators in the system. It should be noted that the notion of emergence introduced here involves no mystical properties apart from those normally ascribed to physical systems.

The analogy is of course that *the I is the virtual regulator of consciousness* that makes the different cognitive control functions get into step. If a subsystem is disconnected, the function of the I is also changed; if all subsystems are disconnected, nothing is left. The I has no existence whatsoever independently of the other components of consciousness, but it is a holistic property of the system. One consequence of this view of the architecture of consciousness is that the study of consciousness cannot totally be reduced to neurophysiology.[14] Even if we knew the function of single neurons in minute details, we would not be able to predict all the properties that the system of neurons will have. In order to reach this goal, we need to apply a system-theoretic perspective.

---

[13] See Brinck and Gärdenfors (1999). The idea suggests Dennett's (1991) multiple drafts model. However, one difference is that Dennett does not consider the interaction between the subject and the environment, what is called the situatedness of the subjects (see Clark 1997).

[14] Sperry (1976), p. 166, writes that consciousness cannot be identified with neural events, but consists of 'holistic configurational properties that have yet to be discovered. We predict that, once they have been discovered and understood, they will be best conceived of as being different from and more than the neural events of which they are composed.'

The unity of the I is not self-evident.[15] All humans go through changes of their inner worlds during their lives. We experience that we have more or less coherent memories from our childhood and that there is continuity in the body that carries the inner world. Nevertheless, one can reflect over whether one is the *same person* now as 10 or 20 years ago.

We have a feeling that the inner world is continuous over time. But this feeling can be fraudulent in the same way as the blind spot in our eye. Our field of vision seems continuous, but it is easy to show that we are blind at certain angles. In a similar vein, we have blind spots in our memory—there are big gaps in our old self. The I is only a reflection through blurry memories. Our reconstructions of the former I are full of self-deception. My I becomes just one part in the story that my brain is inventing this very moment.

But not only the former I is struck by self-deception. It is surprisingly easy to show that the picture of the I that arises in self-consciousness is not always in accordance with what really happens inside us. The gaps in the I are similar to the gaps in the eye. The psychologists Richard Nisbett and Timothy Wilson have run a classic experiment that highlights this.[xxix] In a department store they placed four identical pairs of nylon stockings on a board. The order of the pairs was varied randomly. Customers who passed by were asked to choose the pair they liked best. They were also asked *why* they chose a particular pair. There was a strong *position effect* in their choices: the rightmost pair was chosen four times as often as any other pair. In contrast, the reasons given by the customers for their choices never mentioned the position of the pairs of stockings, but concerned the experienced quality of the stockings. The conclusion that Nisbett and Wilson draw from the experiment is that when people report on their inner processes, introspection does not reach what has really happened, but rather that people construct their judgement on the basis of what *ought to* be the reasons for their choices.

There are individuals who are affected by more drastic problems with their self-experience. One way of describing schizophrenia is to say that the I is no longer a unity. Above all, a schizophrenic patient seems to have problems in separating those perceptions that originate in reality from those that are generated directly in the inner world.

Animals can dread death, but it is most likely only humans who have an *awareness of death*. Chimpanzees do not apparently show sorrow but seem just bewildered by death. When a young chimpanzee dies the mother can carry

---

[15] See, e.g. Humphrey and Dennett (1989).

Figure 5.2 Baboon mother carrying dead baby. (Photo by the author.)

it around for some days before she abandons the body. She seems to be perplexed rather than mourning. I have witnessed the same phenomenon in a troop of Chacma baboons at Cape Good Hope. A female was carrying her dead infant by the tail in her mouth, seemingly relaxed. When she stopped to eat, she left the corpse on the ground, but when she moved on, she picked it up by the tail again. Interestingly, the custom to *bury* individuals appears to be rather recent in the history of hominids. The oldest clearly identified grave found by archaeologists is that of a Neanderthal man who died about 100 000 years ago.

An awareness of death presumes not only that you are aware that you have a consciousness, but also that you realize that this consciousness will end at some point in time. A large part of our religious conceptions derives from the wrestling with this insight. The dream of an eternal life is the expectation that the inner world be so totally detached from its bodily anchorage that it can live on even after the disintegration of the body.

As soon as a child understands that it once will die, its life is changed forever. Deacon asks if our awareness of death may not be an evolutionarily dead end. There is nothing in the limbic system (the part of the brain that handles our emotions) that is adapted to take care of the fear and the sorrow that our awareness of death involves. This is yet another side of the human predicament. We must live with our insights about death, while other animals are mercifully liberated from them. On the other hand, they paint no paintings, write no poems, invent no religions, and do not discuss the meaning of life. Humans are, as Valéry puts it, 'doomed to bell our poemes and our theories— magniloquent and mortified'.

5.7   Free will

"If I hadn't spent so much time studying Earthlings," said the Tralfamadorian,
"I wouldn't have any idea of what was meant by 'free will'. I've visited
thirty-one inhabited planets in the universe, and I've studied reports on one
hundred more. Only on Earth is there any talk of free will."

Kurt Vonnegut: *Slaughterhouse five*

"What do you do when you choose?" I ask Egon.

"I don't choose," he replies. "I just do what I want."

There is an intimate connection between the possibility of a *free will* and the ability to plan for the future. The philosopher Harry Frankfurt says in a classical paper with the title 'Freedom of the will and the concept of a person' that a necessary condition for an individual to be a *person* is that the individual not only wants something but also *wants to want* it.[xxx] Frankfurt calls such wishes 'second-order wants'.

Many animals have a will, but it is presumably only human beings that can reflect on their wishes and *want them to be different*. When we ponder our choices, we are often pleased with them, but not always. The novelist Hjalmar Söderberg writes: 'There is so much I want that I rather want that I did not want.' For example, it is common that a smoker wishes that he or she did not want to smoke. In situations of this type a (first-order) wish is in conflict with a second-order want not to smoke. What is called *akrasia* or weakness of the will is just such situations of conflict where the first-order wish gets the upper hand.

In his analysis, Frankfurt stipulates that to have a free will it is not sufficient that one can choose; one should also be capable of choosing one's will, i.e. one should be able to fulfil one's second-order desires. In other words, one is free to have the will one wants. A drug addict who repeatedly succumbs to his cravings does not have a free will in this sense.

Frankfurt's criterion for free will is based on the existence of detached representations of one's own wishes. This is also the presupposition for anticipatory planning. The converse also holds to some extent: anticipatory planning demands that you can freely choose between trying to satisfy your current wishes or to satisfy the wishes you imagine that you will have in the future.

Animals who plan can *choose* in the sense that they can image different actions and their consequences in their inner worlds and then perform the action that is judged to lead to the best consequences. But this does not entail that they have a *free* will. They need not make any conscious evaluation of the different alternatives and even less reflect upon their choices.

Having a free will presupposes a form of self-awareness in the sense that one must be aware of one's desires to be capable of wanting to have another desire. Kirkegaard expresses the connection in the following way:

> In general, what is decisive with regard to the self is consciousness, that is to say self-consciousness. The more consciousness, the more will; the more will, the more self. Someone who has no will at all is no self. But the more will he has, the more self-consciousness he has too.[xxxi]

The explanation why there is a strong connection between the degree of free will and the level of self-consciousness is that the more freely a human can choose, the more different goals, present and future, she must be able to imagine. In other words, the richer inner inner world you have, the more choices you have. By developing your ability to imagine you increase your possibility to choose freely.

"Are there any arguments that support that we make better decisions because we have a free will?" asks Egon.

"That's a very good question," I answer. "Here, take a banana."

Within economics, statistics, and philosophy one finds several theories of decision making. The best known is the principle that one should choose the alternative that maximizes the expected utility. But none of the theories take into account that conflicts may arise between your current desires and those that you expect to have tomorrow.

In the book *Notes from underground*, Dostoyevsky protests against all forms of utility arguments and that 'reason' should be the guide for our actions. Our free will has a *value in itself* that cannot be traded for other forms of utility. The main character in the book makes all kinds of mistakes and is deliberately evil. This he does just to ascertain that:

> one might even desire something opposed to one's own advantage, and sometimes (this is now my idea) one *positively must do so*. One's very free, unfettered desire, one's own whim, no matter how wild, one's own fantasy, even though sometimes roused to the point of madness—all this constitutes precisely that previously omitted, most advantageous advantage which isn't included under any classification and because of which all systems and theories are constantly smashed to smithereens. Where did the sages ever get the idea that man needs any normal, virtuous desire? How did they ever imagine that man needs any kind of rational, advantageous desire? Man needs only one thing—his own *independent* desire, whatever that independence might cost and wherever it might lead. And as far as desire goes, the devil only knows... .[xxxii]

Despite Dostoyevsky's strong stand for free will, the question remains: what are the evolutionary advantages of being able to choose one's own will, of being able to abstain from what you currently want? The answer, as always, is that a free will increases our fitness.

Our desires have been moulded during an extended evolutionary process where the ecological conditions have been different from what they are nowadays. If we can choose our will, we can better adjust to the new circumstances. To take an everyday example, food rich in sugar content has been scarce during most of the time humans have existed. Since such food is rich in energy, we have developed a craving for ripe fruits and other things rich in sugar. In our modern world, we are rather confronted with a profusion of sugar, and in the long run overconsumption is detrimental to our health. They who can let a second-order want control and choose not to consume excessive amounts of sugar will presumably have a slightly higher evolutionary fitness than those who succumb to the temptations. In this way, one can, for good and for bad, let one's wisdom take command over one's desires. As Paul Valéry says in an aphorism:

> It isn't "novelty" or "genius" that appeals to me, but full possession of oneself—which amounts to this: equipping oneself with the greatest possible number of means of expression so as to attain and grasp that Self, and not to let its native powers run to waste for want of organs at their service.

5.8 Consciousness and morality—why vervets are incapacitated

To treat the evolution of human morality would require a volume of its own. Here I will only take up some connections between consciousness and morality. Already in 1871 Darwin notes in *The descent of man* that moral beings must be capable of reflecting over and evaluating their actions. He is of the opinion that short-term desires like hunger and lust must be suppressed in favour of more long-term values. Darwin recognizes the dilemmas that an anticipatory planner is facing. Humans' ability to foresee our future needs leads to two kinds of complications. First, we have many more alternatives to choose from, because we also must consider future possibilities. Secondly, we can reflect on our own choices and put different kinds of valuations against each other. These two kinds of complication generate a great uncertainty in the chooser—in severe cases an existential insecurity. To alleviate this insecurity humans have a need for guiding principles that help them choose.

It is interesting to note that Darwin considered morality, i.e. the capacity to reflect on one's own behaviour and judge it, as a result of evolution. This idea was revolutionary during a period when most people relied on religious doctrines to give moral guidance—morality was seen as given by God.

"But what *is* morality then?" asks Egon. "Humans seem to worry a lot about the immorality of others. Among my relatives we don't care either about one's own morality or about that of others."

"It is a good question," I answer a bit embarrassed. "One could say that moral principles are detached values."

"You and your detachments! You can use them for all sorts of things, can't you?" Egon grumbles. "Can you explain what you mean?"

Animals can have different goals—needs and desires—and a will to fulfil them. But since they do not have any detached representations of their goals they can not *take a stand on* whether they want to fulfil their goals. Animals who live in a group follow certain social rules, above all those connected with the ranking order within the group. However, these rules do not exist as detached representations with the individuals; they are followed without the animals being aware of the rules.

Piaget claims that a child's moral values do not derive from following the rules of its parents or other authorities, but from its ability to feel *empathy* with others, i.e. the ability to put oneself in somebody else's situation. Such an exchange of roles presupposes that the child has a conception of the other's feelings. But this is not sufficient for morality to emerge. If I want to be moral in relation to you, and not just empathetic, I must make a *conscious choice*—I must have a detached representation of my goal and be able to compare it other possible goals. To be moral hence demands having a self-consciousness and a free will.[16] Mark Twain notes that *Homo sapiens* is 'the only animal that blushes. Or needs to.'

A moral choice can be strictly personal. But if we have decided what to do by reflecting on how somebody else would experience the same situation, it is natural to expect others to do the same thing. Therefore we use language (or possibly some other form of intentional communication) to make others do what we consider that they should do. In my discussion of anticipatory planning, I focussed on the human dilemma. This is illustrated by St. Paul the

---

[16] Immanuel Kant writes in the third part of *Grundlegung zur Metaphysik der Sitten* that one must view oneself as the origin of one's principles, without any influence from outside, in order to consider oneself morally free. Valéry has his own way of formulating the connection between consciousness and morality that is based on the distinction between 'I' and 'me' that was presented in Section 5.5: 'Moral is a badly chosen name for one of the branches of the generalizing policy that encompasses the tactics of the I against itself. In the claims: I am a master over myself, I give in to myself, I allow me, is I and me separated—or not? One could simplify moral analysis to deciding the question of whether the difference between these two pronouns is real or fictitious.'

Apostle who says: 'For what I want to do I do not do, but what I hate I do.'[xxxiii] Moral rules are needed as support for the long-term and overall goals in the struggle between them and our current egocentric desires. A society is created by making the rules explicit as laws or as religious decrees.[17]

"But if I don't want to do as morality says?" Egon asks. "What shall I do then?"

"Well, you may have a problem, in particular if the guards of morality or the laws have pressures to bear on you. This is a problem we are all struggling with."

The choice between co-operating for long-term goals and doing what you are in the mood for right now often leads to a kind of conflict that is called 'prisoners' dilemma' within the theory of games. It means that everybody wins by co-operating, but if everybody else co-operates, every separate individual gains even more by being selfish and not co-operating. But if nobody co-operated, the result is worse for everybody. Paying taxes is a clear example of prisoners' dilemma.

The economist Robert Frank argues that emotions such as shame and love and social values such as confidence and honesty have emerged via evolutionary processes so to avoid short-term gains in prisoners' dilemmas.[xxxiv] If you are to gain by cheating on others, for example by not paying your taxes, the ensuing shame makes the gain feel less and you will therefore avoid the fraud next time. The emotions make us experience that, even in the short run, we gain by co-operating.

"I've never seen the point of being unselfish," Egon declares.

"Well, sociobiological theory says that the *genes* are inherently selfish and try to reproduce in as great numbers as possible.[18] From this it is follows that you should sometimes be altruistic to your children and relatives because it promotes the reproduction of your genes."

"Kids and relatives, yes," frowns Egon. "But I don't see any reason to be unselfish in relation to others around me. I don't understand why people are so well-behaved towards strangers."

Many forms of altruism involve long-range commitments. The strategy of the unselfish is to abstain from a short-tern egoistic choice in order to build up a *trust* that will lead to future involvements in different kinds of co-operation that are more valuable than a momentary capture. Such a strategy is, normally,

---

[17] In the most pure form, one obtains rules like the Golden Rule of Christianity or Kant's categorical imperative: 'So act that you could wish the maxim of your action to become a universal law of human conduct.'

[18] The classical introduction to sociobiology is Richard Dawkins' book *The selfish gene* (1976).

not a conscious choice. Another way of expressing it is that people are unselfish because they worry about their *reputation*—having a good reputation will give them future gains. Being unselfish in the short run is therefore a way of being selfish in the long run.

On the basis of such an investment model, where trust is the currency, one achieves a rational explanation of every-day decency. But it is important to note that the argument builds on two presuppositions. First, anticipatory planning: you are planning already now for future choice situations. You must be able to compare the value of a selfish short-term choice with what can be obtained from future co-operation. Animals live in the present and cannot handle the anticipation that is required for the strategy of decency. Also small children have problems thinking ahead and they are, in the midst of their cuteness, big egoists.

Secondly, the investment model presumes that the unselfish individual lives in a society where you can expect to meet the same people for a long time so that it will be possible to carry through the beneficial co-operation that trust will lead to. During most of the time humans have existed we have lived in small tribes or villages where everybody knows everybody else and where a reputation of being selfish immediately spreads. In such a society the individuals are therefore much more motivated to be altruistic.

Different cultures and religions have formulated many differing and sometimes seemingly odd moral rules. The emotions and drives of humans are biologically controlled and often come in conflict with the moral rules. The balance between the present and future goals makes moral rules that too much violate our direct wishes difficult to maintain. For example, many religions advocate celibacy. If everybody consistently were to practice abstinence, it would naturally be an evolutionary disadvantage for the followers of the religion. Individuals of an alternative religion that encourages reproduction would spread their genes faster.[19] This type of argument shows that moral rules cannot too strongly be in violation of biological principles. As the Roman poet Horace writes, you can drive out nature with a pitchfork, but she will always return. But from this it does not follow that morality is completely

---

[19] However, it does not follow that celibacy for a single individual must result in decreased fitness for the selfish genes of the individual. It is possible that his or her relatives as a consequence will have greater possibilities of reproducing. As an example among mammals, Dawkins (1989), pp. 313–16, presents the African naked mole rats, who have a social structure reminiscent of bees: a single female in the colony gives birth, she mates with two or three males, and the remaining individuals live in celibacy and spend their time supporting the female and her offspring.

determined by biology. By virtue of their fundamental dilemma, humans still have great freedom in their choice of morals.

Responsibility also presupposes self-consciousness and free will, in the same way as morality does. To be responsible means, first, to have an ability to foresee the potential consequences of one's actions. Secondly, one must be able to realize that one can choose differently and to decide to act in different ways—in other words, one must have a free will and thereby also a self-consciousness. Within jurisprudence one makes a distinction between intended and unintentional acts. For example, this division lies behind the distinction between murder and manslaughter.

Small children and animals do not have the mental capacities necessary for being responsible for their actions. To declare somebody incapacitate means exactly that the person is not attributed full capacity to be responsible, which in turn means that their free will and self-consciousness are not fully developed. Vervets are by necessity incapacitated.[20]

"As usual a purely human centred perspective!" Egon sneers.

But one can bring up children, i.e. teach them a 'correct' behaviour, by teaching them how to act in a way that is fit for their cognitive capacities.

"That is not upbringing," Egon protests. "It is dressage."

Notes

  i. Dennett (1978), Chapter 8.
 ii. Humphrey (2002), p. 74.
iii. Humphrey (2002), p. 75.
 iv. Hauser (2000), pp. 108–9.
  v. Menzel, Savage-Rumbaugh, and Lawson (1985).
 vi. E.g. Marten and Psarakos (1994).
vii. Mitchell (1993).
viii. Knight, Power, and Watts (1995).
 ix. Tomasello (1999), p. 94.
  x. Tomasello (1999), pp. 126–8.
 xi. Donald (2001), p. 250.
xii. Luria (1961).
xiii. Gómez (1994).
xiv. See, e.g. Gómez (1994), Proust (1998), Tomasello (1999), pp. 59–70, and Brinck (2000).
 xv. Hauser (2000), p. 212.

---

[20] One could say that 'the Fall', which is about the ability to distinguish between good and bad, occurs when humans develop a free will. That is when we become guilty.

  xvi. Tomasello (1999), p. 132, Brinck (2001).
 xvii. Tomasello (1999), p. 102.
xviii. Brinck (2001).
  xix. Morales, Mundy, and Rojas (1998).
   xx. Tomasello (1999), p. 105.
  xxi. Noble and Davidson (1996), pp. 220–1, Gómez (1994), and Tomasello (1999), p. 233.
 xxii. Bates (1976), p. 277.
xxiii. Brinck (2002).
 xxiv. Tomasello (1999), pp. 89–90.
  xxv. Buber (1970), pp. 73–4. The following quotation is from pp. 78–9.
 xxvi. Meditation VI.
xxvii. Sperry (1976). Popper (1972) has also proposed a similar theory.
xxviii. Wiener (1961).
 xxix. Nisbett and Wilson (1977).
  xxx. Frankfurt (1971).
 xxxi. Kirkegaard (1989), p. 59.
xxxii. Dostoevsky (1989).
xxxiii. Romans 7:15.
xxxiv. Frank (1988).

CHAPTER 6

The dawn of language

In the beginning was silence. During a very long period in the history of human beings there was no spoken language. As mentioned in the introductory chapter, it is estimated that the evolutionary branch of apes that would develop into modern *Homo sapiens* separated from the branch that became chimpanzees at least six million years ago. However, spoken language presumably first developed between 200 000 and 300 000 years ago. Before that hominids were probably communicating with the aid of gestures. Language is thus fresh in the history of humans. Most layers of the human thought structure had emerged in evolution long before we started to speak. Language is just the icing on the cake of thinking.

One of the enigmas in the evolutionary history of humans is how language has emerged. Darwin presents his own theory about the origin of language in the book *The descent of man*. He notes that even if animals only have available a limited number of sound signals, they can use different prosodic patterns that express different moods. But what steps lead from here to human language? Darwin speculates that some form of primitive *song* was first developed that was then followed by voice imitations of different phenomena before we obtained a complete language.

The question of the origin of language has attracted many linguists, from the serious to the charlatans. Even though Darwin's theory of evolution opened new roads, in 1866 the prestigious Societé de Linguistique in Paris forbade all discussions of the subject. The reason for this was that most of what was argued was pure guesswork, since at the time there was so little tangible empirical evidence. Nowadays we have more knowledge about the dawn of language, even though most of the support is indirect. In order to explain the mechanisms behind the evolution of language, I must first introduce a criterion for what I mean by language.

6.1   Signals and symbols

A power rises and rises
from the moment we are born,
—and we are not creatures of a single day.
Our brains are not constructed
to guide wings
but to build languages
and navigate in a different way:
to think is to try
to see in a new way, with polar clarity
—which also means
to grasp the limitation.

Pia Tafdrup: *We are not creatures of a single day*

"In my opinion, animals can communicate excellently," Egon says. "What is it that makes language so different from the signals animals use in their communication?"

Many animal species use complicated systems of signals when communicating. The bees' dance, for instance, is a combinatorial system in which, by dancing in different angles, they indicate the *direction* to the nectar they have found and at the same time by waggling their bodies in different numbers of turns indicate the *distance* to the food source. One can say that the dance has a grammar, and because of this many want to claim that bees have a language.

Another example is vervets that have three different warning calls for leopards, pythons, and birds of prey. It is not difficult to understand the evolutionary value of the warning cries of the vervets. The three types of warning calls are connected with different flight behaviours. If a leopard attacks, the best thing is to flee up in the trees. But since leopards can also climb the vervets must run far out on the branches. This is the worst place to be, though, if an eagle is attacking. Then it is best to hide under a bush.

"Yech, do you have to write about such disgusting animals?" Egon complains dejectedly. His shag bristles up.

If the vervets had only one kind of warning call, they would not know how to best react. The three calls indicate which behaviour is appropriate in the given situation.

A decisive difference between a language and the signals employed by animals is that signals only refer to what is present in the environment of the animal. Bees only dance directly after having returned to the hive when they have found nectar. Vervets only signal when danger is immediate. Neither they nor bees ever tell stories to each other.

"No, they don't live a particularly interesting life, do they?" Egon says sarcastically.

With the aid of a language you can communicate about things that are not here and now or that may not even exist.[1] I submit that language therefore presupposes a rich and complex inner world. In order to formulate this idea more succinctly, I shall distinguish between *signals* and *symbols*. Both signals and symbols are tools of communication that can be expressed in various ways, for example by sounds or gestures. The fundamental difference is that *a symbol refers to a detached representation*, while *a signal stands for a perception or a sensation*.[2] Signals are about the surrounding world, while symbolic language is often about our *inner* world, i.e. about our imaginations, memories, plans, and dreams. The signals of an animal species are more or less identical in all members of the species (barring sexual and age differences). They do not *choose* what to utter. In contrast, a symbol is an arbitrary *convention* that you must learn in order to use it as a communicative tool.

What is called 'body language' is therefore not symbols in this sense, but merely signals. With the aid of our bodily position, our facial expressions and our gesticulation we signal different emotions and attitudes, but these signals do not *refer* to anything in the inner world.

It is neither the complexity of grammar nor the problems of learning a large system that makes language difficult to reach for other animal species, but the fact that it is symbolic.[i] The inner worlds of other animals are not sufficiently rich to manage the complexity of detached representations that language refers to. The ethologist Sverre Sjölander explains elegantly what is missing in animal communication:

> The predominant function of language is to communicate about that which is not here and not now. A dog can 'say': I am angry, I want water, I want to go out, I like you, etc. But it has no communicative means enabling it to 'say': I

---

[1] This idea is related to Hockett's (1960) notion of 'displacement' which is one of the criteria he uses to characterize what constitutes a language. But the claim that symbols refer to detached representations in an inner world is not exactly the same as his. The reason is that he includes the following under 'displacement': 'Any delay between the reception of a stimulus and the appearance of the response means that the former has been coded into a stable spatial array, which endures at least until it is read off in the response' (Hockett 1960, p. 417). His description has a clear behaviouristic ring to it, and it means that every signal that is not an immediate reaction to a stimulus would be counted as an example of 'displacement' according to his criterion. There are, however, plenty of examples of signals that derive from perceptions where there may be longer or shorter delays before the signal is emitted. This does not entail that the signal has any symbolic function whatsoever.

[2] Deacon uses 'symbol' to stand for the mental content that a symbol refers to (see Deacon 1997, p. 443). A symbol for him is thus a special case of a detached representation. Unfortunately, there are researchers who confuse the two meanings of 'symbol'.

was angry yesterday, nor can it 'say': I will be angry if you lock me up tonight again, and I will chew up the carpet. Likewise, the dog can 'say': There is a rat here! but it cannot 'say': There is a rat in the next room.

[...] Clearly, if you live in the present, communicating mainly about how you feel and what you want to do in the moment, the biological signals inherent in each species are sufficient. A language is needed only to communicate your internal representation of what could be, what has been, and of those things and happenings that are not present in the vicinity.[ii]

A spoken word is a *sound gesture* that points to the inner world of the speaker and its aim is that the listener also direct her attention towards what the word is pointing to.[3] Symbols are efficient tools for Gregorian beings who, with their aid, can impart knowledge to each other. The psychologist Ernst von Glasersfeld presents a similar description of language, and he traces the idea to the philosopher Susanne Langer. She makes a clear distinction between signals and symbols:

A term which is used symbolically and not signally does *not* evoke action appropriate to the presence of its object. [...] Symbols are not proxy for their objects, but are *vehicles for the conception of objects*. To conceive a thing or a situation is not the same as to 'react toward it' overtly, or to be aware of its presence. In talking about things we have conceptions of them, not the things themselves; and *it is the conceptions, not the things, that symbols directly 'mean'*. Behavior toward conceptions is what words normally evoke: this is the typical process of thinking.

[...]

The fundamental difference between signs and symbols is this difference of association, and consequently of their *use* by the third party to the meaning function, the subject; signs *announce* their objects to him, whereas symbols *lead him to conceive* their objects. The fact that the same item—say, the little mouthly noise we call a 'word'—may serve in either capacity, does not obliterate the cardinal distinction between the functions it may assume.[iii]

Even if the bees' dances seem to have a kind of grammar, they still consist only of *signals*. In a sophisticated way, the bees describe to each other places where nectar can be found. Given their minute brains, they do this with astonishing precision. The crucial point is that they only use their dances in a *cued* manner, and they only do it immediately after having returned to the hive after a find. Thus, their dances are not symbols according to my criterion. What

---

[3] Tomasello and Call (1997), p. 408, write: 'Indeed, in some formulations a linguistic symbol is nothing more than a social convention by means of which persons who know the convention direct one another's attention to particular aspects of their shared world.' To this I would like to add that the shared world is not only the external, but also primarily the common inner world.

happens is that is that a bee who dances plays back the start of a flight towards the goal, without actually flying off.[4]

Von Glasersfeld adds:

> To qualify as language, the bees' dance would have to be used also *without* this one-to-one relation to a behavioral response (e.g. in comments, proposals, or questions concerning foraging location), and this has never been observed. In short, a communication system that allows for *imperatives* only—no matter how sophisticated and accurate they might be—should not be called a language.[iv]

If symbols refer to the inner world, the meanings of words must be located in the head and not out in the world. This opinion stands in sharp contrast to many philosophical semantic theories that claim that language is about the external world. Even if so-called referential theories seem intuitively plausible, they are faced with problems. One important objection to these theories is that all languages contain words for things that do not really exist, such as 'fairy' or 'centaur'. Nevertheless, we consider that words for fictitious objects have a well-defined meaning about which we can be in astonishing agreement. The explanation for the agreement is that our inner worlds are much the same and they are populated with similar representations. Von Glasersfeld describes the unique character of language in the following way:

> [L]anguage allows us to talk not only about things that are spatially or temporally remote, but also about things that have no location in space and never happen at all. The very fact that we can make *understandable* linguistic statements about space and time, right and wrong, Humpty-dumpty, and the square root of minus one demonstrates rather incontrovertibly that language can deal with items that have nothing to do with 'observable stimuli' or with the 'referents' of the traditional theory of reference in linguistic philosophy.[v]

Symbols referring to something in the inner world of a person can be used to communicate as soon as the listeners have, or are prepared to add, corresponding representations in their inner worlds.[5] What the external world looks like does not, in principle, matter for whether the communication is

---

4 The same point is made by von Glasersfeld (1976), p. 222: 'In my terms, the bees do not qualify for symbolicity, because they have never been observed to communicate about distances, directions, food sources, etc., without actually coming from, or going to, a specific location.' Benveniste (1966), p. 61, says similarly: 'One has never observed that a bee has, for example, conveyed a message to another hive that it has received in its own, which would a be a manner of transmission or relay.'

5 In one article, I present a mathematical model of how the alignment of the inner worlds can arise so that meaningful communication becomes possible (Gärdenfors 1993).

successful. Two prisoners can talk fervently about life on a sunny Pacific island in the pitch dark of their cell.

6.2   ... and icons

Philosopher Charles Sanders Peirce distinguishes between three kinds of signs: indices, icons, and symbols. Indices correspond to what I call signals: signs that refer to something in the current environment. Smoke is a signal for fire. A pigeon can learn that when the green light is on in its cage, it is a signal that food will appear if it pecks on the lever. Peirce's use of the concept 'symbol' corresponds quite well with the meaning I give to it: something that corresponds to a detached representation. In my terminology, an *icon* is a sign that *resembles* the detached representation denoted by the sign.[6] A silhouette of a woman on the door to the ladies' room is an icon for those persons who are expected to enter. A white arrow to the right on a round blue road sign in a traffic circle in Europe is an icon for which direction one is supposed to take. In distinction to symbols, the choice of icons is not arbitrary, but dependent on the resemblance between the sign and what it denotes.

The linguists Elizabeth Barber and Ann Peters describe the difference between signals, icons and symbols in the following way:

> An icon can be interpreted without previous agreement, through general knowledge of the world, and an index [i.e. a signal] through either knowledge of the world or pre-wired instinct. But an arbitrary symbol can only be interpreted through the direct process of agreeing on a convention and then learning it. That is, some preliminary mode of communication is needed to begin making the conventional agreements that underlie arbitrary systems. Icons and indices can serve this bootstrapping function because they can exist without conventional agreement. Thus spoken communication, like writing and sign, had to have begun iconically and/or indexically, and gradually shifted to arbitrariness.

6.3   Linguistic communication and higher-order intentions

> Intelligence is a refined version of the insects' feelers.
> The criterion is not to be able to utter profound remarks
> even lunatics do this—but to be able to listen.

---

[6] This is only marginally related to the religious uses of the notion of an icon. However, the concept is nowadays used in Peirce's way in connection with the design of computer interfaces.

Intelligence presupposes two brains, their interplay.
He who is not coloured by the one he speaks with,
is already on the road to dementia.

Horace Engdahl

A fundamental criterion for a communicative system to be a language is that
it is constituted of symbols. But this is not sufficient to arrive at a language of
the kind humans use to communicate. Another presumption is that the inter-
locutors have well-developed inner worlds. As support for this criterion I shall
briefly present the theory of linguistic meaning proposed by the philosopher
Paul Grice. His initial definition, formulated in the lingo of analytic philosophy,
reads as follows:

'U meant something by uttering x' is true if and only if, for some audience A,
U uttered x intending:

1. A to produce a particular response.

2. A to think (recognize) that U intends (1).

3. A to fulfil (1) on the basis of his fulfilment of (2).

"What?" Egon says puzzled. "Say that once again!"

"Condition 3 means that the listener behaves as the speaker intends because
the listener understands that the speaker intends it."

Although he defines 'meaning', I am more interested in applying the definition to linguistic communication in general. The feature I want to focus on
here is that condition 2 expresses a *third-order intention*: U intends A to think
that U intends something. Gomez even claims that a truly requestive situation
like 'May I have some salt, please?' involves a *fifth-order* level of intentionality:
U *wants* A to *understand* that she *wants* him to *understand* the she *wants*
the salt.[7]

"How complicated," Egon says snidely. "I would just take the salt without
asking."

What is important in Grice's analysis of linguistic communication is that it
establishes that language presumes nested inner worlds—without these we
cannot create the necessary higher-order intentions. At least, we must assume
that U can represent that A in her inner world has a representation of U's inner
world. This is exactly what was required for self-consciousness! Only when one

---

[7] Gómez (1994), p. 68. However, he also claims that the *mutuality* of intentional communication
can be achieved by 'attention contact'. Nested representations of the inner worlds are not
necessary for communication (Gomez 1994, p. 73). I discussed these higher-order forms of
attention in Section 4.2.

Figure 6.1 Nesting of inner worlds.

has this competence can one form third-order intentions of the kind "U *wants* A to *believe* that U *intends* something."

Grice's analysis can be used to explain the difference between how symbolic words are used in linguistic communication and how signals work. Words presuppose that the communicator has third-order intentions, while signals presuppose only first-order intentionality, to the extent they are intentional at all.

If my analysis is correct, the conclusion is that linguistic communication at Grice's level presupposes an individual who has a you-consciousness as well as a self-consciousness. No wonder that language is a very late phenomenon in the evolution of thinking.[vi]

6.4 Animals' linguistic capacity

Many species of animal use their vocal apparatus to communicate. Parrots and other birds can even imitate human voices pretty well. But they just repeat phrases that have been drilled into their heads—they hardly ever create new constructions, which is necessary if their communication is to be called language.[8]

---

[8] An exception is Alex, the African Gray Parrot trained by Irene Pepperberg, who to a limited extent can create new combinations of the words he has learned and who can participate in a proto-dialogue.

Animals cannot *choose* when they shall signal, but this occurs instinctively. Jane Goodall notes that chimpanzee calls are strongly connected with their emotions, to the extent that '[t]he production of a sound in the absence of the appropriate emotional state seems to be an almost impossible task for a chimpanzee'.[vii]

Among mammals it is actually only humans who can deliberately *control* their voices. In our brains, speech is generated in the so-called Broca's area, which is located in the left frontal part of the cortex. The calls of apes and other animals are involuntary. Their voices are controlled by structures in the brain that are located below the cortex, and these structures are evolutionarily much older.

There are evident traces of such involuntary voice reactions in humans as well. For example, we let out cries of pain, fear, and surprise. Maybe the most manifest example is when you have an almost irresistible desire to laugh—you must grit your teeth, hold you hand over your mouth, or turn away.[viii] Sometimes we fail miserably and we burst out in paroxysms of laughter that continue until we are totally exhausted. The first sounds produced by newborns are cries and laughs, and these sounds are fundamental for social communication. Also deaf persons who have never be able to hear laugh in a normal way. Deacon assumes that laughter is an automatic response that indicates that you have cut off the conscious executive control that originates from the frontal lobe in the brain.[ix]

Apes and monkeys in the wild do not use any signals that they *deliberately* produce (they cannot even point). There is virtually nothing to indicate that they have any form of symbolic communication. A gross explanation may be that they have no *need* to talk since they have nothing to talk about. They live in the present (not being anticipatory planners) and hence they need not express themselves about what is not present. Their inner worlds are more limited than ours are. Maybe all they need to communicate can be accomplished with the aid of different forms of signals.

The bees' signalling system is innate, but some animals *learn* to communicate. Many birds must learn their songs by mimicking others. For this reason, there are distinct *dialects* of the songs, for example among white-crowned sparrows and redwings. In certain bird species, for instance blackbirds and nightingales, there are even *generative* structures in the sense that the birds can rather freely extemporate brief song elements into longer sequences. But there is nothing that indicates that the song elements have any independent *meaning* in the way the words of a language have a content.

In contrast to birds, the vocalizations of mammals are innate, and the animals can hardly learn any new sounds. Bringing about the sounds is tightly connected with certain emotional or physiological states.[x] In spite of this, mammals can to a certain extent learn *when* different vocalizations are appropriate.

I experienced an example of this a couple of years ago when I made a trip to southern India, where I visited among other places the nature reserve Nagarhole. One of the great attractions there is herds of the rare wild Indian elephant, but there were also plenty of rhesus macaques.

"But that's where I was born!" Egon shouts. "I was kidnapped from there when I was little and then sold to a circus."

He jumps up and down in front of me and I have never seen him so excited.

"What a coincidence," I say, surprised. "I may have met some of your relatives."

"Did you see my sister Ida? Although she must also be old," Egon says thoughtfully. "But I have nieces and nephews there, don't I?"

"Unfortunately, I did not get to know them that well. But I walked around in the reserve and had several opportunities to study them. A couple of troops were hanging around among the bungalows and they were rather accustomed to people."

Rhesus macaques are closely related to vervets and they have similar warning calls. One interesting episode that I witnessed was when some of the macaques were sitting in a tree eating from its pods. One of the baby macaques spotted a serpent eagle that was circling in the sky above the tree. The youngster gave out a shrill cry that I presume was the warning sound for a bird of prey. The adults looked up and then at the kid and continued calmly to eat. The serpent eagle is not a threat to rhesus macaques.

The rhesus youngster had learned to cry when a dangerous bird of prey comes within sight. But just like human babies, it *over-generalizes* to other similar phenomena and calls out too often. The fact that the adults ignored the signal may have the result that when the kid sees a serpent eagle next time, it has learnt not to emit the warning call for this bird species. Cheney and Seyfarth have carefully studied how vervet youngsters learn to narrow their use of the different warning calls.[xi] However, even among adult vervets certain 'mistakes' occur, i.e. warning calls are emitted for animals that are not dangerous for them. It is better to cry wolf once too many times than once too few, as long as you are credible by and large.

6.5   Kanzi—at the brink of language

"But chimps and gorillas, who are so similar to humans, can they not learn a language?" asks Egon.

One has tried in many ways. When the apes' abilities to learn languages were first studied, researchers tried to teach them to speak. That was a failure because they cannot control their speech organs sufficiently well. Nor can they produce enough variation in the sounds. Later, one tried to teach them sign language. This works better, but each sign must be rubbed in, and they never become very good at combining signs. At best, they master a couple of hundred signs.

Despite all efforts, the apes' linguistic communication is limited. In the best cases, they reach the level of a two-year-old human child. They seldom create combinations of more than two words. Most of what they communicate is about something they want. A typical example is when the chimpanzee Nim Chimpsky signs 'Nim milk, give milk, Laura give Nim milk, more milk'. The apes never *tell* anything—possibly they rat on somebody who has hidden the bananas. One crucial reason why language-trained apes do not tell stories is that narrativity presumes causality: one must keep track of what follows from what in order to tell a story. As we have seen, apes have difficulties understanding causal and temporal connections, in particular such relations as do not involve themselves.

But some years ago a new hero appeared for the researchers: Kanzi. He is a bonobo who has learnt to communicate to a degree far beyond that of any ape before him. He has changed the researchers' view of animals' possibilities to learn language. The primatologist Sue Savage-Rumbaugh, who has trained Kanzi and several other apes, tells his story in the book *Kanzi—The ape at the brink of the human mind*.[9]

The bonobo (*Pan paniscus*) is a species that was identified first in the 1930s as distinct from the common chimpanzee (*Pan troglodytes*). Bonobos are rare, rapidly diminishing in numbers, and they live in a part of Zaire that is difficult to access. The tempers of the two species are different. Bonobos are more social and less aggressive than the common chimp, and they live in larger troops. They use sex in various forms to reconcile and to strengthen social relations. Among chimpanzees, males sometimes kill the young, in particular when a new female with a baby has moved to their troop. But among bonobos no case of infanticide has been observed.

Kanzi grew up with his stepmother Matata at the Language Research Center at Georgia State University. Matata was one of the first bonobos that

---

9 The book is from 1994 and is written together with the science journalist Roger Lewin. More recently she has, together with philosopher Stuart Shanker and linguist Talbot Taylor, discussed Kanzi's communicative capacities more scientifically in the book *Apes, language, and the human mind*.

Savage-Rumbaugh tried to train to communicate with the aid of abstract signs on a computer screen. She was a poor learner in comparison to the chimps that had been trained earlier. During the language training sessions, Kanzi was mostly clinging on her back or was running around playing in the lab.

When Kanzi was two years old, it was decided that Matata should temporarily be moved to another research centre so that she, with the aid of Kanzi's father, could become pregnant again. Kanzi was left alone at the Yerkes Center. It was now that the unexpected discovery was made. Without having been explicitly trained, Kanzi had learnt most of the signs that Matata rather unsuccessfully had been trained on. But he had not previously shown that he could use the signs on the screen. When Savage-Rumbaugh had discovered Kanzi's talent, she added new signs to the screen, in particular signs denoting different places and different kinds of food. He quickly learned the new signs too. Kanzi is a very willing communicator, and he also understands much spoken language, even though he cannot produce it himself, but must express himself with the aid of the signs on the screen or on a portable board.

What is new about Kanzi is that he has learnt the basis of language very much as small children normally do—by *participating* in communication. With this method he requires no special training on separate signs or words. Unlike other apes that were trained according to more behaviouristic methods, his only reward was communication itself and what he could accomplish with the aid of this. The signs that Kanzi learns are used in a natural way in conversations. He also learnt the foundations at a very early age. In contrast, Matata was already a grown-up when her training was started—and then it was too late. After two years of practice involving 30 000 trials she mastered only six signs.

Hence it seems that with the apes, as with humans, there is a critical period during childhood when one can learn fundamental linguistic communication. After this period it becomes much more difficult.[10] This insight opens completely new possibilities for research on apes' language learning. Kanzi is the pioneer. After him his half-sister Panbanisha, among others, have been trained with the same method—with good results. Apes do not learn language in their natural environment, so the learning mechanism supporting their language learning is assuredly also used for other forms of learning. This speaks against

---

[10] A critical period for learning also seems to exist in indigo buntings. These are birds that are born in the spring and migrate to warmer areas during the fall. In their navigation, they are dependent on their knowledge of the stellar map. They learn this map before they even leave the nest, and if they miss the opportunity, they cannot learn it at a later stage.

the claim that there is a module in the brain that is specialized for language learning, as has been argued by many researchers.

But how good is Kanzi's language really? His portable board contains a couple of hundred signs and he uses most of them to communicate. He understands many more spoken words than he can express himself with signs. Nobody decides which words he shall learn, and new signs are added to the board that are thought to be useful to him. He can express much of what he wants—mainly related to food, play, and excursion places—but also what he *intends* to do. But his sequences of signs are almost never more than two or three in a row.

What best shows Kanzi's mastery of language is that he can follow compound instructions he has never heard before. To determine the width of Kanzi's linguistic competence, Savage-Rumbaugh ran an experiment where she tested how well Kanzi understands language in comparison to Alia, who was a two-and-a-half-year-old human child. (Kanzi was nine years old at the time of the test). They were both made to listen to 660 spoken instructions they had never heard before, for example, 'Take the telephone outdoors' and 'Put the ball on the hat'. They could not see the person who uttered the instructions. It was noted how many of the instructions were correctly performed. Kanzi succeeded in 72% of the cases, while Alia's success rate was 66%. Apparently Kanzi's linguistic understanding is at least as good as that of a two-and-a-half-year-old child—or?

Kanzi had problems though—in particular with ambiguous words such as 'can' that are used both as a verb and as a noun. He managed 'Can you put the chicken in the potty?' but failed with 'Can you use the can opener to open a can of Coke?' Savage-Rumbaugh is surprised that he cannot learn the word 'trash', for example when he was asked to empty the trash in his backpack when they were outdoors or to put the banana peel in the trashcan. This is no wonder. Most nouns that Kanzi learns denote food or places or other visually classifiable things. 'Trash', however, refers to a *functional* category—the candy paper or the milk package that was 'candy' or 'milk' some minutes ago has suddenly changed into 'trash'. I conjecture that Kanzi has problems with other functional words that are used to denote visually heterogeneous objects.

"Maybe he just thinks it is boring to clean up," Egon suggests. "You said he is smart, didn't you?"

In her enthusiasm, Savage-Rumbaugh has a tendency to over-interpret Kanzi's linguistic achievements. Even if his understanding of spoken instructions is impressive and goes far beyond what any other ape has accomplished, I hesitate to conclude that he understands language as well as a two-and-a-half-year-old

human child. The sentences used in the experiment with Kanzi and Alia con-
sisted of a few grammatical constructions and they contained a small number
of verbs. An alternative description of his interpretive abilities is that he has
learnt these basic grammatical schemas, with the verb as the central element,
as recipes, and then he is able to replace the nouns in these schemas with other
nouns.[11] For example, Kanzi has problems with conjunctions. When he is
given the instruction 'Show me the milk and the doggie', he does not understand that he is supposed to do two things, but only shows the toy. When
Savage-Rumbaugh then says 'and the milk' he shows it too. She interprets this
as a failure of Kanzi's short-term memory, but there are so many other things
that indicate that his memory is excellent. My hypothesis is that a sentence
with a conjunction does not fit any of the basic recipes that Kanzi has learnt to
master.

There are probably other more fundamental limitations in Kanzi's linguistic
abilities when compared to those of a two-and-a-half-year-old child. But these
are hidden between the lines in Savage-Rumbaugh's writings. A human child
actively seeks knowledge by asking innumerable questions. Among these are
plenty of questions about what things are called. As far as I understand, Kanzi
never asks such questions. He has not grasped the naming game.

A two-and-a-half-year-old has also begun *telling* things. The narrative ability is central for human communication. But there seem to be no examples
showing that Kanzi masters narrativity. We are still waiting for him to tell a
story by the campfire. So, even if Kanzi understands many spoken utterances,
they are coupled to a limited repertoire of communicative functions. They
mainly consist of his obeying requests and expressing wishes. Sometimes he
announces, by using the word 'bad', that he is about to do something he knows
will not be liked. Otherwise he hardly ever uses declarative sentences. In contrast,
a human child soon learns to use language for many types of communication,
for example in games of pretence.

The signs on Kanzi's screen and board are symbols in the sense that they
are arbitrary. This is of course in accordance with how ordinary language
functions—words are seldom similar to their meanings. But Kanzi has also
created some signs himself that he shapes with his hands. For example, when he
wants somebody to open a bottle for him, he makes a turning move with his
hand. These signs are iconic. Iconic signs are, in general, easier to learn than
arbitrary symbols since there is a link between the sign and its meaning. If

---

[11] This is in full accordance with Tomasello's (1999), pp. 138–42 hypothesis that children and apes
learn verbs as 'islands' in the language.

Kanzi had iconic signs on his board, it is likely that he would have been able to learn more and faster. It is also possible that he would have become even more competent if he had been taught sign language instead of pointing to a board that must be carried along. On the other hand, the presence of the signs on the board reminds him of what can be communicated.

The fact that Savage-Rumbaugh and her colleagues use arbitrary symbols is presumably a legacy from the position on how language learning in apes should be studied that has been dominating until recently. According to the linguist Noam Chomsky, language can be seen as an abstract system that is generated from a set of grammatical rules. In line with this position, the primary goal when studying apes' linguistic abilities has been to establish that they can learn grammatical structures.[xii] By and large, one has ignored how language is to be *used*. The results have been meagre, and they have led several primate researchers to claim that apes, let alone monkeys, cannot learn a language. The great insight of Savage-Rumbaugh is not to focus on the apes' grammar but on their communication.

But in the first book on Kanzi, Savage-Rumbaugh is still partly stuck with the traditional view of language. Together with the linguist Patricia Greenfield, she seeks grammatical structures in Kanzi's combinations of signs. They succeed in finding a few such patterns. Kanzi more often places the verb before the object— 'hide nut' instead of 'nut hide' in accordance with a language such as English. When he combines two verbs, for example 'tickle bite' (which does not occur in English), he wants to do the actions in the order he mentions them. However, Kanzi's grammatical patterns are far from consistent, and they tally poorly with the grammatical competence that Chomsky's theory of language postulates.

"Grammar is a luxury to indulge in once you have mastered how to communicate," Egon declares.

Once the focus is on communicative capacities rather than grammatical competence, totally new training methods and research questions become relevant for determining to what extent apes can learn a language. Kanzi has shown that if apes learn a language in the same way as children do, they can reach much further than by using drilling methods. But in spite of his progress, he has some distance left to reach the marvellous natural talents for questions, conversations, and narratives that human children exhibit. As Tomasello and Call write, children have 'a sense of simply sharing experiences with another psychological being, often for no reward outside the sharing itself'.[xiii] Apes do not have this sense.

As far as is known, apes do not use symbolic signs in the wild. But the female chimpanzee Washoe, who was raised by the Gardners and trained in sign language, was, after a miscarriage, put in care of the chimpanzee baby Loulis, whom she adopted. For five years, Loulis was not allowed to meet any human who used sign language. But Washoe shaped Loulis' hand in the manner she had been taught signs by humans. Loulis learnt to use 17 signs during her first 29 months, a figure that rose to 51 after five years. After 15 months, she also produced combinations of two signs. In this way Washoe showed that she can transmit culturally acquired knowledge to her child.

A couple of years ago I met Richard Byrne at a conference on evolution in Uppsala. During a lunch we discussed the linguistic capacities of apes and to what extent one can teach them sign language. I pointed out that we have studied apes by trying to find out how *human* we can make their communication and argued that we should study them according to their own conditions. I suggested that language researchers should live with the apes in their natural environment and try to understand their world of thoughts from the inside—in the way anthropologists do.[12] If you want to teach them a language, it should be easier in an environment where their normal interests are found. Since I knew that Byrne had spent a long time studying the mountain gorillas in the forests of Uganda, I asked him whether he had considered teaching them sign language. He answered: 'No, I would not like to communicate with them. They are only interested in sex and violence.'

Even though Kanzi's linguistic capacities are impressive, his use of symbols is dependent on the context. The symbols mainly express requests that direct the teachers' attention to places, objects, and activities (96% of his productions are requests). In contrast, already at an early age human children use language for purposes other than wishes. The primatologist Jacques Vauclair notes that 'it appears that the use of symbols by apes is closely tied to the achievement of immediate goals, because the referents occur in the context of behavior on their objects'.[xiv] This accords perfectly with the thesis that only humans are anticipatory planners. My tentative conclusion is that one must be able to represent future goals in order to attain a fully detached language.

6.6   How children learn language

Now compare the apes with how children learn language! It is estimated that a normal teenager *understands* about 40 000 words of his or her mother tongue.

---

[12] In analogy with the philosopher Thomas Nagel's classical question 'What is it like to be a bat?' one should ask the question 'What is it like to be a chimp?' that is perhaps easier to answer. (At the end of his book *Wild minds* Marc Hauser asks 'What is it like to be a spider monkey?' Unfortunately, he does not answer the question.)

A little elementary arithmetic shows that children on average learn *ten new words per day* during their youth. Children learn words without effort and completely on their own accord.[xv] During their first years, the discovery of new words is often pure joy. The words stick in their head like flies on flypaper.

Another difference between how human and apes catch words is that the apes must learn the words *in the appropriate context*. If a chimpanzee is to learn the sign for 'milk', there must be milk in the vicinity—it is not enough to talk about the milk spilled yesterday. In a similar way, a dog can be trained what to do when you say 'Sit!' and maybe a few more commands. But the dog does not learn the connections between the different commands. The dog learns by routine while humans *understand* the meaning of words—and can connect different meanings. Deacon claims that the decisive factor is that children understand the *relations* between the different symbols. He argues that this supports their understanding of their meanings.

Children need no *training* in language in the same way as they need to practice how to ride a bike or how to count.[13] Surprisingly quickly they can themselves create combinations of words that nobody has uttered, standing for ideas that nobody has previously thought. Kanzi and some of the other language-trained apes can, to be sure, produce new combinations of the signs they have learnt, but they are far from human children's creativity. And, as Snowdon notes, we should not expect apes to be like children:

> If we were to find a Kanzi that imitated all human cognitive and linguistic abilities, we should probably be asking ourselves what sort of genetic disorder led him to be so short and hairy.[xvi]

Human children also learn new words just by *listening*. By attending to the conversations of others, and later by reading, by tales and stories, children catch words for all kinds of things, even for things and events they have never seen or that do not exist. The linguist Paul Bloom argues in his book *How children learn the meaning of words*, on the basis of extensive empirical data, that most mechanisms that children exploit in their language learning presume that they have a theory of mind. As we have seen, a first step in this direction is the ability to achieve joint attention.

As regards language learning, the most decisive difference between humans and apes is, after all, that we are enormously skilled at interpreting the *intention* behind a linguistic utterance. Human children can understand that the

---

[13] But they are sometimes practicing grammatical forms, for example conjugations of verbs, on their own.

speaker *wants* to inform them about something long before they understand what is said.[14] Apes hear a word or interpret a sign merely as a signal. They cannot enter into the inner world of the speaker. (This is not the same as the capacity to enter into somebody else's feelings that apes apparently manage.)

In brief, the foremost explanation why humans and no other animals have a language is that we have a considerably more developed inner world. Without this capacity, one cannot develop a fully symbolic communication but only use a set of signals. In order to deal with the nested intentions that are used in mature linguistic communication, an inner world that contains a rich and elaborate picture of the inner worlds of others is necessary.

6.7   Miming as intentional communication

> Pantomime without discourse
> will leave you nearly tranquil,
> discourse without gestures
> will wring tears from you.
>
> Jean-Jacques Rousseau

During the historical journey along the short branch of the tree of evolution that separates humans from chimpanzees, something has happened that makes language possible. We have crossed the river Symbolicon and left the signalling world of animals behind. *Homo sapiens* seems to be the only species that uses language in a totally detached manner.

One of the more sophisticated attempts to link the emergence of consciousness and language is presented by the psychologist Merlin Donald in his book *Origins of the modern mind*. There he builds a huge jigsaw puzzle with material from palaeontology, linguistics, anthropology, cognitive science, and neuropsychology.

Donald separates three main stages in the evolution of thought from the time when the paths of hominids and apes parted on route to modern man.[15] These three stages can also be linked to different levels of communication. The first is the *mimetic* stage that is characterized by the ability to bodily enact, to mime, different events. Miming is a form of intentional communication that mainly builds on icons. The second stage, the *mythic* stage, emerges when our ancestors develop the capacity to invent words, that is symbolic expressions.

---

[14] See Tomasello (1998) and Bloom (2000) for an account of a series of experiments that very clearly demonstrate this.

[15] Donald also describes a fourth stage, the episodic stage, that is prior to the other three and that is common to humans and apes.

Out of this capacity then arises the possibility to combine words into stories and myths. The third stage, which Donald calls *externalization of memory*, has occurred comparatively recently and it has no direct anchoring in a biological change. He claims that the emergence of pictures and written language makes it possible to place memories outside human heads (and thereby easier to preserve between generations). Donald is more interested in the evolution of the *cognitive capacities* than in physiological changes or the interpretation of archaeological findings. In this section, I will discuss miming. The second stage will be treated in the following chapter and the third will be presented in Chapter 8.

There are many forms of communication that do not involve spoken language. This is clearly shown by all the sign languages that have arisen in deaf communities all over the world. These languages are not just iconic but also contain symbols; they have fully developed grammars and extensive vocabularies. It is thus perfectly possible to communicate without speech.

The sign languages of the deaf constitute an advanced form of communication, on a par with spoken languages. These languages must be *learned* in the same way as spoken language. But there is a more primitive form of sign communication that is understood by everyone. When we travel to a country where we know nothing of the language, we can explain what we desire by *gestures* or *miming*. By clucking and flapping and by shaping your hands you can explain to the hotel waiter that you want a boiled egg for breakfast.

In the beginning, silence was presumably not total. *Homo erectus* and the other hominids, to be sure, used onomatopoetic sounds as part of the mimed communications. You can cluck like a hen or bark like a dog even if you do not have *words* for the animals. Such sounds function as icons.

Mimed gestures to some extent *resemble* what they refer to, and because of this they are iconic. If you want to sign 'ball', you let your hand form a circle in the air. Presumably, spoken language emerged partly through imitating words, which are also iconic, but in normal language the sounds we use for denoting a concept are arbitrary. The word 'dog' does not resemble a dog. By not using iconic sound signs we achieve greater freedom in creating new sound combinations for the different concepts we want to express, but it also means that we have to *learn* what the words mean.

Chomsky has claimed that there is a special language module in our head that is separated from the rest of the functions of the brain.[16] In this module,

---

[16] In a recent article written with Marc Hauser and Tecumseh Fitch (Hauser, Chomsky, and Fitch 2002), a slightly modified position is presented. In this article, the authors distinguish between

the basic grammatical rules are stored already at birth. According to Chomsky, these assumptions are necessary to explain how children can learn a language so quickly. One of the most frequent arguments in favour of Chomsky's theory of an innate grammar and against the theory that language has developed from a stage of miming is that there are no cultures where one finds vestiges of a sign language. But this is not correct. A sign language exists in parallel with speech in many cultures, for example among some American Indians and among some Australian aboriginals.

Another kind of support for the theory that miming is a part of the evolution of language comes from studies of children: shortly before a child reaches the two-word stage in its language development, it readily combines a word with a gesture to increase its expressive power.[xvii] It can utter 'doggie' and at the same time make a jumping movement with its hand to show that the dog was jumping. Kanzi does the same thing: when he wants to be tickled by a certain trainer, he presses the sign for tickle on his screen and then points to the one he wants to be tickled by.[xviii]

Miming improves the possibilities for co-operation and strengthens social relations. One can show that one wants somebody to fetch water by miming the fetching. A youngster can rat on an older sibling by showing what naughty thing the older has done. One can plan a hunting trip by miming the different phases. Donald ties the emergence of miming to the evolution of *Homo erectus*. This predecessor of ours manufactured advanced tools and engaged in social collaboration, but there are no signs that they had a spoken language.

The most original part of Donald's theory is that he convincingly argues that miming is a necessary precursor of spoken language. Miming is deliberate use of the entire body to communicate one's intentions. The gaze and its direction are also a part of miming. This ability presupposes that the one who is miming can *imagine* the movement before it is executed. You must be able to imagine how your gestures look *to others* in order to succeed in your communication. Hence miming may very well fulfil Grice's conditions for intentional communication. By practicing different gesture schemas, you can learn to perform them at will. Such exercises produce a new form of memories. In this manner, you create new detached representations. Miming also leads to

---

the faculty of language in the broad sense that includes a sensory-motor system, a conceptual–intentional system, and the computational mechanisms for recursion and in the narrow sense that only includes recursion. According to the authors, it is the mechanisms for recursion that provide the capacity to generate an infinite range of expressions. However, they still write as if the mechanisms for recursion form a system that is separate from the sensory–motor system and the conceptual–intentional system.

the brain being able to adjust to handling combinations of movements. Thereby it becomes prepared for spoken language.

Even though some animals are extremely skilful at performing complicated patterns of movements, the movements are not generative in the sense that the animal cannot actively produce new combinations. The play of animal young-sters is stereotypical, but human children invent new games. Studies of the brain reveal that the capacity for motoric combination is located very close to the place for the capacity to form sequences of words—normally in the left hemisphere. In contrast, the right hemisphere of the brain controls the melody of speech, which expresses emotional aspects.

Apes have problems in imitating in the strict sense that I have discussed earlier. They do not even point, at least not if they have grown up in the wild. Even though chimpanzees and gorillas can learn some signs from a sign language, their use of the signs is limited and mostly routine. In brief, apes and other animals do not have the communicative miming capacity that, accord-ing to Donald, was the first great step towards modern humans.

Mimed communication is expressed in, for example, dancing, pretence play, and theatre. The fact that the miming stage is so primitive and a prerequisite for other linguistic capacities may explain our fascination with sports and dance. It is immensely difficult to refrain from kicking when you are watching football on TV—the body is automatically caught up in the movements of others.

Miming is a fundamental capacity that goes deeper than what we normally are aware of. The psychologist Ullin Places notes that '[w]henever vocal com-munication is blocked either because it cannot be heard or, if heard, cannot be understood, human beings of every culture invariably fall back on gesticula-tion'.[xix] Furthermore, speaking is slowed down by the requirement to gesture at the same time, but gestures are not slowed down if you are required to speak.[xx] Another aspect of the same phenomenon is that blind people also ges-ture when they speak—even when they are speaking to other blind people.

Let me illustrate with an experiment run by Justine Cassell, David McNeill, and Karl-Erik McCullough that illustrates the influence of body language on us.[xxi] Subjects watched a video where a person is telling a story about a Sylvester and Tweetie Bird cartoon. The subjects are then asked to retell the story. What they do not know is that there is sometimes a mismatch between what the narrator says on the video and what his gesture indicates. For example, the narrator utters 'Granny whacks Sylvester' but makes a punching gesture at the same time. In about 40% of the mismatch cases, the subject's stories contained inaccuracies in relation to what was actually said on the video. In these cases, the mimed movement apparently had an effect on memory that overrode the spoken statement. The body language used by the subjects when they were retelling the story also confirmed the influence of the narrator's gesture. The experiment indicates that gestures are still strong carriers of meaning, even though we nowadays mainly communicate by speech.

The step from describing gestures to dance and rituals involving body movements is not long. Donald also argues that the first rituals arose during the time when *Homo erectus* existed. The leader of the tribe can mime a planned raid against an enemy group. The women can use a dance to initiate a young girl into adult life. Rites can be used to demarcate the beginning or end of different forms of co-operation within the tribe.

For example, Deacon argues that one of the first symbolic rituals was marriage.[xxii] During the evolution of the hominids two essential changes take place: the diet consists more and more of meat (which is necessary to keep the ever larger brain functioning) and the children demand longer and longer care before they become independent. For a woman who has just become a mother it is difficult to hunt, and this entails that the father of the child must to a higher degree provide for the mother and the child. Since the father thereby invests more in the survival of the child, it is important for him to know that he is really the father of the child. Thus both sexes have evolutionarily motivated reasons for establishing a long-term bond between the woman and the man. A marriage is a prime example of anticipatory planning. For such bonds to be maintained they must be linked to social sanctions. With the aid of a ritual that builds on iconic or symbolic elements, one can mark out such a loyalty bond for the rest of the tribe.

6.8   Keeping time—why chimps do not play in the circus orchestra

Darwin suggests that singing evolutionarily precedes talking.[17] As we shall see, he is probably right in that the prosody of speech, i.e. intonation and rhythm, is more primitive than the words themselves. Singing expresses feelings (sensations) rather than facts about the world (perceptions) or fantasies (imaginations).

"What is so good about singing?" Egon wonders. "For instance, I have never understood the point of opera. And feelings can be shown in others ways, can't they?"

---

[17] Darwin (1871, 1872). Donald (1991), p. 39, is skeptical to the thesis and says that it is difficult to see what additional biological advantage song would convey. Such a possible advantage will be discussed in Section 7.5.

The capacity for miming is enhanced by *rhythm*, in particular when you are miming together. Dancing, which occurs in all human cultures, is based on rhythmic miming. We want to describe the mating displays of cranes as dances, but they cannot keep time. Interestingly enough, the ability to keep time seems to be a uniquely human attribute.[18] Rhythm can be described as symmetry in time. As with rhythm, it seems that animals cannot at all create symmetrical tools.

Some insects, for instance cicadas, make sounds in time. But this ability is purely instinctive and locked to a certain biologically given rhythm (that in some cases turns out to be dependent on temperature). They have no detached control over the beat and hence they cannot vary the rhythm. There have been several attempts to train animals to keep time. Above all chimpanzees have been trained to take part in circus orchestras and the like. But the results have been miserable. The apes love beating on drums and producing sounds with the instruments, but they can never learn to keep time. They cannot *share* the beat. Horses who have been trained to walk in step cannot do this by themselves, but must always be controlled by small signals from the rider.

A wild guess why apes cannot keep time is that it is the same reason why they cannot aim. Simulators are needed also for rhythm: to keep time, the organism must accurately anticipate the time to the next beat.

An evolutionarily valuable aspect of rhythmic movements is that they improve coordination when individuals co-operate. In all human societies one finds work songs, where a common task is performed to the beat given by the song. One hypothesis is that rhythmic movements are also the basis for the first rituals.

The biomusicologist Björn Merker has recently proposed a theory concerning the forces behind the evolution of rhythm in the hominids. The starting point for his argument is that young females among chimpanzees leave the troop where they were born and join another troop. Therefore it is essential for the males of a troop to promote themselves in order to attract the females. Among chimps it is common that the troop give noisy pant-hoots when they have found a tree that is rich in fruit. The function of this behaviour is probably to brag about how rich in assets the territory of the troop is.

The more you hoot and the louder you do it, the more are reached by the message. Merker shows that if everybody shouts in time, then the sound will

---

[18] One possible exception is bonobos. According to an observation by de Waal (1988), pp. 202–3, they have a kind of staccato call not shared with chimps. Bonobos can emit their staccato calls in time with each other. However, a question to be answered is to what extent the apes can *control* their rhythm.

be heard at a far greater distance than if everybody calls for themselves. The sound will be particularly forceful if everybody shouts at the same pitch, i.e. sings in accord. To be able to keep time is also a sign that you can control your voice, and thereby indirectly that you can control your body, which is another side of the promotion.

Chimpanzees live in forests and it is impossible to see other troops at long distances. But the hominids evolved in a savannah type of terrain and were thereby more visible at a distance. If a group made a big kill, they could spread the message about this by shouting in time, but also by moving rhythmically. Dancing goes together with singing. The combination of plenty of food and singing and dancing is an efficient way of making a band of hominids attractive, in particular for young females. Apparently, the party has an evolutionary value. In all societies dance, music, and song are important for meeting a partner. Nobody becomes an idol with the young because you can speak or walk, but because you can sing or dance.

"This is a very sexist story," Egon remarks. "Why is it the males who are supposed to attract the females?"

"Because it is the females who move between the bands. The more females a male can attract to the band, the greater are his chances of siring many offspring."

"But with my relatives it is the males who move between the troops. The important thing for them is to drive out the leading male of a troop."

"Yes, it is true that it is only among the apes, including humans, that one finds female exogeny, i.e. females who move to new bands. So the interesting question is what is the evolutionary force that has led to this change in strategy."

(Egon sighs.)

Foley tells a story that is rather speculative, but which may give part of the explanation.[xxiii] Apes live considerably longer than monkeys. Other monkeys have a fast turnover of leading males—they seldom keep their position more than a couple of years. In contrast, a gorilla male can often dominate a troop for more than 15 years. There are also coalitions between ape males that are based on kinship links. For these reasons a young ape will hardly have any chance to drive out the leading male and his allies—the best way to reproduce your genes is to stay with your father or older brother and hope to inherit his harem. The coalitions one finds in ape troops are therefore based on kinship relations between males, while in monkey species it is the females who form kinship coalitions. Male coalitions are stronger in defending territories. A group of males with a territory rich in food can then loudly advertise and in this way attract females who live under less favourable conditions.

Notes

i. Deacon (1997), p. 23.

ii. Sjölander (1993), pp. 5–6.

iii. Langer (1948), p. 61.

iv. Von Glasersfeld (1977), p. 65.

v. Von Glasersfeld (1977), p. 64.

vi. Donald (1991) discusses this extensively.

vii. Goodall (1986), p. 125.

viii. Deacon (1997), p. 244.

ix. Deacon (1997), p. 421.

x. Deacon (1997), pp. 235–6.

xi. Cheney and Seyfarth (1990b).

xii. Terrace (1982, 1984).

xiii. Tomasello and Call (1997), p. 393.

xiv. Vauclair (1990), p. 319.

xv. For a detailed and lucid presentation of the research on how children pick up the meaning of words, see Bloom (2000).

xvi. Snowdon (1990), p. 239.

xvii. Goldin-Meadow (1999).

xviii. Savage-Rumbaugh and Lewin (1994), p. 161.

xix. Place (2000), Section III.iii.

xx. Feyereisen (1997).

xxi. Cassell, McNeill, and McCullough (1999).

xxii. Deacon (1997), pp. 385–401.

xxiii. Foley (1996).

CHAPTER 7

The origin of speech

The stupidity of humanity has not increased during the course of time,
but its possibility to express its stupidity has become ever greater.

Frans G. Bengtsson

7.1   Why just humans?

"Why do humans *talk*, actually?" Egon ponders.

"You are right that one can communicate in other ways than by speech, for example by gestures."

Jonathan Swift tells the story about Gulliver's travel to Balnibarbi where the learned men communicate by *showing* things to one another. They carry around huge bundles of things and gadgets to be able to exchange as much information as possible. It is not a very handy way of communicating, but it is a possible way.

"Our closest relatives among the apes do not talk—at best they chatter. So one can ask what are the evolutionary forces that have produced *speech* in humans."

"And why have the same forces not worked with apes?" Egon adds.

"Have you also become interested in evolution?"

"No, but I knew you were going to ask that question anyway."

There are some anatomical differences between apes and humans that are relevant. One is that human brains are much larger, in particular the frontal lobe where the higher cognitive functions are located. Certain parts of the brain have been adapted to manage a language with extensive grammar and vocabulary. It is difficult to find any regions in the brain that are totally dedicated to language, but the regions most closely associated with language are *Wernicke's area*, where the analysis of incoming sounds take place, and *Broca's area* that controls the production of speech.

Another evident difference is that the larynx is placed much lower in the human throat. This descent of the larynx has occurred relatively late in the

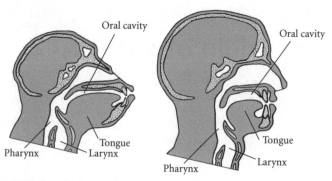

Figure 7.1 Differences in the vocal organs of chimpanzees and humans.

evolution of humans. It is connected with the rise of our own species, *Homo sapiens*, 200 000–300 000 years ago.[i]

The descended larynx makes the mouth cavity larger and, as a consequence, *Homo sapiens* can produce many more sounds, in particular vowels. This anatomical change is the prime reason why the emergence of speech is assumed to have taken place a quarter of a million years ago. But the descended larynx also brings a disadvantage, since the gullet and the windpipe share a common channel. This increases the risk of choking from food that gets into the windpipe. Unlike other apes, we cannot swallow and breathe at the same time.[1] The evolutionary benefits of a spoken language must be large to compensate for such a disadvantage.

The production of consonants also requires subtle control. For example, as regards k, p, t, g, b, d, it is a question of an immensely rapid control of the tongue and the lips. The difference between the sounds may be that the vocal cords being activated with a delay of a few milliseconds. No other primate comes close to such control of the speech organs. We can control the musculature of the tongue and the lips rapidly and in a differentiated manner. The human brain must have specially adapted neural connections to these muscles to manage the planning and supervision of the fast and precise movements that are needed to speak with a fluent stream of words.[ii] Studying the motoric part of cortex, one finds that about a third of the surface is used for the control of mouth, tongue, face, and throat; another third is used by the hands, while the rest of the body shares the last third. Apes use about a tenth

---

[1] Human infants are born with the larynx placed high, though, which makes it possible for them to swallow the breast milk and breathe at the same time. The descent of the larynx begins first at an age of about 18 months and is completed at puberty.

of their motor cortex for tongue and mouth, while hands and feet are assigned a third each.

Humans have a unique talent for constructing a large number of sound combinations (called morphemes by linguists) from a limited number of sounds (phonemes). This word production is also called 'the double articulation'. Linguist Alvar Ellegård explains how it has emerged as follows:

> The double articulation of human speech arose as a necessary consequence of the increasing number of linguistic signs, and the growing demands on quick and more or less automatised production. The brain's reaction to these demands was the double articulation in phonemes and morphemes.[2]

Similar phenomena show up in the sign languages of the deaf. Most of the signs in these languages were originally iconic. But as a sign language gradually develops, the signs can be sorted according to different types that are constituted of some hundred elements.[iii] The building blocks consist of various hand positions and movement components. They can be seen as the counterparts to the phonemes of spoken language. Such a component structure makes the production and interpretation of the signed language more efficient.

Another difference in how humans produce speech sounds in comparison to the apes is that we vocalize almost exclusively at exhalation, while most sounds produced by apes occur with a combination of inhalation and exhalation. To achieve continuous speech it is important to be able to control one's breathing freely. Humans have much stronger voluntary control of their breathing than other animals. The nerve fibres in the spinal column controlling the movements of the chest are also thicker in humans than in chimpanzees. Interestingly enough it turns out that in *Homo erectus* this nerve channel is still rather thin, which suggests that this hominid had not yet full control over its vocal apparatus.[iv]

There are also large *cognitive* differences between humans and apes. We are skilled at *translating* between different senses: already an infant who first touches an object that is hidden under a cloth can, with the aid of its sight, identify the object among many shown in a picture. Coordinating sight, touch, and hearing in this way comes natural for humans, but has turned out to be more difficult for other animals, as I discussed earlier. In passing, it should be noted that this capacity for crossmodality is a necessary prerequisite for the

---

[2] Ellegård (1979), p. 142. He continues: 'the double articulation is a kind of general economy principle for the living organism concerning conveyance of information. The principle applies as soon as an activity or a behaviour reaches a fairly high degree of complexity, at the same time as it must take place rapidly and, above all, unconsciously, automatically' (pp. 142–3, my translation).

use of *metaphors* in language. When, for example, one says that a colour is 'loud', one must be able to see the similarities between the impression made by the colour and a loud sound.

Miming has prepared the way for speech. In the beginning spoken language is not a substitute for miming, but can be seen as an expansion of this capacity: speech can be interpreted as *sound gestures*. Spoken language presumes that you can control your motor functions, above all the facial muscles and the vocal cords. Without such control, you cannot even babble. And babbling is an unavoidable stage in a child's language development. Again, this is a feature that is unique for humans—other apes do not practice the formation of sounds (but there are to be sure birds who rehearse a sizeable repertoire of song themes). One finds a fascinating parallel in deaf children who grow up with sign language. They do not practice their voices, but they practice hand movements—they babble with their hands.[3] Children only babble when they are calm—when they are upset they cry. This indicates that it is the controlling cortex that governs the babbling, while more primitive sounds such as crying are managed by the evolutionarily older parts of the brain, which then override the signals from the cortex.[v]

Donald considers that the capacity to invent new words is the key to the emergence of language. Language is developed to express the conceptual structures that exist in the head in advance of language. He speculates that metaphors play a significant role in this process.

The ability to *utter* the language sounds is not the primary motive power behind the evolution of language, as has been claimed by many. The sign languages of the deaf show that one can manage a complete language using only hands and facial expressions. But there is no society of hearing people that uses only sign language—the advantages of spoken language are too big.[4]

In several ways, speech is more effective than miming as a tool for communication. First, it is easy to use the mouth to form a large number of sound patterns that can be used as signs—in this way we obtain a richer vocabulary than by miming. Another reason is that speech frees the hands for other occupations. If you carry a small child in your arms, it is easier to speak than to use sign language. Humans are the only primates who must carry their infants—those of other apes and monkeys cling to their mothers. A third reason is that

---

[3] Also deaf children start babbling using their voices. They stop, however, after a few months since they do not hear any response.

[4] It should be noted that sign language is controlled by the same parts of the brain as spoken language.

speech functions splendidly in pitch dark, while gestures do not. A fourth reason is that the listener need not have continuous eye contact with the communicator, something that is necessary for sign language. There are hence excellent evolutionary reasons for why speech in the long run drives out miming. But speech is not always the optimal way of communicating. If you use your voice when you are hunting, the kill will be frightened away. In situations of this type, sign language can be more appropriate.

Sports commentators and rap artists produce speech in a rattling tempo that far exceeds the possibilities of miming. Humans' gift of the gab nowadays totally outshines the expressive power of the other body parts. The modern humans' capacity to speak has developed to such an extent that we sometimes wish there were more silence. As the saying goes: 'It takes two years for man to learn to speak, but 50 to learn to keep silent.'

7.2 Consciousness and language

"But must you not have a language in your head before you can express it?" Egon asks. "Must not the *language of thought* develop earlier than miming or speech in the evolution of humans?"

"No, as I have tried to show, it is possible to have many cognitive functions, including self-consciousness, without having a language. And on the other hand, one cannot have a language in my sense without a rich inner world that includes a self-consciousness."

I have argued that animals can plan as soon as there is an inner world where scenarios, actions, and their consequences can be 'displayed'. Such simulations are surely necessary for planning, but they do not require language. For example, consider a slalom skier who, before a race, goes through all the turns of the course and the right bodily movements in her imagination before actually running the race. The brain scientist Marc Jeannerod has shown that the activity patterns occurring in the cortex during such a mental simulation of body movements are very similar to those occurring during a real movement.[vi] But the slalom skier cannot express in words how the legs should move in the piste.

The events in the inner world of humans can be compared to a talking film, while other animals at best experience a silent film. What we experience as an inner monologue (or dialogue) is an evolutionarily later phenomenon that is an *inner simulation of outer speech*. Inner speech should be seen as *a part* of the simulations in the inner world. We imagine saying something without actually doing it. The inner monologue is part of what we *experience* in the inner world. As Valéry puts it: 'I and ME—Dialogue—of one voice/These two unknowns whose discourse is knowledge.'

But how the monologue is *composed* is still wrapped in mystery, in the same way as we are not aware of how we find the words we actually say. Dennett presents the theory that the brain creates a *multiplicity of drafts* of what is to be said and there are then different kinds of filters that let through what best fits with what we think (and that sort out the insults and the obscenities).[vii]

"What's so strange about that?" Egon asks. "How can I know what I think until I hear what I say?"

Chafe points out that 'language itself provides evidence that not everything in consciousness is verbal. Disfluencies show that people often experience difficulty in turning thoughts into words, suggesting that there is more to thought itself than inner speech.'[viii] I agree with Chafe that language is a powerful tool for discovering what goes on in our brains. But we cannot speak about everything that goes on in the brain, only about what happens in our inner worlds.

7.3 The gossip theory

I am sitting scratching Egon's neck—something he likes very much. He thinks so well then, he says.

"If evolution now has produced this wonderful ability to speak, at the cost of this and that, why do people then use it mainly to exchange nonsense and to say mean things about each other?" he asks.

A great part of the time humans spend together they talk. If speech is viewed from an evolutionary perspective, the problem is to describe the selective forces that have led to the emergence of this phenomenon among humans— and only among humans. There is a handy answer: we use language to *inform* each other about what the world looks like. But more recent theories show that it is not obvious that this was the original function of language. The *social function* of language may have been more important.

Some years ago, the psychologist Robin Dunbar presented an unorthodox explanation for the origin of language in his book *Grooming, gossip and the evolution of language*. His goal is to identify the evolutionary forces that have produced language. Dunbar claims that language is not primarily used for communication, but for strengthening the social links between the members of a group. As a form of social cement, the sounds of language may have replaced the kind of grooming that apes and monkeys indulge in. According to Dunbar, language was originally social rather than informative. As we shall see, one consequence of his argument is that *gossip* may have been (and still be) a more important use of language than, for example, information about where a hunting kill is to be found.

The prime cause behind language, according to Dunbar, is that when the size of the hominids' social groups increased, new means for keeping the groups together became necessary. Dunbar reaches this outlook on the role of language by a partly new way of looking at the hominids' evolution. The transition to a life on the savannah must have been extremely tough for the hominids, since they were, among other things, more prone to predators' attacks in the open spaces. To protect themselves they were forced to join together in larger groups.

The problem with large social groups is that they easily result in internal conflicts. Chimpanzees live in bands consisting of about 50 individuals led by an alpha male (bonobos in unified groups of up to 100 individuals). Dunbar estimates that in the societies of primitive humans the group had 150–200 members. It is much more difficult to keep a group of this size together.

During the evolution of humans, the size of the brain increased dramatically. In general, primates have large brains in comparison to other mammals, but *Homo sapiens* has a brain that is nine times as big compared to what can be expected of a mammal with our body weight. The brain is very expensive to maintain—it constitutes 2% of our body weight, but consumes 20% of our energy. One consequence of this is that human beings are the only animals that cannot keep the brain and the stomach fully active at the same time. We do not have the resources to think and digest food simultaneously. How have we, in the struggle for survival, *afforded* to develop such a spendthrift organ? The grey lump of porridge inside our skull must provide us with considerable advantages to compensate for the energy expenditure. The only possibility for the hominids to provide their brains with sufficient energy was to consume more nutritious food. As a consequence of this, their diet was slowly adjusted, from mainly vegetarian to containing more and more meat. Thus the hominids became to an increasing extent competitors to the other beasts of prey.

"Why do you actually need such a large brain?" Egon asks.

When Dunbar compared the size of monkeys' and apes' brains with the sizes of their social groups he discovered that there is a strong correlation between the magnitude of the cortex area and group size. (The solitary orang-utan is an exception.) If this correlation is extrapolated to the size of the human cortex, the prediction becomes that the size of human groups is about 150 individuals.

Monkeys and apes maintain group coherence by grooming each other. When group size increases in the hominid evolution, there will not be enough time to groom everybody you want to have a friendly relationship with.[5] Speech is simply much more efficient for this purpose than grooming. Hence, a large brain is required to master a language that in turn is needed for social coherence. Dunbar claims that the informative function of language has developed later as a by-product of the social function.

"Why has the same thing not happened to chimps and gorillas?" Egon asks.

"Since their groups are smaller, they have enough time to check for fleas in everybody they want to be friends with."

"Yes, that seems to be an eternal problem of humans—to be short of time. Do you have the time to scratch my back now?"

Dunbar examines anthropological and sociological material in order to establish that the natural group size in primitive societies is 150–200 individuals, as his theory predicts. In groups of this size, one can still maintain personal relations with everybody. Even though Dunbar tries to find support from a variety of sources, the impression remains that he chooses a level where the group size fits with his hypothesis. One problem with his argument is that the figure 150–200 is to some extent arbitrary: one can identify human groupings in so-called primitive societies on many different levels from tribes normally consisting of between 1500 and 2000 individuals, to clans with about 150, and to hunting camps that contain five to six families with about 35 persons altogether.

Dunbar claims that humans need a large brain to handle the intrigues and conflicts that arise within the large social group. As we have seen, Machiavellian intelligence is concerned with successful deceiving and at the same time avoiding being deceived. Consistent with this it turns out that there is a strong correlation between the size of the cortex and the ability to deceive.

One ethologist has half-jokingly suggested that the reason why orang-utans are solitary is that they know that they cannot trust each other. The natives on Borneo call the species 'orang hutan', which means 'man in the jungle'. They claim that orang-utans actually can speak, although they are smart enough to keep silent so that they are not put to work.[6]

---

[5] The number of relations to keep track of grows very quickly (factorially) with the size of the group. It is not only my own relations to Tom, Dick, and Harry that are of interest, but also how Tom relates to Dick and Harry.

[6] Cf. Kenneth Grahame who in *The golden age* writes: 'Monkeys ... very sensitively refrain from speech lest they should be set to earn their livings.'

"Maybe the same thing applies to rhesus macaques?" I ask Egon.

"No comment."

If now the social relations among humans (and other apes) are so important, how do you behave to make the right contacts? Apes establish and maintain social ties by grooming each other. One can ask why grooming generates such strong bonds. Part of the explanation seems to be that grooming creates a mild rapture in the one being groomed: it turns out that to be groomed stimulates the production of endorphins in the body (these are the brain's own analgesics). Experiments have shown that if apes are given small doses of morphine, they immediately cease grooming each other.

Grooming also reduces the stress level of the one being groomed. This has direct consequences in the process of natural selection—it has been shown that stressed individuals are less fertile. Another factor that is important for solidarity is that grooming takes time: by investing a lot of grooming time in somebody else, the one being groomed can feel more secure in the alliance.

Chimpanzees who live in bands of 30–50 individuals devote about 20% of the time they are awake to grooming. Dunbar estimates that to achieve the same effect in a group of 150 individuals, one would need 40% of the time for grooming. This would leave too little time for other life-sustaining activities such as sleeping and gathering food. Sometime during human evolution the social stress became too great for grooming to be sufficient.

For this reason there is a strong need for a more efficient way of maintaining social bonds. This is where he places the great innovation: language. A decisive advantage of language is that in a conversation you can 'groom' several persons at the same time and you also have your hands free for other chores (such as taking care of children). But Dunbar shows that a conversational group seldom consists of more than four persons—if it exceeds this number it tends to split.

Together with his students he has made sociological investigations of *what* people in informal groups talk about. It turns out that roughly two-thirds of the time is spent on social topics—you talk about people and their relations. This bias occurs as long as the group contains only one sex. In groups with mixed sexes, one talks about politics, business, or science—men more than women— to impress each other. Gossip is apparently a dominant form of conversation. Sewing circles and pubs therefore fill a fundamental human need.

Dunbar's evolutionary story provides some clues to why humans have a language. Unfortunately, his theory does not say anything about how the various linguistic structures have evolved. For him, language might as well be nonsensical chatter, as long as it functions as a tool for creating social bonds. Furthermore, his theory does not explain why language has *not* evolved among other apes or animals. Even if apes have problems in controlling their voices, there is nothing in Dunbar's theory that explains why they have not developed a form of gossip based on miming.

Gossip, that is so central for Dunbar, requires that you talk about somebody who is not present, but his theory says nothing about how the symbolic structure emerges. It is possible that this arises later in evolution than the social function that Dunbar treats, but what is missing in his theory is a plausible explanation of what has produced symbolic language with its complicated grammatical structure.

In spite of these limitations, Dunbar has contributed a couple of important jigsaw pieces in the story of what happened when we became humans. He emphasizes the role of language as a social lubricant. What is important is not what we talk about but how we say it and to whom. We groom each other's inner worlds, not just our skins. Or as the author Ben Okri writes: 'It is probably because we have so much inside us that community is so important.'

In so-called 'primitive' language, anthropomorphism is common: features from animals and nature are ascribed different human properties.[7] If language has evolved to communicate about social relations, it is no wonder that it becomes anthropomorphic. By attributing human features to the animals you hunt, the hunter can exploit his knowledge about human behaviour to predict how the animal will behave and thereby the hunting becomes more successful. A side effect of such a humanizing of animals is that we attribute them more advanced forms of consciousness than what they really have. (Ockham's razor is an invention of modern ethology.)

Among aboriginals in Australia it is also common to describe the dry landscape by stories about what the mythical 'forefathers' have done there: the few wells are seen as places where the forefathers dug; the trees as places where they left their digging sticks; and deposits of red ochre as traces of their blood. By providing the landscape with such a mythical interpretation, it becomes possible for the aboriginals to *remember* much more geographical information.

7.4   Sharing visions for the future—co-operation begets language

Despite all the merits of Donald's gossip theory, it does not explain why language is *unique* to humans. I will propose another advantage of symbolic

---

[7]   As we have seen, this is presumably a consequence of our thinking about causes being extended from the social to the physical domain.

language that may be evolutionarily more important than those previously suggested: language makes it possible to *co-operate about future goals.*[ix]

Human beings as well as other animals co-operate in order to reach common goals. Even seemingly simple animals like ants and bees co-operate in building complex societies. However, their co-operation is *instinctive*—they have no detached representation of the goal their collaboration is aimed at. For lack of representations, they cannot create new goals of co-operation.

Nevertheless, for many forms of co-operation among animals, it seems that representations are not needed. If the common goal is present in the actual environment, for example food to be eaten or an antagonist to fight, the collaborators need not focus on a joint representation of it before acting.

If, on the other hand, the goal is detached, i.e. distant in time or space or not even existent, then a *common* representation of it must be produced before co-operative action can be taken. In other words, co-operation about detached goals requires that *the inner worlds of the individuals be coordinated.* This cannot be achieved by signalling or by joint attention: symbolic communication is necessary. In my opinion, a major reason for the evolution of language is that it enhances co-operation. Language is the tool by which humans can make their imaginations and desires known to each other. In contrast to animal signalling, language is not bound by the actual. It is based on the use of representations as stand-ins for actual entities. The use of representations replaces the use of environmental features in communication. They liberate the communicators from having to pursue the immediate goals.

Another problem concerning collaboration in order to reach a detached goal is that the *value* of the goal cannot be determined from the given environment, unlike a goal that is already present on the scene. The value of the future goal has to be estimated by each individual with regard to possible outcomes.

Apes seem to lack the cognitive resources that are required for imagining future goals and calculating their values. This is a decisive difference between humans and apes.

Communication by symbols is quite intricate, because the meanings of the symbols are general and defined by interrelation. As mentioned earlier, it has so far not been shown that apes can communicate in a fully symbolic way. Rather, it seems that apes in their natural habitat mainly exploit indexical signalling.

Human language is the prototype example of a symbolic communication system. Clearly, human language paves the way for long-term co-operation and for co-operation towards future goals. As Boysen and Berntson's experiment indicates, it may be difficult to give up a good you possess for a future, but more precious, one.

An important feature of the use of symbols in co-operation is that they can set the co-operators free from the goals that are available in the present environment. The detached goals and the means to reach them are identified and externally shared through the linguistic medium. This kind of sharing gives humans an enormous advantage concerning co-operation in comparison to other species. I view this advantage as a strong evolutionary force behind the emergence of symbolic communication. More precisely, I believe that there has been a co-evolution of co-operation about future goals and symbolic communication.[8]

Language is based on the use of representations as stand-ins for entities, actual or just imagined. Use of such representations replaces the use of environmental cues in communication. If I have an idea about a goal I wish to attain, I can use language to communicate my thoughts. In this way, language makes it possible for us to *share visions*.

There are many kinds of visions. Some of them are about rather concrete goals. For instance, the chief of a village can try to convince the inhabitants that they should co-operate in digging a common well that everybody will benefit from or in building a defensive wall that will increase the security of everybody. The goal requires efforts by the members of the community, but it can still have a positive net benefit for all involved.

Other visions are more abstract and distant and their potential values are hard to assess. Many religions promise an eternal life after death, if you just behave according to certain norms. Such a vision is a temptation to many, even though it is impossible to know whether it can be fulfilled. An eloquent leader can depict enticing goals and convince the supporters to make radical sacrifices, even though the visionary goals are extremely uncertain. However, in deprived circumstances the visions may seem especially promising.

To show the evolutionary importance of co-operation for future goals, recall Deacon's suggestion that the first form of symbolic communication is marriage agreements.[x] He argues that there was strong evolutionary pressure in hominid societies to establish relationships of exclusive sexual access. He says that such an exclusive sexual bond 'is a *prescription* for future behaviors'. A symbolic pair-bonding relationship implicitly determines which future behaviours are allowed and not allowed. These expectations concerning future behaviour do not only include the pair, but also the other members of the social group who are supposed not to disturb the relationship by cheating.

---

8   Cf. the 'ratchet effect' discussed by Tomasello (1999), pp. 37–40.

Anybody who breaks the symbolic agreement risks punishment from the entire group.

How can such a symbolic marriage be established in a hominid society that does not yet have a language? Deacon points to the role of rituals. To turn a communicative signal into a symbol demands that the users shift attention from a concrete representation in the environment to a detached meaning, often with future reference. Such a transition involves a re-learning that involves changing the coupling between a sign and a concrete reference into a new coupling between the sign and the detached symbolic meaning. Repeating an interwoven set of signals in ritualistic circumstances is a way of attaining this transition from signals to a network of symbols with inter-related meanings. Tokens such as ritual clothing, bodily decorations and scarrings can in this manner turn from circumstantial signals to ritual symbols. After the ritual, the tokens serve as a reminder of the agreement concerning future goals that was established during the ritual.

Recent research on animal cognition has, to a large extent, focused on the *deceptive* capacities of different species—often in terms of Machiavellian intelligence. This tendency has spilled over to the debate on the evolution of human cognition. However, a general conclusion to be drawn from this chapter is that, as regards the human species, the development of advanced and flexible forms of co-operation is more important when explaining the evolution of language.

Advanced co-operation demands access to detached representations, and the capacity to communicate about such representations. Therefore, the efficiency of communication about a detached goal will be a bottleneck in changing the strategic situation of the group. The core argument of this section is that without the aid of symbolic communication, we would not be able to share visions about the future. We need it in order to convince each other that a future goal is worth striving for.

I believe that the benefits of advanced co-operation are so extensive that they are the major evolutionary forces behind the emergence of symbolic language. In this sense, co-operation begets language.

Unlike Dunbar's theory, the ideas presented here also explain why only humans have language. Being able to co-operate about future goals requires detached representations of goals as well as a theory of mind. As far as we know, both these cognitive capacities are uniquely human.

7.5 Language as a social marker

Machiavellian intelligence has many facets. When language evolves it becomes much easier for humans to lie and deceive. We end up in an intricate game where it is important to keep the right balance between telling the truth and lying (or at least not telling the whole truth). Every poker player knows that truth is not always the best strategy—it will inexorably be exploited by the opponents. It is necessary to bluff occasionally. And conversely, you should not be too credulous and blindly trust others.

Language can be used both by the good and the evil. But the role of language as a social lubricant to a certain extent counteracts misuse. The chimpanzee Yeroen groomed Nikkie to form an alliance with him. Modern man also primarily uses language to create different kinds of coalitions.

There are other features of language that support its function to create collaborating groups. One persistent problem in a society is to be able to impede spongers who try to exploit the resources that are generated by different forms of co-operation. A sure-fire method is to only form alliances with persons you really trust. Blood is thicker than water: it turns out that also among other primates it is more common to enter into alliances with relatives than with others.

When the social groups are growing during the evolution of hominids to contain many more than your relatives, you must be able to determine whether somebody belongs to your group so that cheaters are not let in. Gossip is, of course, an effective method of blocking spongers, but it is not sufficient in large societies. Dunbar claims that *dialects* develop as markers of group affiliation. It is extremely tough to flawlessly learn a new dialect as an adult, and your dialect is therefore a valuable indicator that you belong to the group and hence are a reliable partner to co-operate with.

A biblical example of language as a social marker is the word 'shibboleth' as is told in the Book of Judges. The Gileadites were at war with the Ephraimites, and to distinguish friend from foe the Gileadites asked any unknown person they encountered how they pronounced 'shibboleth'. If anybody said 'sibboleth', he was considered an Ephraimite and killed immediately.

Today people migrate over much larger distance than in the old days. Our society is no longer built around the tribe or village community that dominated for millennia. To an increasing extent we are living far from our relatives. The old conditions for co-operation within the group have thereby drastically changed. Our hereditary language functions unfortunately still make it difficult for us to trust somebody with a divergent dialect, let alone a different language. Hence the possibilities to create secure forms of co-operation in modern society are constrained by the behavioural and emotional patterns that have been rooted by evolution. But by becoming aware of our biologically controlled prejudices, we will hopefully defy them.

7.6   Motherese

The psychologist Lev Vygotsky proposed already in the 1930s that a child's cognitive development and its linguistic development in their first stages are separate processes, but that the developmental lines in normal cases eventually meet so that 'thought becomes verbal and speech rational':

> The preintellectual roots of speech in child development have long been known. The child's babbling, crying, even his first words, are quite clearly stages of speech development that have nothing to do with the development of thinking. These manifestations have generally been regarded as a predominantly emotional form of behavior. Not all of them, however, serve merely the function of release. Recent investigations of the earliest forms of behavior in the child and of the child's first reactions to the human voice ... have shown that the social function of speech is already clearly apparent during the first year, i.e., in the preintellectual stage of development.[xi]

Dunbar's gossip theory is supported by some studies of the interaction between mother and infant. The way mothers talk to their children is sometimes called 'Motherese'. Distinguishing features are that the pitch of the voice is high and that the stresses are exaggerated. For fathers it is regrettable that infants can more easily perceive the pitch of women and children than the lower male voice.

The emotional role of communication with small children has been highlighted by the linguist Anne Fernald, who has conducted studies comparing how mothers and infants in different cultures communicate.[xii] Of course, the mothers use different phonemes, different words, and different nursery rhymes when talking to their infants. However, it turns out that if the intonation patterns—the tones of voice—are considered, one finds *four* fundamental structures:

1. The mother can *encourage* the infant to do something ('can you get it?') with rising pitch.
2. She can *reward* the child for something it has done ('good girl') with falling pitch.
3. She can *warn* or *forbid* the child and then the phrasing is often short sound thrusts ('no, no, no').
4. Finally she can *comfort* the child and then the melody of the speech shows a soft, billowing pattern ('Poor Eddy').

These four sound patterns seem to occur in all cultures, independently of which language is used to express the messages to the infants. (An interesting link to animal communication is that in many species warnings consist of sound thrusts.) Interestingly enough, Fernald's results to some extent justify Darwin's song theory of the evolution of language. The important feature is the *emotional* content, rather than which words are used. This further supports the notion that a fundamental function of language is to express feelings. To be sure, feelings are tightly connected to social relations. The informative function of language has presumably evolved much later. As Donald writes about infants' learning of language:

> They know about the 'prosodic', or emotional, features of speech a very long time before they can understand its meanings. Later they use this knowledge as an attentional hook to help them home in on the intended meaning of what they hear. The speaker's tone of voice tells the infant where and when to look and marks the significance of the utterance. The situational context usually provides the meaning. This reduces the difficulty of tracking the content hidden in words and sentences.[xiii]

Furthermore, the psychologist Colwyn Trevarthen has shown that the communication between a mother and her infant exhibits distinct *rhythmic* patterns.[xiv] Even if they cannot yet pronounce any real words, the infants learn very quickly when it is their 'turn' to say something. Mother and child practice such turn taking, among other things by nursery rhymes such as 'Itsy Bitsy Spider' that often involve bodily actions on the child's part. Rhythmic nursery rhymes of this kind are found in all cultures.

As adults, we depend on language as a carrier of information and we are seldom aware of its more basic functions. It is said that the pen is more powerful than the sword. The question is whether speech is even more powerful— a skilled orator can seduce masses. The emotional charge of speech is still more influential than the informative content. The problem is that we are seldom aware of *how* a speaker steers our emotions. Rhetoric education teaches a few tricks, but there is still much to learn about the mechanisms of persuasion.

7.7   Protolanguage

Even if early *Homo sapiens* were the first with a spoken language, it surely took a long time to develop a language with an advanced *grammar*. One can roughly divide the building blocks of language into two groups: grammatical and semantic. The semantic components are those that carry most of the meanings, while the grammatical are used to compose the semantics and to eliminate ambiguities.

The long transition from miming to a fully developed language with a grammar has presumably passed through several intermediate stages. The linguist Derek Bickerton argues in his book *Language and species* that there was a stage in the evolution of language when a *protolanguage*, containing only the semantic components of language, was used.[9] In support of his thesis he shows that there still are four different types of language that have a very simplified grammatical structure and that resemble each other.

The first type is the stage children normally pass between 18 and 24 months when their language consists of two-word sentences. Here are some typical examples (with their linguistic function marked within parentheses):

Big train; Red book	(*attribution of qualities to objects*)
Adam checker; Mommy lunch	(*possessive relations*)
Walk street; Go store	(*location of actions*)
Adam put; Eve read	(*relation of agents to actions*)
Put book; Hit ball	(*relation of actions to patients*)

This form of communicative system clearly presupposes detached representations that have been coded by symbols, i.e. words. The meanings of the simple words are already anchored in the children's heads. But such a system of phrases with few words contains no grammar.

The second type of evidence for a protolanguage builds on apes that are taught sign language. They never learn a language with a grammar, but halt at a level that is reminiscent of children's two-word stage. Also Kanzi's linguistic capacities seem to be a good example of protolanguage. The following examples are signed utterances produced by the chimpanzee Washoe. Their linguistic form and content corresponds very well to children's two-word stage:[xv]

> Drink red; Comb black
> Clothes Mrs. G.; You hat
> Go in; Look out
> Roger tickle; You drink
> Tickle Washoe; Open blanket

"Washoe speaks like Tarzan," Egon comments.

The third type of data comes from 'closet children', i.e. children who have been deprived of normal language communication during the first years of

---

[9] Bickerton (1990), p. 174, submits that the transition from protolanguage to fully grammatical language is 'catastrophic' in the sense that the complete language emerges as the result of a mutation in a single individual. In my opinion, his arguments for such a direct transition are very weak. Barber and Peters (1992), pp. 343–4, and Jackendoff (1999) present interesting theories about a gradual development of grammar in early *Homo sapiens*.

their lives. Bickerton tells the story of Genie, who had been locked up in her room until she was 13.[xvi] She had perfectly normal intelligence, but she could never learn language completely in spite of great efforts to teach her. She did not reach much further than a two-year-old as far as grammar is concerned.

The last type of empirical evidence that Bickerton offers concerns when two cultures with unrelated languages meet. Then so-called pidgin languages develop that also have a structure resembling two-word sentences. After the first generation, a pidgin language that has been adopted by children who speak it from the beginning can transform into a so-called Creole language with a fully developed grammar. But if a pidgin language is only used in sporadic meetings, for example in trading, it can remain at the same immature level during many generations. Bickerton presents the following example of a dialogue between a Russian who wants to sell flour and a buying Norwegian. The dialogue is translated from Russonorsk—a pidgin language that has developed in trading contacts between Russian and Norwegian sailors. (Note that the Norwegian uses 'buy' also in the sense of 'sell'.)[xvii]

> R: What say? Me no understand.
> N: Expensive, Russian—goodbye.
> R: Nothing. Four half.
> N: Give four, nothing good.
> R: No, brother. How me sell cheap? Big expensive flour on Russia this year.
> N: You no true say.
> R: Yes. Big true, me no lie, expensive flour.
> N: If you buy please four *pud* (measure of 36 lbs.) If you no buy—then goodbye.
> R: No, nothing brother, please throw on deck.

On the basis of the material from these four areas, Bickerton concludes that:

> There is a mode of linguistic expression that is quite separate from normal human language and is shared by four classes of speakers: trained apes, children under two, adults who have been deprived of language in their early years, and speakers of pidgin.[xviii]

As regards the position of protolanguage in relation to the evolution of hominids, Bickerton's theory is that *Homo erectus* mastered a protolanguage and it is not until *Homo sapiens* that one finds a language with a grammatical structure. This theory seems to be compatible with Donald's thesis that *Homo erectus* communicated by miming, in particular if sounds are included in miming. The difference is that mimed signs and sounds are iconic, while Bickerton writes about protolanguage as if it builds on symbolic expressions. But in principle one can conceive of an evolutionarily earlier variant of protolanguage, where words are just iconic (independently of whether they are mimed or spoken). The transition from iconic expressions to arbitrary symbols has presumably been gradual.[10]

7.8 The role of grammar

The grammar of a natural language is a complicated system. Nevertheless almost all children learn the constructions of their mother tongue. Chomsky argues that the feedback that is given to a child during its youth is far from sufficient to distinguish between all possible grammatical systems. According to him, children can simply not learn all grammar from the beginning. Chomsky therefore has claimed that there is necessarily a system of *innate* grammatical rules.

But Chomsky's early view on language has been heavily criticized during recent years. First, he only focuses on grammatical rules and cares little about the meaning of language (semantics) and even less about how it is used in communication (pragmatics). A great deal of children's language learning can be explained with the aid of these factors. Secondly, Chomsky supposes that grammar is stored in the brain as a kit of rules that function in way similar to programming instructions in a computer. But it is far from certain that there is such a system of rules. Just because we can explain many aspects of human linguistic competences by using certain rules, it does not follow that these rules actually exist in the heads of the language users. Here is an analogy: a swinging pendulum moves according to Galileo's law, but this does not mean that the law in any sense is stored in the pendulum.

To understand why it is not necessary to store a number of rules in the brain in order to know a language I want to go back to how termites build their hills as was described earlier. The termites only follow the principle of placing their clay balls where the smell is strongest. The physical laws of the environment then lead to the development of the complex hill.

Human language may have developed in an analogous way—as a termite hill of thoughts. Instead of clay balls we drop speech balloons. One balloon often brings out others. The utterances will adjust to one another so that the

---

[10] Lyons (1988), p. 159, adds the following argument: 'Iconity, of which onomatopoeia in spoken languages is the most obvious example, is generally regarded as one of the 'design-features' which separates non-linguistic, or pre-linguistic, systems of communication from fully fledged languages. But iconity, more generally defined as non-arbitrariness of the association of form and meaning, is [...] not a matter of yes or no, but of more or less; and there is much more iconicity in "ordinary" natural languages, at all levels of their structure, than the conventional wisdom in linguistics would have us believe.'

balloons form patterns. Eventually, patterns of balloons have created pinnacles and arches of meanings that we must follow when want to say something new. In this way, language obtains a self-organizing structure that is *common* for all speakers. What looks like grammatical rules are just the arches that emerge as a result of the fundamental cognitive conditions for human communication. Hence Chomsky's idea of innate rule is not called for. Because of historical coincidences, different societies will construct their own version of the linguistic castle in the air, even though the principles of construction are the same.

According to this position language *emerges* from the utterances of the speakers. Once the linguistic structure has developed it will strongly direct which speech acts are meaningful. And once language is established it becomes a tool that can be used for other purposes than communication. It can serve as a banister for thinking so that our thoughts do not lose their way in the dusk of the convolutions of the brain. We formulate our thoughts in speech or write them down on paper. The very formulation locks the thought in a mould that can then be regarded from the outside and be used as support for new thoughts.

The neurobiologist Deacon is also critical of Chomsky's outlook on language. He starts out from the metaphor that *language is a parasitic symbiont*.[11] Language infects the brain, but forms a kind of symbiosis with it. Language would not survive without humans, but humans also benefit greatly from language. The language parasite has adapted to the environment where it lives—above all language must easily be spread to a child's brain. Therefore languages are adapted to the learning mechanisms of children (it is much more difficult to learn a language later in life).[12] A language that has a structure that is too complicated to learn will not survive for many generations.

But how much of language is then genetically determined and how much is learned? Chomsky claims that the most fundamental grammatical rules are innate. However, different languages vary greatly and they *change* rapidly—*very* rapidly from the perspective of natural selection. In contrast to Chomsky, Deacon argues that for a language trait to be innate it must be applicable in all variations of language. From this it follows that only the most adamant

---

[11] Deacon (1997), p. 112. This view is preceded by Christiansen (1994), p. 126, who writes that: 'Following Darwin, I propose to view natural language as a kind of a beneficial parasite—i.e., a nonobligate symbiont—that confers some selective advantage onto its human host without whom it cannot survive.'

[12] Deacon also claims that this mechanism explains how a Creole language with a well-developed grammar can arise so quickly from a grammarless pidgin language (Deacon 1997, p. 139).

language structures can be innate. The kind of universal grammar advocated by Chomsky does not belong to the kind of structures that would be favoured by natural selection. It is therefore highly incredible that grammatical rules are innate (if there are any rules in our heads at all).

"Grammar is complicated," Egon says. "Can't you do without it completely?"

"Yes, I have described how you can communicate pretty well using a protolanguage."

The question remains, however: what is the evolutionary explanation for the fact that all human languages contain elements that do not directly carry meaning, but help to structure language? Why is protolanguage insufficient? The psychologist Charles Snowdon who in a survey of animals' linguistic capacities presents a clue: 'Bonobos and chimpanzees seem to be more limited in the topics that they find interesting to communicate about.'[xix] In my opinion, this derives from a fundamental difference between humans and other apes: Our inner worlds are much richer and more complex than those of apes. We have many more 'meanings' to communicate—our dream castles have more towers and pinnacles. Earlier in this book, I have highlighted the factors that constitute the background to humans' complex inner world.

The anthropologist Thomas Schoenemann has also argued that grammatical structure arises from the need to communicate a complex semantics.[xx] As Gregorian beings we must supply the symbols of language with a syntactic order to make the exchange of inner worlds more efficient. Schoenemann shows that many common grammatical constructions can be explained as deriving from such a need. Since grammar partitions language into *phrases* it becomes easier to understand which words go together and thereby one can more quickly understand a spoken utterance.

One great communicative advantage is that syntactic markers make the message less *ambiguous*. If a two-year-old comes home from kindergarten and tells 'not eat fish', we do not know whether the child has not eaten the fish (or did not want to eat it) or it is the fish in the aquarium that did not eat the candy offered by the child. To understand the two-year-old's utterance, we must put it in a *context*—words alone are not sufficient. Grammatical markers result in a language that is much more *independent* of the context. In this way language itself carries more of its meaning. In other words, grammar leads to more detached linguistic constructions (once again confirming the general trend in the evolution of thinking). A special case is that grammar makes language more independent of the *present*, since, for example with the use of tenses, we can more easily mark whether we speak about the past, the present, or the (hypothetical) future.

Savage-Rumbaugh and Rumbaugh accentuate the evolutionary need for communication that is independent of context:

> It will also be argued that syntax, rather than being biologically predetermined, is a skill which arises naturally from the need to process sequences of words rapidly. As overall intelligence increased, spurred by the ever-increasing use of language for planning future activities, communications became increasingly complex and increasingly independent of context. When complex ideas began to require groups of words for their expression, it became essential to devise a means to specify which of the words in a group modified (or were related to) which other words. Syntactical rules were developed to solve this dilemma. Such rules were the inevitable outgrowth of complex symbolic communication involving multiple symbols.[xxi]

Vygotsky's thesis that the primary role of language is emotional and social, rather than purely informative, is supported by Dunbar's gossip theory that builds on a different empirical foundation. And the thesis that speech and thought develop independently is supported by the fact that Genie never reached full command of language although her thinking and general intelligence were normal. Her linguistic development was hampered during a critical period and could never be regained. Barber and Peters write, fully in line with Vygotsky: 'It therefore looks as though the acquisition of the *meaningful* parts of language (vocabulary and semantics) are dependent on Cognition, whereas development of the *grammatical system* of Language is relatively independent of it.'[xxii]

A second explanation of the emergence of grammar, which probably cannot be totally separated from the first, is that along with hominids' societies becoming more multifarious, the more there was to gain from *quick and efficient communication*. A system that is constructed from symbols can be built up in a more *systematic* fashion than a purely iconic system. Words can be reused as recycled parts in a regularly constructed pattern. Even if single icons are easier to learn than arbitrary symbols, it is simpler to create *new combinations* in a regular symbolic system.[13]

"What did the first language look like, then?" Egon asks.

---

[13] Compare Barber and Peters (1992), p. 311. Ellegård (1979), p. 143, also says that standardized word order 'can be regarded as an emanation of the same economy principle of the brain that leads to the double articulation: the tendency to create building blocks (word classes and phrases) to construct an otherwise messy and intractable variety of different wholes (sentences).'

For many linguists it has been an axiom that there has been an *Ursprache*, an original language that all other languages have developed out from. But Ellegård opposes such an original language:

> There is no reason to believe that there ever existed any uniformity in these respects within the budding humanity. Just as little should one believe that the vocabulary was ever common to everybody. A common original language is as incredible a hypothesis as the view that humanity descends from a single pair. Already the spread of Australopithecus over the entire African continent and that of Homo erectus over the entire Old World makes such an assumption unreasonable. To be sure, language evolved in a similar way over the whole area, simply because the conditions for its emergence were similar.[xxiii]

Some researchers, though, claim, with support from genetic analyses, that *Homo sapiens* descends from a very small population, even if it did not consist of only Adam and Eve. But even if this were true, language transforms so rapidly that it would be meaningless to try to trace an original language. New Creole languages that have been created do indeed show similarities with the languages they originate from, but they also have many unique features. Even though we see a rapid death of many languages in the world, *totally new* languages still come into existence. For example, the deaf population in Nicaragua has only since the 1970s been given the opportunity to go to schools suited for their handicap. Within this population a sign language has rapidly evolved, including a complete grammatical structure that does not show any direct relationship with any other spoken or signed language.

7.9 Myths and narratives

> Language is like a cracked kettle on which we beat out tunes for bears to dance to, while all the while we long to move the stars to pity.
>
> Gustave Flaubert: *Madame Bovary*

Donald argues that one of the most important uses of language was to express *myths*. Myths exist in all cultures and they have been more important in earlier stages than they are for modern humans. He writes that 'language is not about inventing words. It is about telling stories in a group. *Languages are invented on the level of narrative, by collectivities of conscious intellects.*'[xxiv]

In my understanding, the function of myths is to serve as carriers of *common knowledge*. They provide an excellent method for preserving the painfully acquired knowledge of others. Myths, sagas, and fairy tales have been important carriers of culture. They have also contained much of the knowledge accumulated by a society. Ellegård expresses the thought as follows:

> What advantages were brought by such a narrative language for our hunting flocks? I have already spoken of the greater precision that is achieved when conventional rules can express relations that earlier were left to be read from the context or from pantomime. The precision makes the linguistic story as efficient a ground for action as direct experience. The narrative ability hence means that the groups who master it can base their actions on a much wider experience than others.[xxv]

Being able to *narrate* involves more than knowing a language. Narration presumes a memory with a conception of time and causation that makes it possible to *order* the elements into a coherent story. The key phrase of a story is 'and then...'. Children with autism, even those with good linguistic competence, have difficulties in narrating in a normal way and Kanzi cannot do it either. Hence, the ability to narrate involves yet another step in the evolution of language. And myths require the narrative form. It is difficult to know which forms of narration arose first. It is possible that miming and dance have been used for certain narrative functions before spoken language emerged.

One problem concerning the economy of thinking is that before the existence of external media all knowledge and all myths must be kept in the head. Our limited memory demands that our thoughts have a special structure. The media researcher Walter Ong writes:

> You know what you can recall.... How could you ever call back to mind what you had so laboriously worked out? The only answer is: Think memorable thoughts. In a primary oral culture, to solve efficiently the problem of retaining and retrieving carefully articulated thought, you have to do your thinking in mnemonic patterns, shaped for ready oral recurrence.... Hence the mind must move ahead more slowly, keeping close to the focus of attention much of what it has already dealt with. Redundancy, repetition of the just-said, keeps both speaker and hearer surely on the track.[xxvi]

Knowledge is valuable and it is needed so that we can choose the right actions. As Ong demonstrates, the knowledge that has been arduously acquired in a society needs great care to guarantee that it can be transferred.

Myths make us even more advanced Gregorian beings. Their narrative form makes them easy to remember, which enhances their transferability. Myths often present fictive worlds, inhabited by gods and fictional beings.

"You humans seem to have a predilection for unreal worlds above the reality you live in," Egon sneers.

"That's true, but it doesn't matter much whether the myths directly correspond to anything in the real world as long as they transmit an experience that can be used for real."

Myths are also tools for transmitting knowledge about *causal relations* to new generations. The fictive, often magical worlds contain elements that provide explanations for weather, solar eclipses, illness, hunting luck, etc. In light of the interrogation lamps of modern science, many of these explanations seem obviously incorrect. But they may have been sufficiently successful and easy to learn to function under more primitive circumstances, and thereby they may have survived for countless generations.

Myths also contain elements that explain the moral rules of a culture. One finds out *why* one should behave in a certain way. The myths thereby give power to the moral rules.[xxvii] He who controls the myths thereby has strong steering power in relation to the rest of the group. Donald notes that a conquering culture always imposes its myths on the defeated culture.[xxviii] And the defeated culture resists the thought invasion as long as possible, since you lose a great part of your identity if you lose your myths.

7.10 Language in the brain

> This strange brain ... where language constantly is prosecuted.
>
> Paul Valéry

In modern brain research the language acquisition device that Chomsky postulates cannot be found. Instead it seems that the language ability is tightly woven together with the other functions of the brain—linguistic competencies are spread over large parts of the brain. It builds on older cognitive functions, above all the capacity to plan and execute *sequences* of actions—a capacity that is also tapped in other domains such as tool making and miming.

If the brain is viewed from an evolutionary perspective, it also becomes difficult to explain why there should be a special unit for language. It is normally supposed that the evolution of an organ proceeds in small steps. It therefore seems unreasonable that a language centre that is separated from the rest of the brain should emerge.

"But must not the brain be rebuilt to handle grammar as it becomes more complicated?" Egon pursues.

It is difficult to find any unequivocal areas of the brain where language governs, since the functions of the brain are extremely *plastic*, in particular during the first years of our lives. If a certain part of the brain is damaged, the chances

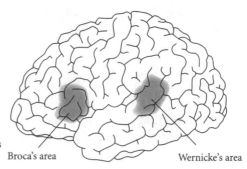

Figure 7.2 The locations of Broca's and Wernicke's areas.

Broca's area

Wernicke's area

are good that another part can take over its function. For example, with a child that has an accident or illness destroying the language centres in the left hemisphere, the right hemisphere can learn to take over the language functions. There are also considerable individual variations in how different areas of the brain are used.

Most clearly, the language faculties are linked to *Wernicke's area* in the temporal lobe of the cortex, where the analysis of the language sounds takes place, and to *Broca's area* in the lower back part of the frontal lobe where the production of spoken language is controlled. Both these areas are normally located in the left hemisphere, but there are exceptions (for example in a minority of left-handers). Wernicke's area can be regarded as an outgrowth of the auditory cortex. Its function is to separate out the different language sounds, the *phonemes*, from the sound stream that reaches the ear. Damage to Wernicke's area causes problems in understanding speech. But the ability to read sometimes remains even after such an injury.

There is a strong connection between the ability to perform complicated movement patterns, above all hand movements, and the language capacity. The connection does not only hold for speech—deaf people also lose the ability to use sign language after injuries in the left hemisphere.

Tool making presumes that one can perform a *series* of hand movements. This competency preceded spoken language in the evolution of humans.[xxix] From a neurological point of view, the left hemisphere normally controls the construction of the sequences. In order to create a new tool, already known sequences of actions must be combined in a new manner. The so-called *motor theory* of language claims that when the hominids eventually had learnt to use symbols, the practical ability to combine hand movements was exploited to produce sequences of symbols: First short sequences—two-word sentences—and then gradually longer sequences with special effects in the form of grammatical markers. Apes only have a rudimentary ability to create sequences, something that may explain why they never pass beyond protolanguage.[xxx] In accordance with the view that language is a benign virus, the cognitive scientist Elizabeth Bates has suggested that language is a 'parasitic' system that has been super-imposed on areas in the brain that originally were developed for more basic motor tasks.[xxxi] From this perspective it is no wonder that language and ges-turing run so closely together—language 'leaks' into the motor functions.

"Ha! Speech is an incontinent form of communication," Egon mocks. "No wonder one finds so many comparisons between speech and lower bodily functions."

"You drivel rather well yourself," I moan. "May I continue?"

Playing involves combining sequences of known elements into new combi-nations of actions with objects that are often used symbolically.[xxxii] Piaget has emphasized that play and imitation are inevitable for the development of the capacity to manage symbols.

In support of the motor theory it can be noted that from the beginning the part corresponding to Broca's area in the brain of an infant is used both for manipulating objects and for controlling language. At the end of the second year, the area is split into two parts where only the lower is specialized for advanced language functions.[xxxiii] The psychologist Micael Corballis writes that 'brain-imaging studies strongly suggest that Broca's area still plays a role in integrating hand movements with vision, a role that in humans has become confined to the left side of the brain but that has nothing to do with vocal language.'[xxxiv]

Also the right hemisphere has certain roles for language. Among other things, it governs the *intonation* in speech. Persons who as a result of a stroke or for other reasons have injuries in the regions of the right hemispheres that corres-pond to the language regions on the left side produce a droning form of speech.

There are some anatomical differences between the two hemispheres. *Planum temporale* at the upper rim of the temporal lobe, where Wernicke's area is located, is normally much larger on the left side. One explanation for this is that the two hemispheres develop for different periods of time and are assigned different tasks. The right side specializes on visual and spatial functions. The left grows for a longer period during a stage that is critical for language learning. If a child, for some, reason, does not receive any linguistic practice during this period it will never learn a complete grammar, but instead speak something that resembles protolanguage.

In humans the left hemisphere is larger than the right, which presumably results from the language mechanisms being placed there. Interestingly enough a certain hemispheric asymmetry is found already in *Homo habilis*. As Deacon points out, the specialization of the hemispheres should be seen as a *result* of the co-evolution of language and brain and not as a cause of it.[xxxv]

7.11   Where are the meanings of words?

Wernicke's and Broca's areas can be said to handle the input and output of language. But language is not just to be heard and spoken—it must also be *understood*. It turns out that many different parts of the brain are involved in the understanding of word and sentences.

The grammatical and the semantic constituents of language are handled at different locations in the brain. Grammatical parts are primarily generated in the frontal lobes. Injuries in Broca's area result in a kind of *aphasia* so that one can no longer produce grammatical sentences. But one can still *decide* whether sentences that are heard or read are grammatically correct. One consequence of this is that it is not possible to posit a set of 'grammatical rules' in Broca's area (and as I have argued it is not likely that the brain contains any system of rules anywhere).

When it comes to semantic words the picture is still muddled, but here it seems that the parietal and temporal lobes, i.e. the rearward parts of the cortex, are important. When you understand an expression, you create an 'image' of the meaning. One hypothesis is that such an understanding actually involves the same kind of process that occurs in the brain when you interpret a real picture.[14]

In the lower part of the parietal lobe, information from vision, hearing, and touch merges. This part of the human brain is much larger than in related species, and it is probably necessary for the formation of abstract concepts. It also has strong connections to Wernicke's area. Damage to the parietal lobe results in problems understanding nouns and adjectives. For example, the meanings of colour words are managed in a rather dedicated part of the visual association cortex. Injury to this region makes it impossible for a person to speak about colours of objects.

Following Chomsky, many linguists have seen language as an independent cognitive module. But psychologists who do research on learning have long

---

[14] In Gärdenfors (1999) I give an outline of so-called cognitive semantics, where one of the basic tenets is that the meanings of words are represented in the brain as 'image schemas'. Also see Damasio and Damasio (1992) for a clear description of how linguistic meanings are handled in the brain.

considered that language is a development of previous cognitive abilities. As I have tried to show, this idea also receives support from modern neuroscience.

As an example of results that support the idea, the neurobiologist Doreen Kimura shows that in clinical cases, aphasia (loss of language function) is often related to apraxia (loss of intentional movements). Such losses are sometimes caused by strokes in the association cortex of the left hemisphere.[xxxvi] As I have described, this hemisphere is dominant when it comes to the production of series of actions—motor actions as well as linguistic actions (which are a special case of motor actions).

Even in deaf persons who develop problems in signing with their hands, the cause can be traced to the speech areas on the left side. As I have argued earlier, signing and miming have presumably developed from a form of iconic communication before symbolic spoken language became possible. I have also introduced Donald's thesis that it was the capacity of miming that gave *Homo erectus* a communicative advantage in relation to earlier hominids. Kimura concludes that the left hemisphere 'is particularly well adapted, not for symbolic function *per se*, but for the execution of some categories of motor activity which happened to lend themselves readily to communication.'[xxxvii] In brief, language cannot be separated from other cognitive functions.

Notes

i. See, e.g. Bickerton (1990), Donald (1991), Deacon (1992), and Lieberman (1992).
ii. Deacon (1997), pp. 247–9.
iii. Bergman (1977).
iv. Walker and Shipman (1996).
v. Deacon (1997), p. 251.
vi. Jeannerod (1994).
vii. Dennett (1991).
viii. Chafe (1995).
ix. This section is based on Brinck and Gärdenfors (2001).
x. Deacon (1997), pp. 399–407.
xi. Vygotsky (1976), p. 81.
xii. Fernald (1992).
xiii. Donald (2001), p. 230.
xiv. Trevarthen (1992).
xv. Bickerton (1990), p. 114.
xvi. Bickerton (1990), pp. 114–18.
xvii. Bickerton (1990), pp. 121–2.
xviii. Bickerton (1990), p. 122.
xix. Snowdon (1990), p. 222.

xx. Schoenemann (1999).

xxi. Savage-Rumbaugh and Rumbaugh (1993), pp. 86–7.

xxii. Barber and Peters (1992), p. 328.

xxiii. Ellegård (1979), pp. 143–4.

xxiv. Donald (2001), p. 292.

xxv. Ellegård (1979), p. 144.

xxvi. Ong (1982). The quotation fragments are from pp. 33–40.

xxvii. Chase (1999), p. 40.

xxviii. Donald (1991), p. 258.

xxix. Corballis (1989). See also Allott (1991) and Tomasello (1991).

xxx. See also Barber and Peters (1992), p. 174, and Donald (1991), pp. 70–5.

xxxi. See Corballis (1999), pp. 144–5.

xxxii. Vauclair and Vidal (1994).

xxxiii. Mueller (1996), p. 620.

xxxiv. Corballis (2002), p. 48.

xxxv. Deacon (1997), pp. 309–11.

xxxvi. Kimura (1976).

xxxvii. Kimura (1976).

CHAPTER 8

Externalizing the inner world

> One must be indulgent towards Man
> —think of the era during which he was created.
>
> Alphonse Allais

Many animal species live in complex social groups, but it is only humans who live in cultures. The hominids, and in particular *Homo sapiens*, have undergone an enormous development in an evolutionarily very short time. Such a development would not be possible without cultural transfer of knowledge. Tomasello and Call write:

> In attempting to characterize human cognition as a special case of primate cognition, therefore, the challenge is to find a small difference that made a big difference—a small change, or set of changes, that transformed the process in fundamental ways. In our view, the only possible candidate for such an adaptation, or set of adaptations, is one that changed cognition from a basically individual enterprise to a basically social-collective enterprise. Human cognition is what it is because human beings are adapted for cultural life and all that entails.[1]

Handing down culture between generations results in a particular type of evolutionary process that saves the individuals great efforts and many risks. Gregorian individuals can piggyback on the collected experiences of their parents and their ancestors.

Homo sapiens has also spread over much larger parts of the surface of the planet than any other primate. To succeed with this, we must manage exploiting a great variety of foodstuffs. These we collect from enormously varying environments, from the !Kung San people's desert life in southern Africa, to life-long vegetarianism in India, to the Inuits who live almost exclusively on seal meat. This flexibility in diet puts high demands on the *abilities to learn*.

---

[1] Tomasello and Call (1997), p. 401.

The growing generation must learn what can be eaten, where food can be found, and how it is to be prepared. Knowledge about tools and techniques for obtaining food and its preparation becomes a fundamental part of culture that each new generation must acquire.

The most important factor, though, is that *Homo sapiens* is alone in having a language that is an immensely powerful tool for cultural transfer. Via linguistic communication, vast possibilities open up for us as Gregorian beings to take part in the lives of others. In this sense language opens up new worlds.

However, humans have developed yet another fundamental technique for transmitting experience between individuals, namely to place knowledge in the *external* world with the aid of different media. This final chapter is about what an evolutionary perspective on thinking implies for modern humans and their relationship to externalized knowledge.

A detailed account of cultural and technical development falls outside the covers of this book. Hence this chapter will be rather rhapsodic. The emphasis will be on how the evolution of external media, above all writing, has effected the cognitive powers of humans. I shall show that the detachment of different kinds of representations continues. We have come so far that the representations are unloaded from the brain and placed in the world. In the last step on the evolutionary ladder, thinking to some extent leaves the humans themselves. This simplifies the task of the evolutionary detective, since the traces become easier to follow.

8.1   External memories

The boundary between inner and outer world is not sharp. Already when we are sharing memories with others via language and myths we locate our inner worlds outside ourselves—in the inner worlds of *others*. Another possibility to transfer knowledge between the inner worlds is to utilize the external world to create representations of one's inner world. The author Kristian Petri writes about how the Penan people on Borneo give names to the jungle:

> A turn of the river can carry the name of a special person or an event that took place a long time ago. Trees, rivers, stones: the entire jungle is an immense cultural landscape, invisible for others than the initiated. The jungle is the history of the Penans, their living memory that speaks of events and social relations. So when a person travels through the jungle he revives the landscape, creates it anew by naming it. The jungle is the memory of an entire people, a way of memorizing. This is one of the great tragedies involved in the felling. It is not only the possibilities for the Penans to obtain food and fuel

that is torn away, but their complete history that is not written down since it consists of the trees, the stones, the rivers, and the water falls.

If one is punctilious, one can say that the Penans do not create the landscape but rather their *memories* when they are moving through it—the trees are just keys to the memories.

We have now come to Donald's third transition to modern man that, according to him, occurred about 50 000 years ago. Then humans began *storing* symbols from the inner world in the external world and not just in their own and others' heads. (The Penans in Petri's text only *name* the world.)

This development can be seen as yet another step on Dennett's ladder (after the four he allows for: Darwinian, Skinnerian, Popperian, and Gregorian). Let us call those who can locate their knowledge in the external world *Donaldian beings*. The important novelty is that the use of external memories means that *representations are detached from human minds*.

It is not clear what was the earliest way of storing knowledge in the external world. The oldest find of anything that could be a *sculpture* comes from Berekhat Ram in Israel. The figure has been dated as being more than 100 000 years old, but archaeologists dispute the extent to which the figure actually is made to be depicting.

Another form is pictures that we find for example in cave paintings, rock carvings, and ceramic patterns. Such objects presume that one can create rich inner representations of the pictures *before* they are placed in the outer world. For example, the 15 000-year-old animal images in the paintings in the cave of Lascaux must have been painted without having any model available. A third early form of external storage is *calendars* of different kinds that have been important for keeping track of seasons and when the rites connected to them should be performed. Some of the early inscriptions on bones have been interpreted as such calendars.

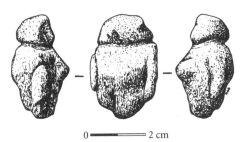

0 ⟺ 2 cm

Figure 8.1 The figure from Berekhat Ram from three angles.

Unfortunately, many of the early forms of external memories have not been preserved for posterity. One example of what was important as a tool for transferring culture comes from the Walbiri people in Western Australia. They use drawings in the sand as a kind of running notation while they are telling their myths.[i] Some graphical elements, for example circles and lines, function as symbolic elements, but most of the drawings are iconic representations. These drawings can be seen as an extension of the miming capacity—not only the body but also the world, that is the sand surface, is used during the narration. We still use similar narrative tools, for example when we describe the road to somebody. The linguistic road description is supplemented with a sketch on a piece of paper where the most important landmarks are represented, often in a very schematic manner.

The Donaldian beings' ability to create and use external memories does not directly correspond to any physiological alteration of the human brain. We have discovered how to develop new memory systems faster than evolution can change our brains.[2] Still the outer memories influence our way of thinking. They support certain talents, above all literacy, but also abstract thinking. The plasticity of the human brain makes it possible to practice such abilities. It is probably an increased specialization of the two brain hemispheres that makes it so easy for modern humans to manage information that is stored in external media. The talent to deal with external memories can have developed at the cost of oral talents and visualization. It is possible that culture in the long run will affect natural selection and thereby slowly change the organization of our brains.

"I remember what I want to remember," Egon says obstinately. "If I have forgotten something, it was not worth remembering."

Locating our thoughts in external media not only aids communication, but is also a tool for the single individual. The human memory capacity acquires a new role with the development of external memories. One can use words and pictures to *ease the load on* thinking. External media can, above all, be used to support one's memory—short-term as well as long-term. In a culture without external media, high demands are placed on the individuals' memories. The limitation of working memory means that a culture without a written language must use special tricks to remember knowledge. In such a culture certain memory experts develop: bards, storytellers, shamans, etc.

---

[2] External memories can possibly be counted as a fourth level of memory system following after Tulving's partitioning into procedural, semantic, and episodic memory.

For example, there is an account of how a tribe of Australian aboriginals survived a long period of extreme draught. One of the elders in the tribe lead them for half a year, without the support of maps or anything similar, through a series of more than 50 waterholes over a distance of more than 600 kilometres, even though he had only visited a few of these waterholes and then decades ago. He had learnt where they were located through the song cycles that together with totemic dance rituals constitute the aboriginals' myths of the 'animal ancestors'. Bruce Chatwin tells about these memory traditions in a romanticized form in his book *The songlines.*

Plato already exhibits a divided opinion as regards the role of written language as a support for memory. On the one hand, it is by writing down the dialogues that his philosophical doctrine becomes the first one that is fully preserved to posterity. On the other hand, he considers that writing *impoverishes* memory. In the dialogue *Phaidros* he lets Socrates say:

> He would be a very simple person, and quite a stranger to the oracles of Thamus or Ammon, who should leave in writing or receive in writing any art under the idea that the written word would be intelligible or certain; or who deemed that writing was at all better than knowledge and recollection of the same matters?

In societies with external memories, the old memory experts disappear and the importance of myths diminishes. The reason is that working memory can do with taking in the external information piece by piece. The brain can then wander through 'information space' in the same way as it, housed in a body, wanders through real space. When we read, the thoughts are 'played' by the text of the book in roughly the way music is played by a tape recorder. In a sense, our thoughts are made to resonate with the text. In education, pieces learnt by heart will therefore play ever lesser roles. What we in the modern world call education actually mainly involves learning to handle the external memory systems.

During modern times we have seen an enormously rapid development of new types of external memories in the form of books, photos, records, computers, etc. In societies with external memories, memory experts are no longer needed. Instead we use encyclopaedias or the Internet. Andy Clark formulates it elegantly: 'Our brains make the world smart so that we can be dumb in peace!'[ii] Impregnating our environment with meaningful knowledge reduces the burden on internal memory.

Given the abundance of information stored on external media that exists in the modern world, it has become more and more important to be able to *find* knowledge than to have it available in one's head. School and working life reward those who can quickly browse different information channels. Perhaps there is an evolutionary pressure towards a new species: *Homo zappiens.*

Present day human thinking has become strongly dependent on outer media. Philosopher Bo Dahlbom and computer scientist Lars-Erik Janlert write that just as you cannot do very much carpentry with your bare hands, there is not much thinking you can do with your bare brain.[iii] Just as our society would break down if our machines stopped working, our thinking would practically disappear if our intellectual tools were not available. We would not be able to reflect if we did not have words, books, pictures, computers, algebra, legal systems, etc. It can even be said that there is no sharp border between the thinking human and the 'thinking' world. Consciousness leaks out into the world.

As Dennett points out, this effect may explain why old people often seem bewildered when they are moved to a hospital, even though no physical change occurs to them.[iv] When inner memory is blunted with age, a lot of old peoples' thinking becomes dependent on signals from their home environment that help them solve everyday problems—the clothes hang where they have always hung in the wardrobe, the coffee tin is at its right place, etc. When the old are moved to an unfamiliar environment, they lose their habits. They lose their external memory and are thereby in practice cut off from a part of their consciousness. They are struck by the same kind of memory loss as when the Penans' forests are felled.

The constitution of our bodies is partly influenced by the artefacts we create. In cultures where you sit on chairs your leg muscles will have different lengths than in those where you squat. Chair people cannot squat more than a short while and squatters find chairs uncomfortable. In analogy with this it can be asked to what extent the constitution of our thinking is affected by the artefacts we use. Can we with our Western thought muscles understand how you think squatting?

"Or how you think climbing," Egon puts in.

8.2   The development of writing

The conditions for myths and other stories change when the external world can be exploited to transmit knowledge. The first stories to be placed outside the heads of people are based on *pictures* representing focal moments in the story. The picture medium is purely visual and static. But it is perfectly possible to use pictures to tell stories; for example a hunting story can be drawn as a series of pictures. Such a series can also function as a support for memory in an oral tradition. A historically later example is tapestries that tell about warfare or religiously important events. A characteristic feature of pictures and other later external media is that the audience need not (or should not even) be *present* when the story is created.[3]

It is mainly through *writing* that stories located on external media have led to thorough changes for us.[4] Modern writing is visual, but symbolic rather than depicting, and, in the same way as a picture, static. In contrast, speech is auditory and dynamic.

The development of writing is a fascinating story. Three stages can be discerned: from picture to ideographic icons and then to alphabet. A first step in the development of writing can have been that a picture was replaced by a *sequence* of pictures that correspond to the different stages in a story or a myth. The Lascaux cave in France is one of the most famous places for early painting. There one finds some complex paintings that can possibly be interpreted as descriptions of hunts or myths.

Cuneiform, which was the first form of writing, did not originally have any narrative functions but was used for *accounting* in trading. But most of the cuneiform signs have an iconic origin that eventually becomes stylized. For example, oxen were first drawn as complete figures, but were later reduced to a simplified ox head. In addition to purely figurative signs, symbols for numbers were added. These were among the first purely *symbolic* external representations.

Learning to read and write cuneiform is analogous to learning a *new* language.[v] The signs (that become more and more arbitrary) represent meanings that only exist in the inner world. The link between a sign and its meaning must be learned in the same way as you learn a word in a foreign language.

Another early written language, the hieroglyphs, also began as standardized pictures of things. It was an ideographic representation. In contrast to cuneiform, hieroglyphs could be used to express all kinds of linguistic messages including narrations. Soon hieroglyphs also came to include representations for *phonetic* elements, above all syllables. Sometimes this took the form of a *rebus* so that the sign standing for a word that is pronounced in a particular way is also used for some other content that corresponds to a word with the same pronunciation (compare 4U: 'for you'). Such combinations of ideographic elements with phonetic rebuses are still in use in Chinese writing.

---

[3]   Ong (1982), p. 100, writes: 'Writing is a solipsistic operation. I am writing a book which I hope will be read by hundreds of thousands of people, so I must be isolated from everyone.'

[4]   Ong (1982), p. 77, says: 'More than any other single invention, writing has transformed human consciousness.'

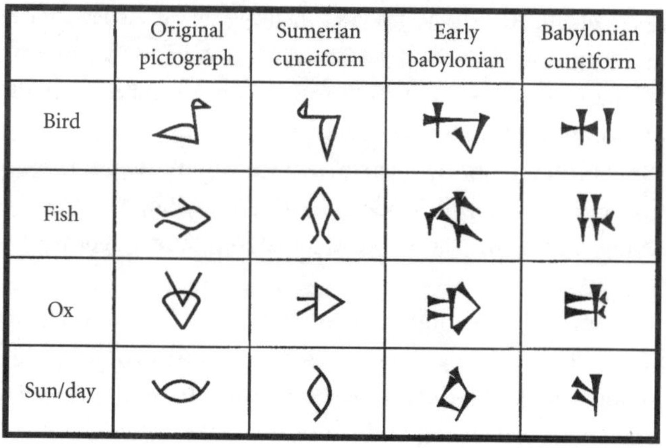

	Original pictograph	Sumerian cuneiform	Early babylonian	Babylonian cuneiform
Bird				
Fish				
Ox				
Sun/day				

Figure 8.2 The development of cuneiform from picture to stylized signs.

The last stage of writing is the transition to a *phonetic* representation. With time, cuneiform developed into a representation where each sign stood for a syllable. It is difficult to say when the first purely phonetic alphabet arises where every sign represents a language sound—the transition from iconic representation has been gradual. Learning to read and write using a phonetic alphabet is, in contrast to earlier forms of writing, not the same as learning a new language, but learning a new *code* for the language you already know. The first Phoenician alphabet contained 22 consonants, but no vowels (it is mainly the consonants that determine the meaning of a word in Semitic languages). The Greeks later added vowels since they carry meaning in Greek and they were thereby needed to reduce the number of ambiguities.

8.3   The influence of writing on thought

To locate thoughts *outside* your head by writing them down means that the fleeting thoughts are locked up in the external medium. A West African prince describes his first meeting with the written word in the following way:

> The one crowded space in Father Perry's house was his bookshelves. I gradually came to understand that the marks on the pages were *trapped words*. Anyone could learn to decipher the symbols and turn the trapped words loose again into speech. The ink of the print trapped the thoughts; they could no more get away than a *doomboo* could get out of a pit.[vi]

The signs place our thoughts in the world. Memory is relieved since we need not keep the formulations in our heads: we can recall them by reading the text. Writing also increases the possibilities to coordinate our actions.

A language normally appears in many dialects. When a phonological representation for a language is selected, the dialect to be represented must be chosen. An alphabetic writing, a 'grapholect', will thereby function as a *norm* for the spoken language. As a consequence, the differences between the dialects in different villages or tribes are toned down and are replaced by the phonetic norm of the written language. Because of this, it is only when it becomes possible to spread texts in a large number of copies that *national languages* emerge. Previously there have only been more or less discernable regional dialects. This is a clear example of the political importance of writing.

The same mechanism does not work for ideographic written languages. Chinese dialects are so different over all that it would have been difficult to introduce a uniform phonetic alphabet for them, but since the words are represented as ideas and not as sounds, all Chinese can understand the same writing.

Ong points out that writing results in a larger vocabulary:

> Literate users of a grapholect such as standard English have access to
> vocabularies hundreds of times larger than any oral language can manage.
> In such a linguistic world dictionaries are essential.[5]

Spoken language is tied to a certain context and is expressed with intonation and facial expressions that can be much more charged than the 'literal' message. All this is lost when language is fixed to a sheet of paper. Marshall McLuhan reminds us that until the Middle Ages reading was tantamount to reading aloud—the written text was transformed into an oral performance. It is only later that reading becomes *silent*. Thereby the mouth is decoupled from the reading process. Reading becomes something that occurs in the inner world.

It is not until we acquire an alphabetic writing that we become *aware* of the phonetic structure of language and its grammatical construction. It is writing that makes it possible to reflect on the structure of language rather than the other way around.[vii] The psychologist David Olson writes: 'Ironically, learning to read is learning to hear speech in a new way.'[viii] Writing means a new kind of detachment of language from humans themselves.

Similar patterns can be found in children's language development. Children do not learn the meaning of 'letter', 'word', and 'sentence' until they learn to read. The linguists Lisbeth Hedelin and Erland Hjelmqvist tested whether children remember verbatim what is said or just the content of the utterance.[ix]

---

[5] Ong (1982), p. 14. On p. 31 he writes: 'Try to imagine a culture where no one has ever "looked up" anything. In a primary oral culture, the expression "to look up something" is an empty phrase'.

The experiment revealed that only at the age of six could children clearly distinguish between a verbatim repetition and a paraphrase.

Olson summarizes:

> What literacy contributes to thought is that it turns the thoughts themselves into worthy subjects of contemplation.... [W]riting and reading played a critical role in producing the shift from thinking about things to thinking about representations of those things, that is, thinking about thought. Our modern conception of the world and our modern conception of ourselves are, we may say, by-products of the invention of a world on paper.[6]

One cause of this new awareness is that the thoughts that are expressed in writing are detached from their *context*. Ong writes:

> Once print has been fairly well interiorized, a book was sensed as a kind of object which 'contained' information, scientific, fictional, or other, rather than, as earlier, a recorded utterance.[x]

Before the Middle Ages writing only functioned as a *support* for memory— it was never a *replacement* for memory. The content of what was treated existed in the mind and not in the text. The idea that written language carries an *autonomous meaning* that is independent of the author and the reader is established first in the Middle Ages—that is when writing is assigned a *literal* meaning, which does not change with a change in context.

Olson demonstrates that the idea that writing is just a transcription of speech is a myth. There are essential differences between the structure of written and spoken language. Grammatical markers become important for the unambiguousness of writing. For example, written language uses more words than speech in the narration of a story.

At the outset, writing does not itself show how it should be *taken*. Olson argues that written language must *compensate* with different means for the part of the spoken message that is imparted by intonation, rhythm, facial expressions, and body language.[xi] Writing must also recreate the context that surrounds an oral performance. The reader of a text must supply it with a meaning. For example, he demonstrates that linguistic markers for speech acts such as 'claim', 'doubt', 'deny', 'confirm', and 'interpret' are introduced in writing first during the Middle Ages or even later. Such markers are not needed in

---

[6] Olson (1994). The quotes are from p. 277 and p. 282. Ong (1982), p. 24, notes similarly: 'The new way to store knowledge was not in mnemonic formulas but in written text. This freed the mind for more original, more abstract thought.' This will be shown, for example, by how the Greeks developed geometry and other sciences, as I shall discuss in the following section.

an oral tradition where sentence melody and other expressive forms make it clear which kind of speech act is performed.

When written language was developed about 5000 years ago it was primarily used for book keeping in business and in juridical contexts. It took time before writing was used to take down oral stories, and then it was only used as a support for oral narration. It is only in connection with the printed book that writing develops its own narrative forms, with the novel as the prime example. Ong writes:

> [A]n oral culture has no experience of a lengthy, epic-size or novel-size climactic linear plot. It cannot organize even shorter narrative in the studious relentless climactic way that readers of literature for the past 200 years have learned more and more to expect—and, in recent decades, self-consciously to depreciate.[xii]

In connection with the art of printing there is also an upturn in the use of maps, diagrams, schemas, and similar visual representations.[xiii] Such representations influence our way of viewing the world. Olson writes: 'Cook's voyages are, therefore, not to be seen simply as putting the world on paper but of exploring the world *from the map's point of view*.'[xiv] As we shall see in the following section, external representations of these kinds are also important for the development of science.

8.4   Science: the world of theories

Humans are extremely skilled at finding *causal relations* in the world. A trivial example is that we learn that after lightning comes thunder. But we often learn the relations implicitly—as 'tacit' knowledge. We do not have any detached representations of them. The question is how such tacit knowledge best can be transferred to other Gregorian and Donaldian beings. As mentioned before, some of the tacit knowledge shows up in myth, religion, and morality. For example the rule that pork is 'unclean' in Jewish and Muslim religions derives from the fact that pork often contained trichinae that made people sick.

Many of the causal connections concern the changing seasons. Arduously acquired knowledge about the seasonal variations of food becomes much easier to transmit if one can keep track of the seasons. Humans have no senses for such long time spans, so we need tools for this. Different kinds of calendars are found among the earliest external representations. In a similar vein, knowledge about astronomy is important for the agricultural cycles. Astronomy also makes possible more advanced forms of navigation. It is important to note that calendars as well as navigational tools *amplify* the capacity for anticipatory planning.

Some of the external representations are gigantic. Stonehenge in England, which is about 4000 years old, can be viewed as a giant device to enhance vision.[xv] The construction creates an abstract model of astronomical movements. The size of the machine makes it possible to read the different positions on the canopy of heavens with great precision. The astronomical observations made at Stonehenge cannot be made with a naked eye. This provides us with a first example of how *instruments* liberate humans from the imperfections of their senses. This is a general trend within science: the instruments that are developed within different disciplines result in objective observations that detach us from the limitations of our senses and enhance their sensitivity. Saying that observations are objective means that they are in principle available for everybody.

In ancient Greece one could for the first time avail oneself of several advanced systems of external symbols. The Greek alphabet was the first to include signs for vowels as well as consonants. They used numeral systems and geometric figures. Eventually, this led to the development of abstract geometry and mathematical *proofs*. A proof is a formal argument that is universally valid—it does not matter who produces it and when. It must be convincing in itself, detached from the linguistic form it happens to be dressed in. Humans have always been able to reason, but it is now they begin reasoning about reasoning. In connection with the development of geometry and mathematics, *abstract thinking* emerges—a kind of thinking that is amplified by being preserved with the aid of external symbolic representations.

Donald points out that it is the Greeks who first break with *mythical* thinking.[xvi] Hippocrates, the father of medicine, is for example the first to separate the art of medicine from religion. The Greeks can do this since they are the first to distinguish between mythical and non-mythical.[xvii] The main scientific contribution of the Greeks was not to discover new facts but to create a *theory of knowledge* where one can speak about 'argument', 'logic', and 'proof'. The separation of science from religion then continues in the rise of one discipline after the other. One of the latest steps in this divorce was when Darwin replaced the biblical creation story with the evolutionary process as an explanation of the origins of humans.

The Greeks also created scientific discussion, the 'disputation'. Instead of a proclaiming presentation such as in myths or religious dogmas, arguments and counter-arguments are now presented and one tries to *defend* a thesis. This results in a totally new attitude towards what knowledge is. It can be said that the scientific discussion brings in the 'you' in the judgement of what is knowledge. Not just the opinion of the single individual is counted when it is determined whether something is knowledge, but it is also required that it is reflected in the inner worlds of others. The method of discussion was then transferred to written language. A good example is Thomas Aquinas' *Summa Theologica*. The author begins by posing a question and then presents objections against answering the question in a particular way. Thomas then rebuts these objections and presents his own arguments for the answer to the question.

Until the Middle Ages, this discussing method is mainly used for philosophical and religious issues and when interpreting different holy or classical scriptures. But the method of critically discussing is eventually transferred to the budding science. Instead of asking questions concerning holy scriptures, the scientist asks Nature questions. Philosophers and scientists such as Francis Bacon, Galileo Galilei, and Robert Boyle write about studying the *Book of nature*. The 'you' that is argued against is no longer another individual but Nature herself. The logic of disputing is replaced by that of the *experimental* investigation. It is thought that Nature answers a loud 'no' or a feeble 'yes' to the question of the experiment. However, there are large similarities between the two strategies for seeking knowledge: For example, Olson points out that in the same way as theological exegetics distinguishes between literal and hidden meaning in the text, Galileo and Boyle distinguishes between 'facts' and 'hidden causes'.[xviii]

Olson demonstrates convincingly the crucial role *maps* and *diagrams* have had on the development of science. The world is put on paper. Ong writes:

> Only after print and the extensive experience with maps that print
> implemented would human beings, when they thought about the cosmos or
> universe or 'world', think primarily of something laid out before their eyes, as
> in a modern printed atlas, a vast surface or assemblage of surfaces ... ready to
> be 'explored'.[xix]

The influence of maps on thinking is an excellent example of how external representations can expand and alter our inner worlds.

As regards diagrams, Galileo, for example, describes his laws of motion with the aid of geometrical tools. Thereby the laws of motion can be presented as models on paper. Descartes' invention of *the system of coordinates* as a tool for representing mathematical functions has had a revolutionary influence within the sciences, above all as a tool in education. Exploiting external representations has become ever more dominant within science. Scientific education consists to a large extent in learning to handle different kinds of symbolic notations. Olson summarizes:

> The paper world, therefore, did not simply provide a means for accumulating and storing what everyone knew. Rather it was a matter of inventing the conceptual means for coordinating the bits of geographical, biological, mechanical, and other forms of knowledge acquired from many sources into an adequate and common frame of reference. This common frame of reference became the theoretical model into which local knowledge was inserted and reorganized.[xx]

Modern science provides us with theories that contain theoretical entities that bring out the 'hidden' causes of different phenomena. Newton's notion of *force* is a classic example. With the aid of the theoretical variables, we can make calculations of extremely different kinds. The calculation methods lead to the science of engineering that has come to replace the 'tacit' knowledge of craftsmen, where knowledge normally was not expressed in words or with the aid of external methods.

With the aid of theoretical models science has created new worlds for us—worlds that no longer need to be inside us, but are handled by different forms of symbol systems in external media. During the last few decades we have obtained a powerful tool for the control and manipulation of artificial worlds, namely the *computer*. More and more scientific activity is handed over to these artefacts. They collect data, calculate statistics, and can even be used to find mathematical proofs. Above all, we can use computers to *simulate* different virtual worlds. The computer has increasingly become a tool for planning. Machines have in this way taken over a part of the role that the inner worlds of humans used to play. But we have still not seen computers that have an inherent motivation or that can reflect over their own knowledge process.

8.5   Drifting thought—and the selfish meme

> A scholar is just a library's way of making another library.
>
> Samuel Johnson

"It sounds rather woolly to say that you place thoughts in the world," Egon says. "They are in the heads of somebody, aren't they—if they exist at all? You write almost as if thoughts had their own life."

"The question is what could be meant by saying that thoughts have a life of their own. In the final chapter of his book *The selfish gene*, Dawkins submits the idea that in the world of thoughts there exists a kind of counterpart to the genes in the biological world."

"You are putting the cart in front of the horse," Egon remarks sarcastically. "Can he really 'submit' an idea?"

The genes of thought Dawkins calls *memes*. In the same way as genes spread between generations, certain memes can spread to new heads. He also imagines that they are recombined and that there is a selection among the memes so that some better succeed in multiplying than others. It need not be a particular kind of meme that is successful—among those with the highest rate of spreading one finds popular songs that everybody is humming. Other memes fall on barren rock and it does not matter how good their creator thinks they are and how much effort he takes in communicating them—they simply do not strike roots in any other heads and therefore they do not 'survive'.

If the analogy between genes and memes holds water, it would be possible for thoughts to form an evolutionary system themselves. The question is whether they can become completely independent of having humans as carriers (and thereby go beyond Donaldian beings). There is already the phenomenon of computer viruses that 'live' in an electronic world and have a lifestyle that in many ways resembles that of biological viruses. There are also experiments involving computer structures that are based on so called genetic programming. These structures are supposed to live an independent 'life' on the Internet and spread copies and mutations to computers all over the world.

As Dawkins points out himself, the problem of the analogy between genes and computerized memes is that there are no physical bearers of memes that let them 'share a fate'. The computers that are hosts to the memes have no 'motivation' to let the programming structures live on and spread, while a biological organism is highly motivated to have its genes multiply. Given the artificial bearers of memes that are available now, the analogy between genes and memes is not complete. Humans are still necessary to keep thoughts alive.

8.6   Detached identity

During most of the time that humans have existed, we have lived in small tribes or villages with a couple of hundred inhabitants where everybody knows everybody else. Through the agency of natural selection, village life has left its mark on our way of being.

In the village the individual is given an identity through its social relations to the others in the group. A person becomes known as 'the cook's son' or 'the butcher's mother' rather than by his or her name. The individuals cannot be viewed as detached from their social relations. He or she is given an *outer* identity. The group has a well-known ranking order that seldom changes. In the village society, shame has a central role as a controlling mechanism. Social psychologists call such a construction a *Gemeinschaft*.

In the traditional society there is a need to sometimes upset the outer identity by changing the social relations. For example, in certain feudal regions it was a tradition that the prince acted as a servant to the servants one day each year. In other places, carnivals are organized where you dress yourself up as somebody else and change identities for a couple of days. Moral rules are temporarily dissolved and you are let off being ashamed. Paradoxically, it seems that such traditions increase the unity of a society. They show how crazy the world would be if the prince was not the ruler and if there was no morality.

Village community has gradually been replaced by life in ever-larger societies. Nationalism grows strong in the 19th century, partly because of the national languages that have been created with the aid of printing. It creates a national identity for us that has largely knocked out the identity created in a Gemeinschaft: 'I am so happy that I am Swedish' gets greater weight than 'I am so happy that I come from Cowtown'.

Rather than a Gemeinschaft, the urban world creates a *Gesellschaft* that is based on economic and political relations.[7] In such a society we do not have a personal relation to most of the people we meet. It is no longer necessary to be ashamed of how you behave. This leads to the disintegration of the social identity.

"But what will happen to the village morality in the long run then?" Egon asks.

"McLuhan says that with the aid of communication technology we will create a 'global village' where our social relations are maintained with a select band independently of geographical distances—something he predicted long before the existence of mobile phones."

During the last millennia culture has evolved very rapidly. We are badly adapted to the modern environment. Many artefacts and social patterns go beyond the cognitive proficiencies that have been chiselled out during thousands of year of tribal life. We are still rather well mannered in the urban world. For example, people queue kindly even among total strangers. This is presumably due to the fact that our genetically built-in village mentality still vetoes blatantly selfish behaviour. On the other hand, humans are the only animals who create social networks where you collaborate with strangers. Such an

---

[7]   McLuhan (1964), p. 16, writes: 'We are no more prepared to encounter radio and TV in our literate milieu than the native of Ghana is able to cope with the literacy that takes him out of his collective tribal world and beaches him in individual isolation. We are as numb in our new electric world as the native involved in our literate and mechanical culture'.

extended co-operation would probably not be possible without symbolic communication and a well-developed system of norms.

In this book I have argued that during their biological evolution humans have acquired an increasingly richer inner world. Above all, we have developed a self-consciousness, which means that we can become aware of our own thoughts. Moreover, we can also put ourselves in somebody else's inner world and imagine what they think about us. The self is partly created by viewing yourself through the eyes of others. You see your own inner world as in a mirror. This gives rise to the *inner* identity—the acquaintance with your own inner world. Animals do not have such a self-conception and hence they do not have any inner identity.

Sometimes the outer identity comes in conflict with the inner. I do not want to or cannot perceive myself as others do. If one can tolerate such a discrepancy, it can be a way of fulfilling the expectations of the group and at the same time looking after one's own needs. However, tensions between the outer and the inner identities are also the strongest source of shame.

In the era of electronic communication we can change identities like chameleons, for example when we are chatting over the Internet. We can dress up in virtual masks—without shame. We can play with multiple identities and juggle several inner worlds against each other. Authors and actors have always done this, but nowadays anybody can become an actor in cyberspace. The communication with other alter egos is still primarily based on words, but it is already possible to add pictures, movies, sounds, and soon maybe even tactile experiences. With the aid of technology we can create virtual carnivals that dissolve the identities of real life.

8.7   The open person

> O my soul, do not aspire to immortal life,
> but exhaust the limits of the possible.
>
> Pindar

Above the entrance to the aula of Uppsala University is written: 'Thinking freely is great, but thinking rightly is greater'. In this book I wanted to show that in an evolutionary perspective on thinking, the converse is more correct: thinking rightly is great, but thinking freely is greater.

My main thesis has been that the appearance of an inner world has made possible the emergence of more advanced forms of thinking. Higher cognitive capacities such as planning, self-consciousness, free will, and language presuppose such an inner world. During the development of thinking, humans have achieved an ever-higher degree of *independence* of what happens in their current surroundings. The activities of the brain have become detached from the direct control form the senses. Thought can lift and fly its own way.

In *Nichomachean ethics*, Aristotle writes about the goals of humans. According to him happiness does not consist in enjoyment or bodily pleasures, but in virtuous activities. People who do not develop their abilities to the highest degree possible, whether in art, politics, or science, do not fulfil themselves completely as human beings. Happiness is activities in harmony with virtue, and the highest virtue is contemplation. Contemplation can lead to the cultivation and refinement of one's inner world. He writes:

> [T]he activity of reason, which is contemplative, seems both to be superior in serious worth and to aim at no end beyond itself, and to have its pleasure proper to itself (and this augments the activity)...and as all the other attributes ascribed to the supremely happy man are evidently those connected with this activity, it follows that this will be the complete happiness of man, if it be allowed a complete term of life....[xxi]

The freedom of human thought consists in other things than being detached from the environment. More important is that we, in contrast to other animals, can freely create *new* inner worlds. Thinking is open in its nature. To a high degree, we are the masters of our inner world—at least we experience it in this way—and we may as artists, poets, or scientists strive to expose them to others. The quest for knowledge is a part of human nature that cannot be emphasized enough. It is our biological fate that we cannot refrain from continuing investigating the worlds of thoughts. As the Swedish poet Tomas Tranströmer expresses it in his poem *Roman arches*:

> A faceless angel embraced me
> and whispered through my whole body:
> 'Don't be ashamed that you are a human being, be proud!
> Within you vaults open endlessly behind vaults.
> You'll never be completed, and that's as it should be.'

Epilogue

"In any case I am complete," Egon says, but I cannot hear whether he is ironical or melancholic.

"This is also complete," I gasp. "The book, that is."

"It became a good book, didn't it?"

"Thank you very much for your support. You have been a great source of material."

"Yes, I played my role well, didn't I?"

"What role?" I exclaim, flabbergasted.

"You don't believe I am as stupid as I seem, do you? I have just pretended to be like a normal rhesus so to give you good examples for your theoretical points. And I have got quite a lot of peanuts and bananas during the writing."

"So you have been monkeying around all the time!"

"Of course. You have written yourself that you cannot have a language unless you have all the other cognitive capacities. How could I have put all my smart questions otherwise?"

"No, that's true, but . . . I thought you were an exception."

"How could I be if your analysis is correct?"

"But how have you then obtained your linguistic abilities and your intelligence?"

"Well, you tell me. Maybe you know better than I," Egon replies and screws up his eyes.

"Do you want another banana?"

"No thank you. I'd rather that you scratch my back."

Notes

i. Munn (1973).

ii. Clark (1997), p. 180.

iii. Dahlbom and Janlert (to be published).

iv. Dennett (1996), pp. 138–9.

v. Lecours (1996), p. 221.

vi. McLuhan (1964), p. 81

vii. Olson (1994), p. 68.

viii. Olson (1994), p. 85.

ix. Hedelin and Hjlemquist (1998).

x. Ong (1982), p. 124.

xi. Olson (1994), p. 111.

xii. Ong (1982), p. 140.

xiii. Olson (1994), Chapter 10.

xiv. Olson (1994), p. 212.

xv. Donald (1991), p. 338.

xvi. Donald (1991), pp. 342–3.

xvii. Lloyd (1979), p. 232.

xviii. Olson (1994), p. 269.

xix. Ong (1982), p. 73.

xx. Olson (1994), p. 232.

xxi. *The Nicomachean ethics* 1177b 18–20 and 1177b 23–4.

References

Allott, R. (1991). The motor theory of language. In von Raffler-Engel, W., Wind, J., and Jonker, A., eds., *Studies in language origins*, Vol. 2. John Benjamins, Amsterdam, pp. 123–57.

Axelrod, R. (1984). *The evolution of cooperation*. Basic Books, New York, NY.

Balkenius, C. (1995). *Natural intelligence for artificial creatures*. Lund University Cognitive Studies 37, Lund.

Balkenius, C. and Morén, J. (1998). Computational models of classical conditioning: A comparative study. In Pfeifer, R., Blumberg, B., Meyer, J., and Wilson, S., eds., *From animals to animats 5: Proceedings of the Fifth International Conference on Simulation of Adaptive Behavior*. MIT Press, Cambridge, MA.

Barber, E. J. W. and Peters, A. M. W. (1992). Ontogeny and phylogeny: what child language and archeology have to say to each other. In Hawkins, J. A. and Gell-Mann, M., eds., *The evolution of human languages*. Addison Wesley, Redwood City, CA, pp. 305–51.

Baron-Cohen, S., Leslie, A. M., and Frith, U. (1986). Does the autistic child have a 'theory of mind'? *Cognition* 21, 37–46.

Barsalou, L. W. (2000). Perceptual symbol systems. *Behavioral and Brain Sciences* **22:4**, 577–660.

Bates, E. (1976). *Language in context*. Academic Press, New York, NY.

Bennett, J. (1988). Thoughts about thoughts. *Behavioral and Brain Sciences* **11**, 246–7.

Benveniste, É. (1966). *Problèmes de linguistique générale*, Vol. 1. Gallimard, Paris.

Bergman, B. (1977). *Tecknad svenska*. Liber, Stockholm.

Bickerton, D. (1990). *Language and species*. The University of Chicago Press, Chicago, IL.

Bischof, N. (1978). On the phylogeny of human morality. In Stent, G. S., ed., *Morality as a biological phenomenon*. University of California Press, Berkeley, CA, pp. 48–66.

Blair, R. J. R. (1995). A cognitive developmental approach to morality: investigating the psychopath. *Cognition* **57**, 1–29.

Bloom, L. (2000). *How children learn the meanings of words*. MIT Press, Cambridge, MA.

Boesch, C. and Boesch, H. (1990). Tool use and tool making in wild chimpanzees. An analysis of hammer transports for nut cracking. *Primates* **25**, 160–70.

Boysen, S. and Bernston, G. (1995). Responses to quantity: perceptual versus cognitive mechanisms in chimpanzees (*Pan troglodytes*). *Journal of Experimental Psychology and Animal Behavior Processes* **21**, 82–6.

Brentano, F. (1973). *Psychology from an empirical standpoint*. Routledge and Kegan Paul, London.

Brinck, I. (2000). Demonstrative reference and joint attention. Manuscript.

Brinck, I. (2001). Attention and the evolution of intentional communication. *Pragmatics and Cognition* **9(2)**, 255–72.

Brinck, I. (2002). The pragmatics of imperative and declarative pointing. Manuscript.

Brinck, I. and Gärdenfors, P. (1999). Representation and self-awareness in intentional agents. *Synthese* **118**, 89–104.

Brinck, I. and Gärdenfors, P. (2001). *Co-operation and communication in apes and humans*. Lund University Cognitive Studies 88, Lund. (Revised version to appear in *Mind and Language*.)

Brunet, M. *et al.* (2002). A new hominid from the Upper Miocene of Chad, Central Africa. *Nature* **418**, 145–51.

Buber, M. (1970). *I and Thou*. T. & T. Clark, Edinburgh.

Butterworth, G. and Jarret, N. L. M. (1991). What minds share in common is space: spatial mechanisms serving joint visual attention in infancy. *British Journal of Developmental Psychology* **9**, 55–72.

Byrne, R. W. (1995). *The thinking ape: Evolutionary origins of intelligence*. Oxford University Press, Oxford.

Byrne, R. W. (1998). The early evolution of creative thinking: evidence from monkeys and apes. In Mithen, S., ed., *Creativity in human evolution and prehistory*. Routledge, London, pp. 110–24.

Byrne, R. W. and Russon, A. E. (1998). Learning by imitation: a hierarchical approach. *Behavioral and Brain Sciences* **21**, 667–84.

Calvin, W. H. (1982). Did throwing stones shape hominid brain evolution? *Ethology and Sociobiology* **3**, 115–24.

Calvin, W. H. (1983). *The throwing Madonna*. McGraw-Hill, New York, NY.

Cassell, J., McNeill, D., and McCullough, K.-E. (1999). Speech-gesture mismatches: Evidence for one underlying representation of linguistic and nonlinguistic information. *Pragmatics and Cognition* **7**, 1–33.

Chafe, W. (1980). The deployment of consciousness in the production of a narrative. In Chafe, W. L., ed., *The pear stories: Cognitive, cultural, and linguistic aspects of narrative production*. Ablex, Norwood, NJ, pp. 9–50.

Chafe, W. (1995). Accessing the mind through language. In Allén, S., ed., *Of thoughts and words*. Imperial College Press, London, pp. 107–25.

Chase, P. G. (1999). Symbolism as reference and symbolism as culture. In Dunbar, R., Knight, C., and Power, C., eds., *The evolution of culture*. Edinburgh University Press, Edinburgh, pp. 34–49.

Cheney, D. L. and Seyfarth, R. L. (1990a). Attending to behavior versus attending to knowledge: examining monkey's attribution of mental states. *Animal Behavior* **40**, 742–53.

Cheney, D. L. and Seyfarth, R. L. (1990b). *How monkeys see the world: Inside the mind of another species*. University of Chicago Press, Chicago, IL.

Cheney, D. L., Seyfarth, R. L., and Silk, J. B. (1995). The responses of female baboons (*Papio cynocephalus ursinus*) to anomalous social interactions: evidence for causal reasoning? *Journal of Comparative Psychology* **109**, 134–41.

Christiansen, M. H. (1994). *Infinite languages, finite minds, connectionism, learning and linguistic structures*. University of Edinburgh, Edinburgh.

Clark, A. (1997). *Being there: Putting brain, body and world together again*. MIT Press, Cambridge, MA.

Collingwood, R. J. (1972). *Essay on metaphysics*. Gateway, Chicago, IL.

Connolly, J. A. and Doyle, A. (1984). Relation of social fantasy play to social competence in preschoolers. *Developmental Psychology* **20**, 797–806.

Corballis, M. C. (1989). Laterality and human evolution. *Psychological Review* **96**, 492–505.

Corballis, M. C. (1999). The gestural origins of language. *American Scientist* **87**, March–April, 139–45.

Corballis, M. C. (2002). *From hand to mouth: The origins of language*. Princeton University Press, Princeton, NJ.

Cosmides, L. and Tooby, J. (1992). Cognitive adaptations for social exchange. In Barkow, J., Cosmides, L., and Tooby, J., eds., *The adapted mind: Evolutionary psychology and the generation of culture*. Oxford University Press, Oxford, pp. 163–228.

Coussi-Kourbel, S. (1994). Learning to outwit a competitor in mangabeys (*Cercocebus torquatus torquatus*). *Journal of Comparative Psychology* **108**, 164–71.

Craik, K. (1943). *The nature of explanation*. Cambridge University Press, Cambridge.

Dahlbom, B. and Janlert, L.-E. (to appear). *Computer future*. Book manuscript.

Damasio, A. R. (1995). *Descartes' error: Emotion, reason and the human brain*. G. P. Putnam's Sons, New York.

Damasio, A. R. and Damasio, H. (1992). Brain and language. *Scientific American*, September 1992, 63–71.

Darwin, C. (1871). *The descent of man, and selection in relation to sex*. Appleton, New York, NY.

Darwin, C. (1872). *The expression of the emotions in man and animals*. Murray, London.

Dasser, V. (1988). Mapping social concepts in monkeys. In Byrne, R. W. and Whiten, A., eds., *Machiavellian intelligence: Social expertise and the evolution of intellect in monkeys, apes and humans*. Clarendon Press, Oxford, pp. 85–93.

Davenport, R. K. (1976). Cross-modal perception in apes. In Harnad, S. R., Steklis, H. D., and Lancaster, J., eds., *Origins and evolution of language and speech*. *Annals of the New York Academy of Science* **280**, 143–9.

Davis, L. H. (1989). Selfconsciousness in chimps and pigeons. *Philosophical Psychology* **2**, 249–59.

Dawkins, R. (1976, 1989). *The selfish gene*. Oxford University Press, Oxford. Second edition 1989.

Deacon, T. W. (1992). Brain-language coevolution. In Hawkins, J. A. and Gell-Mann, M., eds., *The evolution of human languages*. Addison Wesley, Redwood City, CA, pp. 49–83.

Deacon, T. W. (1997). *The symbolic species*. Penguin Books, London.

Dennett, D. (1978). *Brainstorms*. Bradford Books, Cambridge, MA.

Dennett, D. (1981). True believers: the intentional strategy and why it works. In Heath, A. F., ed., *Scientific explanation*. Clarendon Press, Oxford, pp. 53–78.

Dennett, D. (1988). Why creative intelligence is hard to find. *Behavioral and Brain Sciences* **11**, 253.

Dennett, D. (1991). *Consciousness explained.* Little, Brown and Company, Boston, MA.

Dennett, D. (1995). *Darwin's dangerous idea.* The Penguin Press, London.

Dennett, D. (1996). *Kinds of minds.* Basic Books, New York, NY.

de Waal, F. B. M. (1982). *Chimpanzee politics.* Jonathan Cape, London.

de Waal, F. B. M. (1988). The communicative repertoire of captive bonobos (*Pan paniscus*) compared to that of chimpanzees. *Behavior* **106**, 183–251.

de Waal, F. B. M. (1995). Bonobo, sex and society. *Scientific American* **272**, 58–64.

Dewan, E. M. (1976). Consciousness as an emergent causal agent in the context of control system theory. In Globus, G., Maxwell, G., and Savodnik, I., eds., *Consciousness and the brain.* Plenum Press, New York, NY, pp. 181–98.

Donald, M. (1991). *Origins of the modern mind.* Harvard University Press, Cambridge, MA.

Donald, M. (2001). *A mind so rare: The evolution of human consciousness.* Norton and Company, New York, NY.

Dostoevsky, F. (1989). *Notes from underground.* Norton and Company, New York, NY.

Dunbar, R. (1996). *Grooming, gossip and the evolution of language.* Faber and Faber, London.

Ellegård, A. (1979). Om det mänskliga språkets ursprung. *KVHAAs årsbok*, pp. 131–48.

Epstein, R. (1982). Representation: a concept that fills no gaps. *Behavioral and Brain Sciences* **5**, 377–8.

Epstein, R., Lanza, R. P., and Skinner, B. F. (1980). Self-awareness in the pigeon. *Science* **212**, 695–6.

Fagen, R. (1981). *Animal play behavior.* Oxford University Press, Oxford.

Farah, M., Soso, M. J., and Dashieff, R. M. (1992). Visual angle of the mind's eye before and after unilateral occipital lobectomy. *Journal of Experimental Psychology: Human Perception and Performance* **18**, 241–6.

Fernald, A. (1992). Meaningful melodies in mothers' speech to infants. In Papousek, H., Jürgens, U., and Papousek, M., eds., *Nonverbal vocal communication: Comparative and developmental approaches.* Cambridge University Press, Cambridge, pp. 262–82.

Feyereisen, P. (1997). The competition between gesture and speech in dual-task paradigms. *Journal of Memory and Language* **36**, 13–33.

Foley, R. (1996). *Humans before humanity: An evolutionary perspective.* Blackwells, Oxford.

Frank, R. H. (1988). *Passions within reason.* Norton, New York, NY.

Frankfurt, H. (1971). Freedom of the will and the concept of a person. *Journal of Philosophy* **68**, 5–20.

Frith, U. (1994). *Autism: Explaining the enigma.* Blackwells, Oxford.

Frith, U. and Happé, F. (1999). Theory of mind and self-consciousness: what is it like to be autistic? *Mind and Language* **14**, 1–22.

Gallese, V., Ferrari, P. F. and Umiltà, M. A. (2002). The mirror matching system: A shared manifold for intersubjectivity. *Behavioral and Brain Sciences* **25**, 35–6.

Gallup, G. G. (1977). Self-recognition in primates. *American Psychologist* **32**, 329–38.

Gallup, G. G. (1988). Toward a taxonomy of mind in primates. *Behavioral and Brain Sciences* **11**, 255–6.

Garcia, J. and Koelling, R. A. (1966). Relation of cue to consequence in avoidance learning. *Psychonomic Science* **5**, 123–4.

Gärdenfors, P. (1993). The emergence of meaning. *Linguistics and Philosophy* **16**, 285–309.

Gärdenfors, P. (1994). How logic emerges from the dynamics of information. In van Eijck, J. and Visser, A., eds., *Logic and information flow.* MIT Press, Cambridge, MA, pp. 49–77.

Gärdenfors, P. (1995). Speaking about the inner environment. In Allén, S., ed., *Of thoughts and words.* Imperial College Press, London, pp. 143–51.

Gärdenfors, P. (1996a). Cued and detached representations in animal cognition. *Behavioural Processes* **36**, 263–73.

Gärdenfors, P. (1996b). Language and the evolution of cognition. In Rialle, V. and Fisette, D., eds., *Penser l'esprit: Des sciences de la cognition à une philosophie cognitive.* Presses Universitaires de Grenoble, Grenoble, pp. 151–72.

Gärdenfors, P. (1997). The role of memory in planning and pretense. *Behavioral and Brain Sciences* **20**, 24–5.

Gärderfors, P. (1999). Some tenets of cognitive semantics. In Allwood, J. and Gärdenfors, P., eds., *Cognitive semantics: Meaning and Cognition,* John Benjamins, Amsterdam, pp. 19–36.

Gillberg, C. and Peeters T. (1998). *Autism: Medical and educational aspects.* Whurr Publishers, London.

Glenberg, A. M. (1997). What memory is for. *Behavioral and Brain Sciences* **20**, 1–19.

Goldin-Meadow, S. (1999). The role of gesture in communication and thinking. *Trends in Cognitive Sciences* **3**, 419–29.

Gómez, J. C. (1994). Mutual awareness in primate communication: a Gricean approach. In Parker, S. T., Mitchell, R. W., and Boccia, M. L., eds., *Self-awareness in animals and humans.* Cambridge University Press, Cambridge, pp. 61–80.

Gómez, J. C. (1998). Some thoughts about the evolution of LADS, with special reference to TOM and SAM. In Carruthers, P. and Boucher, J., eds., *Language and thought: Interdisciplinary themes.* Cambridge University Press, Cambridge, pp. 76–93.

Goodall, J. (1986). *The chimpanzees of Gombe: Patterns of behavior.* Harvard University Press, Cambridge, MA.

Gopnik, A. (1998). Explanation as orgasm. *Minds and Machines* **8**, 101–18.

Gopnik, A. and Astington, J. W. (1988). Children's understanding of representational change, and its relation to the understanding of false belief and the appearance-reality distinction. *Child Development* **59**, 26–37.

Gopnik, A. and Graf, P. (1988). Knowing how you know: young children's ability to identify and remember the sources of their beliefs. *Child Development* **59**, 1366–71.

Gopnik, A. and Meltzoff, A. N. (1997). *Words, thoughts, and theories.* MIT Press, Cambridge, MA.

Grice, P. (1957). Meaning. *The Philosophical Review* **66**, 377–88.

Grice, P. (1969). Utterer's meaning and intentions. *The Philosophical Review* **78**, 147–77.

Grush, R. (1997). The architecture of representation. *Philosophical Psychology* **10**, 5–23.

Grush, R. (1998). Wahrnehmung, Vorstellung und die sensomotorische Schleife. In Esken, F. and Heckmann, H.-D., eds., *Bewußtsein und Repräsentation.* Verlag Ferdinand Schoeningh, Paderborn.

Gulz, A. (1991). *The planning of action as a cognitive and biological phenomenon.* Lund University Cognitive Studies 2, Lund.

Hammond, G. R. (1990). Manual performance asymmetries. In Hammond, G. R., ed., *Cerebral control of speech and limb movements*. North-Holland, Amsterdam, pp. 59–77.

Hauser, M. (1997). *The evolution of communication*. MIT Press, Cambridge, MA.

Hauser, M. (2000). *Wild minds: What animals really think*. Penguin Books, London.

Hauser, M., Chomsky, N., and Fitch, T. (2002). The faculty of language: What is it, who has, and how did it evolve? *Science* **298**, 1569–78.

Hawkins, R. D. and Kandel, E. R. (1984). Steps towards a cell-biological alphabet for elementary forms of learning. In Lynch, G., McGaugh, J. L., and Weinberger, N. M., eds., *Neurobiology of memory and learning*. Guilford, New York, NY, pp. 385–404.

Hedelin, L. and Hjelmquist, E. (1998). Preschool children's mastery of the form/content distinction in communicative tasks. *Journal of Psycholinguistic Research* **27**, 421–52.

Held, R. and Hein, A. (1963). Movement-produced stimulation in the development of visually guided behavior. *Journal of Comparative and Physiological Psychology* **56**, 872–6.

Hesslow, G. (2002). Conscious thought as simulation of behaviour and perception. *Trends in Cognitive Sciences* **6(6)**, 242–7.

Heyes, C. (1998). Theory of mind in nonhuman primates. *Behavioral and Brain Sciences* **21**, 101–15.

Hockett, C. F. (1960). The origin of speech. *Scientific American* **203(3)**, 88–96.

Holsanová, J. (2001). *Picture viewing and picture description: Two windows on the mind*. Lund University Cognitive Studies 83, Lund.

Hume, D. (1739, 1978). *A treatise of human nature*. Selby-Bigge/Nidditch Edition, Oxford University Press, Oxford.

Humphrey, N. K. (1993). *A history of the mind*. Vintage Books, London.

Humphrey, N. K. (2002). *The mind made flesh*. Oxford University Press, Oxford.

Humphrey, N. K. and Dennett, D. (1989). Speaking for our selves: an assessment of multiple personality disorder. *Raritan* **9**, 68–98.

Jackendoff, R. (1999). Possible stages in the evolution of the language capacity. *Trends in Cognitive Sciences* **3**, 272–9.

James, W. (1890). *The principles of psychology*. Henry Holt, New York, NY.

Jeannerod, M. (1994). The representing brain, neural correlates of motor intention and imagery. *Behavioral and Brain Sciences* **17**, 187–202.

Johnson, M. (1987). *The body in the mind: The bodily basis of cognition.* University of Chicago Press, Chicago, IL.

Kawato, M. (1999). Internal models for motor control and trajectory planning. *Current Opinion in Neurobiology* **9**, 718–27.

Keating, C. F. and Heltman, K. R. (1994). Dominance and deception in children and adults: are leaders the best misleaders? *Personality and Social Psychology Bulletin* **20**, 312–21.

Kimura, D. (1976). The neurological basis of language qua gestures. In Whitaker, H. and Whitaker, H. A., eds., *Current trends in neurolinguistics.* Academic Press, New York, NY.

Kirkegaard, S. (1989). *Sickness unto death.* Penguin Books, London.

Knight, C., Power, C., and Watts, I. (1995). The human symbolic revolution: a Darwinian account. *Cambridge Archeological Journal* **5:1**, 75–114.

Lachman, R. and Lachman, J. L. (1982). Memory representations in animals: some metatheoretical issues. *Behavioral and Brain Sciences* **5**, 380–1.

Langer, S. (1948). *Philosophy in a new key.* Penguin Books, New York, NY.

Lecours, A. R. (1996). The origins and evolution of writing. In Changeux, J.-P. and Chavaillon, J., eds., *Origins of the human brain.* Clarendon Press, Oxford, pp. 213–35.

Leslie, A. M. (1987). Pretense and representation: the origins of 'theory of mind'. *Psychological Review* **94**, 412–26.

Lewis, C. and Osborne, A. (1990). Three-year-olds' problems with false beliefs: conceptual deficit or linguistic artefact? *Child Development* **61**, 1514–19.

Lieberman, P. (1992). On the evolution of human language. In Hawkins, J. A. and Gell-Mann, M., eds., *The evolution of human languages.* Addison Wesley, Redwood City, CA, pp. 21–47.

Llinas, R. and Pare, D. (1991). On dreaming and wakefulness. *Neuroscience* **44**, 521–35.

Lloyd, G. E. R. (1979). *Magic, reason and experience.* Cambridge University Press, Cambridge.

Lorenz, K. (1977). *Behind the mirror: A search for a natural history of human knowledge.* Methuen, London.

Luria, A. R. (1961). *The role of speech in the regulation of normal and abnormal behavior*. Liveright, New York, NY.

Lyons, J. (1988). Origins of language. In Fabian, A. C., ed., *Origins: The Darwin College Lectures*. Cambridge University Press, Cambridge, pp. 141–66.

Machiavelli, N. (1513, 1999). *The prince*. Penguin Classics, London.

Månsson, J. (2000). *Occluding contours: a computational model of suppressive mechanisms in human contour perception*. Lund University Cognitive Studies 81, Lund.

Marten, K. and Psarakos. S. (1994). Evidence of self-awareness in the bottlenose dolphin (*Tursiops truncatus*). In Parker, S. T., Mitchell, R. W., and Boccia, M. L., eds., *Self-awareness in animals and humans*. Cambridge University Press, Cambridge, pp. 361–79.

McLuhan, M. (1964). *Understanding media*. McGraw-Hill, New York, NY.

Meltzoff, A. N. (1985). The roots of social and cognitive development: models of man's original nature. In Field, T. M. and Fox, N. A., eds., *Social perception in infants*. Ablex, Norwood, NJ, pp. 702–9.

Meltzoff, A. N. (1988). The human infant as *Homo imitans*. In Zentall, T. R. and Galef, B. G., eds., *Social learning: Psychological and biological perspectives*. Lawrence Erlbaum, Hillsdale, NJ, pp. 319–41.

Meltzoff, A. N. (1996). The human infant as imitative generalist: a 20-year progress report on infant imitation with implications for comparative psychology. In Galef Jr, B. G. and Heyes, C. M., eds., *Social learning in animals: The roots of culture*. Academic Press, New York, NY, pp. 347–70.

Menzel, E. W. (1973). Chimpanzee spatial memory organization. *Science* **182**, 943–5.

Menzel, E. W. (1974). A group of chimpanzees in a 1-acre field: leadership and communication. In Schrier, A. M. and Stollnitz, F., eds., *Behavior of nonhuman primates*. Academic Press, New York, NY, pp. 83–153.

Menzel, E. W., Savage-Rumbaugh, S., and Lawson, J. (1985). Chimpanzee (*Pan troglodytes*) spatial problem solving with the use of mirrors and televisad equivalents of mirrors. *Journal of Comparative Psychology* **42**, 454–62.

Merleau-Ponty, M. (1962). *Phenomenology of perception*. Routledge and Kegan Paul, London.

Mitchell, P. (1997). *Introduction to theory of mind: Children, autism and apes*. Arnold, London.

Mitchell, R. W. (1993). Mental models of mirror-self-recognition: two theories. *New Ideas in Psychology* **11**, 295–325.

Mitchell, R. W. (1994). Multiplicities of self. In Parker, S. T., Mitchell, R. W., and Boccia, M. L., eds., *Self-awareness in animals and humans.* Cambridge University Press, Cambridge, pp. 81–107.

Mithen, S. (1996). *The prehistory of the mind: A search for the origins of art, religion and science.* Thames and Hudson, London.

Morales, M., Mundy, P., and Rojas, J. (1998). Following the direction of gaze and language development in six-month-olds. *Infant Behavior and Development* **21**, 373–7.

Müller, R.-A. (1996). Innateness, autonomy, universality? Neurological approaches to language. *Behavioral and Brain Sciences* **19**, 611–75.

Munn, N. D. (1973). The spatial presentation of cosmic order in Walbiri iconography. In Forge, A., ed., *Primitive art and society.* Oxford University Press, Oxford.

Murray, E. A. (1990). Representational memory in nonhuman primates. In Kesner, R. P. and Olton, D. S., eds., *Neurobiology of comparative cognition.* Lawrence Erlbaum, Hillsdale, NJ, pp. 127–55.

Nagel, T. (1974). What is it like to be a bat? *Philosophical Review* **83**, 435–50.

Nisbett, R. E. and Wilson, T. D. (1977). Telling more than we can know: verbal reports on mental processes. *Psychological Review* **84**, 231–59.

Noble, W. and Davidson, I. (1996). *Human evolution, language and mind.* Cambridge University Press, Cambridge.

Oakley, K. P. (1961). On man's use of fire, with comments on tool-making and hunting. In Washburn, S. L., ed., *Social life of early man.* Aldine Publishing Company, Chicago, pp. 176–93.

Oakley, K. P. (1985). Animal awareness, consciousness and self-image. In Oakley, D., ed., *Brain and mind.* Methuen, London, pp. 132–51.

Olson, D. R. (1994). *The world on paper.* Cambridge University Press, Cambridge.

Ong, W. J. (1982). *Orality and literacy.* Routledge, London.

Pepperberg, I. (1990). Conceptual abilities of some non-primate species, with an emphasis on an African grey parrot. In Parker, S. T. and Gibson, K. R., eds., *'Language' and intelligence in monkeys and apes.* Cambridge University Press, Cambridge, pp. 469–507.

Perner, J., Leekam, S., and Wimmer, H. (1987). Three-year-old's difficulty with false belief: the case for a conceptual deficit. *British Journal of Developmental Psychology* **5**, 125–37.

Perner, J. and Lopez, A. (1997). Children's understanding of belief and disconfirming visual evidence. *Cognitive Development* **12**, 367–80.

Perner, J. and Lang, B. (1999). Development of theory of mind and executive control. *Trends in Cognitive Sciences* **3**, 337–44.

Piaget, J. (1954). *The construction of reality in the child*. Basic Books, New York, NY.

Piaget, J. and Inhelder, B. (1956). *The child's conception of space*. Routledge and Kegan Paul, London.

Place, U. (2000). The role of the hand in the evolution of language. *Psycholoquy* *11.007*.

Popper, K. R. (1972). *Objective knowledge: An evolutionary approach*. Oxford University Press, Oxford.

Povinelli, D. J. (2000). *Folk physics for apes: The chimpanzee's theory of how the world works*. Oxford University Press, Oxford.

Povinelli, D. J. and DeBlois, S. (1992). Young children's (*Homo sapiens*) understanding of knowledge formation in themselves and others. *Journal of Comparative Psychology* **106**, 228–38.

Povinelli, D. J. and Eddy, T. J. (1996). What young chimpanzees know about seeing. *Monographs of the Society for Research in Child Development*, Vol. 61. Chicago, IL.

Power, C. (1999). 'Beauty magic': the origins of art. In Dunbar, R., Knight, C., and Power, C., eds., *The evolution of culture*. Edinburgh University Press, Edinburgh, pp. 92–112.

Premack, D. (1996). Cause/induced motion: intention/spontaneous motion. In Changeux, J.-P. and Chavaillon, J., eds., *Origins of the human brain*. Clarendon Press, Oxford, pp. 286–308.

Premack, D. and Woodruff, G. (1978). Does the chimpanzee have a theory of mind? *Behavioral and Brain Sciences* **4**, 515–26.

Proust, J. (1998). Can nonhuman primates read minds? *Rapport no. 9807*. CREA, Paris.

Risteau, C. (1991). Aspects of the cognitive ethology of an injury-feigning bird, the piping plove. In Risteau, C., ed., *Cognitive ethology: The mind of other animals*. Lawrence Erlbaum, Hillsdale, NJ, pp. 91–126.

Russell, J., Mauthner, N., Sharpe, S., and Tidswell, T. (1991). The 'windows task' as a measure of strategic deception in preschoolers and autistic subjects. *British Journal of Developmental Psychology* **9**, 331–50.

Savage-Rumbaugh, E. S. and Lewin, R. (1994). *Kanzi: The ape at the brink of the human mind*. Wiley, New York, NY.

Savage-Rumbaugh, E. S. and Rumbaugh, D. M. (1993). The emergence of language. In Gibson, K. R. and Ingold, T., eds., *Tools, language and cognition in human evolution.* Cambridge University Press, Cambridge, pp. 86–108.

Savage-Rumbaugh, E. S., Shanker, S. G., and Taylor, T. J. (1998). *Apes, language and the human mind.* Oxford University Press, Oxford.

Schoenemann, P. T. (1999). Syntax as an emergent characteristic of the evolution of semantic complexity. *Minds and Machines* **9**, 309–46.

Shultz, T. R. (1982). Rules of causal attribution. *Monographs of the Society for Research in Child Development* **47**(1).

Silberberg, A. and Fujita, K. (1996). Pointing at smaller food amounts in an analogue of Boysen and Bernston's (1995) procedure. *Quarterly Journal of Experimental Psychology* **66**, 143–7.

Singer, W. (1999). The observer in the brain. In Riegler, A., Peschl, M., and von Stein, A., eds., *Understanding representation in the cognitive sciences.* Plenum, New York, NY, pp. 253–6.

Sjölander, S. (1984). *Nya tankan on gamla hjärnor.* Brombergs, Stockholm.

Sjölander, S. (1993). Some cognitive breakthroughs in the evolution of cognition and consciousness, and their impact on the biology of language. *Evolution and Cognition* **3**, 1–10.

Sjölander, S. (1999). How animals handle reality—the adaptive aspect of representation. In Riegler, A., Peschl, M., and von Stein, A., eds., *Understanding representation in the cognitive sciences.* Plenum, New York, NY, pp. 277–81.

Sjölander, S. (2002). *Naturens budbärare.* Nya Doxa, Nora.

Snowdon, C. T. (1990). Language capacities of nonhuman animals. *Yearbook of Physical Anthropology* **33**, 215–43.

Sperry, R. W. (1976). Mental phenomena as causal determinants in brain function. In Globus, G., Maxwell, G., and Savodnik, I., eds., *Consciousness and the brain.* Plenum Press, New York, NY, pp. 163–77.

Stone, W. L., Ousley, O. Y., and Littleford, C. D. (1997). Motor imitation in young children with autism. *Journal of Abnormal Child Psychology* **25**, 475–85.

Taylor, C. K. and Saayman, G. S. (1973). Imitative behaviour by Indian ocean bottlenose dolphins (*Tursiops aduncus*) in captivity. *Behaviour* **44**, 286–98.

Taylor Parker, S., Mitchell, R., and Boccia, M., eds. (1994). *Self-awareness in animals and humans.* Cambridge University Press, Cambridge.

Terrace, H. (1982). Why Koko can't talk. *The Sciences*, December 1982, 8–10.

Terrace, H. (1984). Animal cognition. In Roitblat, H. L., Beve, T. G., and Terrace, H. S., eds., *Animal cognition*. Lawrence Erlbaum, Hillsdale, NJ.

Thouless, R. H. (1931). Phenomenal regression to the real object, II. *British Journal of Psychology* **22**, 1–30.

Tolman, E. C. (1948). Cognitive maps in rats and men. *Psychological Review* **55**, 189–208.

Tomasello, M. (1991). Processes of communication in the origins of language. In von Raffler-Engel, W., Wind, J., and Jonker, A., eds., *Studies in language origins*, Vol. 2. John Benjamins, Amsterdam, pp. 85–97.

Tomasello, M. (1996). Do apes ape? In Galef Jr, B. G. and Heyes, C. M., eds., *Social learning in animals: The roots of culture*. Academic Press, New York, NY, pp. 319–46.

Tomasello, M. (1998). Reference: intending that others jointly attend. *Pragmatics and Cognition* **6**, 229–43.

Tomasello, M. (1999). *The cultural origins of human cognition*. Harvard University Press, Cambridge, MA.

Tomasello, M. and Call, J. (1997). *Primate cognition*. Oxford University Press, Oxford.

Tomasello, M., Call, J., Warren, J., Frost, T., Carpenter, M., and Nagell, K. (1997). The ontogeny of chimpanzee gestural signals: a comparison across groups and generations. *Evolution of Communication* **1**, 223–53.

Toth, N. (1985). The Oldowan reassessed: a close look at early stone artifacts. *Journal of Archeological Science* **12**, 101–20.

Trevarthen, C. (1992). An infant's motives for speaking and thinking in the culture. In Heen Wold, A., ed., *The dialogical alternative*. Scandinavian University Press, Oslo, pp. 99–137.

Tulving, E. (1985). How many memory systems are there? *American Psychologist* **40**, 385–98.

van Lavick-Goodall, J. (1968). The behaviour of free-living chimpanzees in the Gombe Stream reserve. *Animal Behaviour Monographs* **1**, 161–311.

Vauclair, J. (1987). A comparative approach to cognitive mapping. In Ellen, P. and Thinus-Blanc, C., eds., *Cognitive processes and spatial orientation in animal and man: Volume I: Experimental animal psychology and ethology*. Martinus Nijhoff Publishers, Dordrecht, pp. 89–96.

Vauclair, J. (1990). Primate cognition: from representation to language. In Parker, S. T. and Gibson, K. R., eds., *'Language' and intelligence in monkeys and apes*. Cambridge University Press, Cambridge, pp. 312–29.

Vauclair, J. and Vidal, J.-M. (1994). Discontinuities in the mind between animals and humans. Paper presented at the conference on *Cognition and Evolution*, Berder, March 1994.

von Glasersfeld, E. (1976). The development of language as purposive behavior. In Harnad, S. R., Steklis, H. D., and Lancaster, J., eds., *Origins and evolution of language and speech. Annals of the New York Academy of Science* **280**, 212–26.

von Glasersfeld, E. (1977). Linguistic communication: theory and definition. In Rumbaugh, D. M., ed., *Language learning by a chimpanzee: The LANA project*. Academic Press, New York, NY, pp. 55–71.

von Uexküll, J. (1985). Environment and inner world of animals. In Burghardt, G. M., ed., *Foundations of comparative ethology*. Van Nostrand Reinhold Company, New York, NY, pp. 222–45.

Vygotsky, L. (1976). *Thought and language*. MIT Press, Cambridge, MA.

Walker, A. and Shipman, P. (1996). *The wisdom of the bones*. Alfred Knopf, New York, NY.

Weir, A. A. S., Chappell, J., and Kacelnik, A. (2002). Shaping of hooks in New Caledonian crows. *Science* **297**, 981.

Westergaard, G. C., Liv, C., Haynie, M. K., and Suomi, S. J. (2000). A comparative study of aimed throwing by monkeys and humans. *Neuropsychologica* **38**, 1511–17.

Whiten, A. and Byrne, R. W. (1988). Tactical deception in primates. *Behavioral and Brain Sciences* **11**, 233–44.

Whiten, A., Custance, D. M., Gómez, J. C., Teixidor, P., and Bard, K. A. (1996). Imitative learning of artificial fruit processing in children (*Homo sapiens*) and chimpanzee (*Pan troglodytes*). *Journal of Comparative Psychology* **110**, 3–14.

Wiener, N. (1961). *Cybernetics*. MIT Press, Cambridge, MA.

Wimmer, H. and Hartl, M. (1991). Against the Cartesian view on mind: young children's difficulty with own false beliefs. *British Journal of Developmental Psychology* **9**, 125–38.

Wimmer, H., Hogrefe, G.-J., and Perner, J. (1988). Children's understanding of informational access as a source of knowledge. *Child Development* **59**, 386–96.

Woodruff, G. and Premack, D. (1979). Intentional communication in the chimpanzee: the development of deception. *Cognition* **7**, 333–62.

Index